# Saviors or Sellouts

# Saviors or Sellouts

The Promise and Peril
of Black Conservatism,
from Booker T. Washington
to Condoleezza Rice

CHRISTOPHER ALAN BRACEY

BEACON PRESS
BOSTON

Beacon Press
25 Beacon Street
Boston, Massachusetts 02108-2892
www.beacon.org

Beacon Press books
are published under the auspices of
the Unitarian Universalist Association of Congregations.

11  10  09  08    8  7  6  5  4  3  2  1

This book is printed on acid-free paper that meets the uncoated paper
ANSI/NISO specifications for permanence as revised in 1992.

Text design and composition by Yvonne Tsang
at Wilsted & Taylor Publishing Services

LIBRARY OF CONGRESS CATALOGING-IN-PUBLICATION DATA

Bracey, Christopher Alan
Saviors or sellouts : the promise and peril of Black Conservatism, from Booker T. Washington to Condoleezza Rice / Christopher Alan Bracey.
p. cm.
Includes bibliographical references and index.
ISBN 978-0-8070-8375-8
1. African Americans—Politics and government. 2. Conservatism—United States—History. 3. African Americans—Intellectual life. 4. United States—Race
relations—Political aspects. 5. United States—Politics and government—History.
I. Title.
E185.B798 2008
323.1196'073—dc22                                    2007026297

*This book is dedicated to
my newborn son, Lawson,
and my lovely wife, Susan—
my citadel of pride and
joyous sanctuary, respectively.*

# Contents

# Introduction

## Facing Reality: Black Conservatism's Growing Appeal and Why It Matters

What exactly does it mean to be a black conservative, and why would anyone choose to become one?

This is the kind of question that rarely elicits a serious response. Depending upon the source, it can come off as cynical, accusatory, and politically loaded. Over the years, I have asked this question of self-proclaimed black conservatives in a variety of formal and informal settings—sometimes in jest, but mostly with earnest intention. Responses have been predictably wide ranging. The interminable pregnant pause. The wry smile. The incredulous glance. Mild deflection, followed by an inquiry into my own personal politics. The cautious and thoroughly caveated explanation. The full-blown ideological rant. Rarely, if ever, have I come away from such exchanges substantively and intellectually satisfied.

There was a time when the answer to this question was largely inconsequential. In the mid-twentieth century, black conservatives resided at the periphery of American culture and politics. The influence of black conservatives and the ideas they espoused had little demonstrable effect on the trajectory of American politics and race relations. Liberals commanded the black political and cultural stage, and the answer to this question, to the extent that it was ever asked, was largely ignored.

As twenty-first-century Americans, however, we find ourselves in a radically different posture. Black conservatives are quickly becoming the most visible and prominent voices within African American politics, culture, and society. The rising tide of black conservatism will invariably shape policy that will define the social, political, and economic future of African Americans as well as other socially disfavored groups. As the effects of black conservatism begin to reverberate through the body politic, what was once viewed as a largely irrelevant query will assume newfound significance. For individuals who take social justice matters seriously—especially those that affect the African American community—the ability to secure progressive change in American race relations will increasingly hinge upon the depth of one's understanding and engagement with the source of black conservative ideals in general, and the black conservative perspective on racial empowerment in particular. We face a new political reality in this country. We need a serious and satisfying answer to this question, and we need it now.

In these pages, you will find an answer (or, perhaps more precisely, answers) to this question and many others regarding black conservatism. However, I want to make clear at the outset that this book is *not* written with the idea of improving conservative philosophy, enhancing its appeal among African Americans, or accelerating the explosion of black conservatism on the national political scene. There exist more than a sufficient number of ideologues, political pundits, and special interest groups eager to advance that particular agenda.

The fact is that ideological posturing often promotes a closing-ranks mentality that works to stifle sincere, constructive, and intelligent engagement across ideological lines. This breakdown in communication undoubtedly complicates governance in our larger democratic community, but it risks a particular form of devastation within the black community. We live in a society in which people of color, and African Americans in particular, not only continue to struggle to realize their full political, social, and economic potential, but risk losing the societal gains achieved by previous generations. For those who take seriously the attainment of political, social, and economic empowerment for all African Americans, ideological posturing of this sort and the crisis of communication that ensues are luxuries that we simply cannot afford.

By contrast, this book *is* written to promote a much needed public conversation among conservatives and liberals regarding the rising tide of black conservatism within American politics and, in particular, how this conservative movement relates to the long-standing efforts by liberals to secure racial empowerment for African Americans. As a professor of law and African and African American studies who has dedicated his professional life to exploring the possibilities for achieving racial justice in American society, I have a deep and abiding respect for the freedom struggle of African Americans. The bulk of my research and writing focuses on racial discrimination, structural oppression, and the toll that each takes on the lives of everyday people. And I am especially interested in what law, politics, and public policy can (and cannot) do to achieve racially just outcomes in American life.

I began this project, like many liberals, essentially baffled by the modern conservative stance on race matters and their relentless critique of liberal public policy measures designed to achieve racial justice. Conservatism, at least as commonly understood today, is fundamentally at odds with what many African Americans have understood to be the best strategy for racial empowerment. Most liberals who write about modern black conservatives dismiss them as fabricated and inauthentic voices that simply are not committed to racial justice and empowerment. This kind of response is not only unsatisfying on a personal level, but leaves that critical question unanswered: namely, What exactly does it mean to be a black conservative, and why would anyone choose to become one? It raises a host of other important questions as well. For instance, what is the source of these conservative ideas? Can we say that there is such a thing as a black conservative tradition in American politics? If so, what is the history of that tradition? What sort of influence did this black conservative tradition have on freedom struggles in the past? And perhaps most important, why does conservatism prove appealing to an increasing number of African Americans today?

Ideological posturing cannot begin to answer these questions. Such questions can be addressed only when we come to know and appreciate the virtues and vices of black conservatism and create space for serious and robust dialogue on the promise and limits of racial empowerment from the ideological Right.

As I began to research this book, I found little, if any, serious discussion by liberals of what appears to be a rather obvious conservative trend in modern black America. This lack of sincere engagement with black conservatives, though perhaps understandable in some ways, left me wanting to know more about black conservatives and their understanding of racial empowerment. As I dug deeper, I quickly realized that racial empowerment, at least historically, was not the exclusive domain of liberals. Indeed, a more nuanced reading of the freedom struggle in this country reveals a strategy for racial empowerment sourced from both liberal and conservative political traditions.

This is something that is often overlooked by scholars and commentators, and in my mind suggests that it would be a mistake to dismiss the conservative political tradition as presumptively antithetical or irrelevant to the task of racial empowerment. Instead, I believe it vital that we all understand and appreciate the important historic role of black conservatism in promoting racial empowerment in this country and give this tradition its proper respect.

But to be clear: although I argue that we should not summarily dismiss black conservatism, I am not suggesting that we should heap unqualified praise upon the tradition. Indeed, sincere engagement with the black conservative tradition demands that one not only understand and appreciate the best of this tradition, but *interrogate and critique* it as well. As detailed in the chapters of this book, historic forms of black conservatism, viewed in their proper context, were not unqualifiedly positive modes of racial empowerment. They entailed real sacrifices and trade-offs. For instance, traditional black conservatives believed that blacks must achieve economic stability before pursuing social and political equality. The development of black businesses and institutions certainly produced economic growth within black communities. But early black conservatives failed to see that social and political rights were necessary to stabilize and secure the enjoyment of those gains. Limited material success did nothing to ameliorate the growing social and political isolation experienced by blacks, and did even less to protect blacks against lynchings, beatings, threats of racial violence, and everyday acts of racial callousness. It is vital that both conservatives and liberals appreciate the complex manner in which these ideas can be understood to advance as well as undermine prospects for racial empowerment.

Modern black conservative thought similarly suffers from blind spots and deficits of political imagination. Furthermore, as detailed in the later chapters of this book, modern black conservatism diverges from traditional black conservatism in a number of important ways—some of which may lead traditional black conservatives to view their modern counterparts as "inauthentic" or perhaps even outside the tradition. Whereas traditional black conservatism is "organic" in that it developed and remains largely supported from within the black community to promote racial empowerment, much of what we understand to be modern black conservatism is "inorganic" in that it is nurtured and sustained by political actors, think tanks and research institutes, and media outlets outside the black community. For instance, many modern black conservatives advocate limited government and emphasize individual freedom over group empowerment—two positions commonly endorsed by white conservatives that are rooted in the Goldwater revival of white conservatism in the mid-twentieth century. It is important to appreciate the critical departures of modern black conservatism from its historic counterparts because they reveal modern black conservatism to be susceptible not only to external liberal critique but to *internal* critique from traditional conservatives on grounds wholly independent of the liberal critique of conservative racial policy.

## 2006 Midterm Election

The more immediate point worth emphasizing here is that modern black conservatism, though susceptible to an assortment of criticisms, is plainly on the rise in American political life. The 2006 midterm election appeared to signal a triumph of liberal democratic ideas over the prevailing conservative and militaristic agenda set by leading Republicans in the late twentieth and early twenty-first centuries. The apparent shift away from prevailing conservatism was fueled in large part by disenchantment with lack of progress in the "war on terrorism" in Afghanistan and Iraq, disillusionment with policies that deepened wealth and income disparities, and disdain for arrogant and corrupt political practices cloaked in the language of morality. The dramatic assumption of control by Democrats over both houses of Congress and a number of state governorships and local legislatures was a surprising victory for liberals and a devastating blow to modern conservatives. America had spoken, and it had apparently chosen a liberal path for the country's future.

In the midst of this groundswell of liberal outpouring, we witnessed the ascension of two important African American figures on the Democratic landscape. Deval Patrick, who served as head of the Civil Rights Division of the Department of Justice during the Clinton years, won an unprecedented race to become the first African American governor of the State of Massachusetts. At the same time, Barack Obama, a freshman senator from Illinois, swept onto the national political scene as the new face of the Democratic Party, working effectively as a fundraiser and catalyst for political change in contested races across the country. Although "Patrick Fever" remains largely confined to New England, the same cannot be said of enthusiasm for Obama. His national popularity continues to grow, and, in the minds of many, his prospects for securing the Democratic nomination for president in the 2008 election may soon eclipse those of his chief rival, New York Senator Hillary Rodham Clinton.

Many liberals generously interpreted the rise of Patrick and Obama and Democratic electoral triumphs across the nation as indicative of the inevitable decline of modern conservatism. And though it would be a mistake to conclude that American conservatism no longer presents a viable political strategy, there is little doubt that conservatives will have to close ranks, regroup, and redeploy in innovative ways if they are to achieve any traction in the 2008 election cycle.

But if the midterm election gave liberals reason to celebrate, it also provided reason for puzzlement, if not genuine concern. African Americans, the long-standing loyal constituency of the Democratic Party, publicly and unapologetically broke ranks. In Maryland, the Republican challenger for the traditionally Democratic seat in the U.S. Senate was the first African American lieutenant governor of the state, Michael Steele. To the surprise of many, Steele's senatorial bid received public support from sports and entertainment luminaries such as hip-hop mogul Russell Simmons, boxing promoter Don King, and retired heavyweight champion Mike Tyson. Although Steele lost the general election to his Democratic opponent, he received 25 percent of the African American vote. Steele is more popular than ever within Republican circles, and since the election has been considered for a host of national appointments, including chairman of the Republican National Committee and secretary of Housing and Urban Development.

Michael Steele, however, is but one of the cadre of next-generation black conservatives that are quickly moving to the center stage of American politics. In Michigan, Keith Butler made a strong albeit unsuccessful showing in the August 2006 Republican primary in his quest to unseat Democratic incumbent Debbie Stabenow. In Pennsylvania, Professional Football Hall of Fame wide receiver Lynn Swann led a highly publicized but ultimately unsuccessful challenge to Democratic legend Ed Rendell for the governorship of Pennsylvania. Republican Secretary of State Kenneth Blackwell, in the neighboring swing state of Ohio, likewise made a highly credible showing in the gubernatorial election in his state.

Despite their losing efforts, these individuals demonstrate that the ranks of black conservatives have swelled far beyond Colin Powell, Condoleezza Rice, and Clarence Thomas. At the same time, there appears to be a small-scale conservative renaissance taking place within the ranks of black voters, exemplified by the outcomes of two state ballot initiatives —both of which should give Democrats further pause. The 2006 anti–affirmative action referendum in Michigan, bankrolled by African American conservative Ward Connerly—the same man who spearheaded similarly successful efforts in California and Washington—passed with 58 percent of the vote. In Virginia in the fall of 2006, blacks broke with traditional liberal coalitions to support a ban on same-sex marriage with 56 percent of the black vote—a percentage roughly equal to the corresponding percentage of the white vote.

Popular elections tell only a portion of the story. The most prominent writings on American race relations in recent years are all by self-proclaimed conservatives: John McWhorter's *Losing the Race: Self-Sabotage in Black America;* Shelby Steele's *The Content of Our Character: A New Vision of Race in America* and *White Guilt: How Blacks and Whites Together Destroyed the Promise of the Civil Rights Era;* and Thomas Sowell's *Black Rednecks and White Liberals.* Even comedian Bill Cosby seems to have embraced conservatism with newfound fervor, offering a scathing critique of African American cultural practices that he deems destructive to the black community. Enter the blogosphere, and one finds a small but vibrant and growing community of black conservatives eager to present and exchange ideas on conservative strategies for racial empowerment.

When asked why he supported Steele, Tyson said that although he had formerly thought of black Republicans as "sellouts," he abandoned that view after researching Steele's record as lieutenant governor. "We have to open our eyes more," remarked Tyson. Statistics show that an increasing number of African Americans have come to share the same political sentiment over the past quarter-century. In 1972, less than 10 percent of African Americans identified themselves as conservative.[1] In 2004, nearly 30 percent, or 11.2 million African Americans, self-identified as conservative.[2] By contrast, the number of blacks who self-identified as liberal declined to 13 percent.[3] Twenty-first-century African Americans support conservative policy in record numbers—60 percent of blacks support school voucher programs; 50 percent support the privatization of Social Security investment accounts; and nearly 65 percent oppose the legalization of gay marriage.[4] In the 2004 presidential election, the black vote for George Bush was more than 30 percent above what it was in the 2000 election.[5]

The significance of this trend may be lost on many liberals, but not on leading African American Democrats such as Barack Obama. In June 2006—well before the midterm election—Senator Obama chastised fellow Democrats for failing to "acknowledge the power of faith in the lives of the American people," and declared that the Democratic Party must begin to compete for the support of evangelicals and other churchgoing Americans. Obama made good on his intentions following the success of the midterm election, accepting an invitation to speak at Saddleback Church, one of the largest Evangelical megachurches in the country and home to leading Evangelical pastor Rick Warren, author of the profoundly influential Christian text *The Purpose Driven Life*. Obama appeared alongside Senator Sam Brownback of Kansas, a longtime favorite of the religious Right, and addressed more than a thousand Evangelical pastors and religious leaders at the church summit. If Obama's appearance hinted at the potential for recalibration of the political loyalties of churchgoing Americans, it also plainly professed a personal acknowledgment on his part that a deepened appreciation of the values held by conservatives would soon become an increasingly relevant component of successful Democratic governance.

Most liberals, however, continue to bask in the afterglow of the midterm election. And they do so at their own peril. When Democrats finally peer through the celebratory haze of this midterm election, they will undoubtedly be surprised at the political change taking place right beneath their noses. Despite having vanquished their conservative political opposition, Democrats will discover that conservative ideas live on and indeed flourish in the lifeblood of their most loyal constituency. They will find that, for an increasing number of African Americans, conservatism has become a credible and compelling alternative to traditional liberal modes of political, cultural, and economic empowerment.

In the wake of this discovery, liberals will have no choice but to respond to the rising tide of conservatism within black political thought. They must learn to engage with these ideas in the spirit of intellectual curiosity, reasoned debate, and a sincere interest in exploring the myriad pathways to racial empowerment. Indeed, the future of their relationship with their most loyal constituency, continued electoral success, and ability to govern effectively depend upon it.

## Black Conservatism:
## Modern Invention or Historic Tradition?

For better or worse, black conservatives have been and continue to be objects of both curiosity and scorn. A conservative is commonly defined as someone "disposed to maintain existing views, conditions, or institutions." From the standpoint of both the historic and contemporary black experience, it seems contradictory, if not unimaginable, for an African American to be conservative in this sense. Yet over the past twenty-five years, black conservative thought has witnessed a remarkable growth in popularity as an increasing number of blacks publicly embrace and espouse political conservatism. This alone may provide a reason for questioning whether this common definition captures fully the richness and complexity of the black conservative political tradition. But given the increasing prominence of black conservatives in social, political, and economic life, and the shift to the right in American politics more generally, it is imperative that we reflect upon the principles and ideas that underlie black conservative thought and the critical implications they pose for African Americans seeking new political alternatives and strategies in the post–civil rights era.

When it comes to understanding modern black conservatism, most commentators identify the Fairmont Conference in 1980 as the most crucial moment of its genesis. Organized by leading white Republicans one month after Ronald Reagan's successful bid for the American presidency, the Fairmont Conference brought together leading conservative thinkers, black and white, who were thought to be particularly sympathetic to the emerging Republican agenda for managing American race relations. The objectives of the conference were clear: to establish a cohort of prominent blacks who could speak to a new conservative thrust in domestic race relations policy, with the hope that these new voices would emerge as viable alternatives to the leaders of the civil rights establishment. The conservative Institute for Contemporary Studies hosted the event in San Francisco, and attorney Edwin Meese, then legal counsel to the president, and Tony Brown, a black conservative journalist, organized and edited the proceedings.

The influence of this conference on black politics proved quite dramatic. Philosophical conservatives, who ordinarily resided at the periphery of African American and white society, were summarily legitimated through the bestowal of governmental largess, private funding, and national public exposure. Consider the career trajectory of some of the black participants—Clarence Thomas, Clarence Pendleton, Samuel Pierce, Thomas Sowell, Glenn Loury, and Walter Williams. Shortly after the conference, the Reagan administration appointed several of these men to top government positions. Clarence Thomas was named to head the Equal Employment Opportunity Commission, Clarence Pendleton was named chairman of the Civil Rights Commission, and Samuel Pierce went to Housing and Urban Development. Sowell, Loury, and Williams obtained positions at conservative think tanks such as the American Enterprise Institute, Cato Institute, and Hoover Institution that fell in line behind the Republican Party's new African American strategy. With the government support and financial backing of the white conservative elites, black conservatism gained exposure and political momentum at a remarkable pace.

Predictably, scholars and historians reflecting upon the rapid ascension of black conservatives in the modern era tend to view black conservatives as not only a relatively recent development, but marginal, fabricated, and distinctly lacking an organic black constituency. Contemporary black conservatives are viewed as somewhat *sui generis,* if not simply contrived—either as a needed and salutary break from the civil rights establishment, or as outsiders devoid of any authentic contact with African American political traditions. Even among commentators who acknowledge historic expressions of conservatism within black politics, modern black conservatism is either excluded from this legacy or is grafted onto black political and social thought. In either case, black conservatism is viewed as a fringe and inauthentic voice of African American community interests.

This prevailing view of black conservatism, however, obscures the important, and often overlooked, legacy of black conservatives that has existed since the founding of the Republic. Indeed, from the founding until the early twentieth century—nearly 150 years—conservatism was the dominant mode of black political engagement with white society. Black conservatism, like any other intellectual movement, is perhaps best understood as a shifting, organic mood or consciousness developed over time by African Americans in response to specific lived conditions. In this sense, what it means to be a black conservative is necessarily contingent upon the political and cultural climate of a particular historic moment. Nevertheless, black conservatism has proved remarkably durable and consistent over the years, and modern black conservatism ought to be viewed as part of this important black political tradition.

The failure to appreciate black conservatism as a bona fide intellectual movement has particularly tragic consequences. As an initial matter, it has the effect of denying the intellectual and human agency of black conservatives. Black conservatives, past and present, have developed a distinctive political consciousness designed to promote black success in the face of tremendous obstacles. The prevailing view of black conservatives denigrates unnecessarily these historic and contemporary efforts by blacks to lead fulfilling and self-directed lives. The failure to recognize the historic tradition of black conservatism also reinforces the prevailing perception of blacks as a cultural and political monolith. An acknowledgment of the extended legacy of black conservatism highlights the rich diversity within African American political thought—a feature commonly overlooked in the historical and contemporary political literature. Finally, a narrow, ahistorical view of black conservatism not only renders twenty-first-century black conservative thought largely unintelligible from a cultural/political perspective, but leaves its enduring appeal among blacks essentially unexplained. By contrast, a deeper appreciation of the intellectual and cultural connections that modern black conservatives share with the larger political tradition of black conservatism helps to explain why black conservatism remains a coherent and compelling alternative for many African Americans.

In these pages, I want to advance a deepened account of black conservatism as an intellectual movement. I want to provide a framework for understanding black conservatism that not only links modern conservative figures to their historic counterparts but contextualizes the meaning of black conservatism by offering an account of what it means to be a black conservative that is contingent upon the political and cultural climate of a particular historic moment. In this way, one comes to understand black conservatism as a legitimate, organic intellectual tradition rather than a marginal and fabricated political oddity.

## Precepts of Black Conservatism

Defining black conservatism, or any intellectual movement for that matter, is a notoriously difficult task. To be sure, there is no single definition that adequately captures the philosophical complexity, analytic diversity, and pragmatic eclecticism that constitute black conservative thought. Of course, this difficulty merely underscores an important point that is overlooked in most discussions about ideology and politics: namely, that the dividing lines between categories of political points of view are rarely as crisp as we like to imagine.

Moreover, black conservatism, like any intellectual movement, takes shape against the backdrop of prevailing political, social, and economic realities. Regional and temporal variation profoundly shapes what it means to be a black conservative within any particular historical moment. Black conservative thought and what it means to be a black conservative are highly contingent, but perhaps no more so than any other intellectual movement or political tradition.

Despite the elusiveness of a categorical definition, one can nevertheless establish a framework for discussing black conservative positions by focusing upon its basic themes or precepts. Perhaps the most fundamental of these are a deep respect for the culture and institutions of American society and Western civilization and an abiding belief that blacks, through their own efforts, can thrive within American society. This is not to suggest that black conservatives are insensitive to or indifferent toward racism. Nor are black conservatives necessarily opposed to government intervention designed to make possible black political, social, and economic advancement. Rather, black conservatives choose to focus upon the prospect of individual, self-directed achievement in lieu of government action and formal legal redress. At bottom, black conservatives possess what might be described as an abiding faith in the benevolence of the American social order—a firm conviction that racism is fundamentally incompatible with the best of the American tradition of freedom, equality, and democracy.

Accordingly, black conservatives tend to adopt a posture of pragmatic optimism. They tend to accentuate the positive but remain firmly anti-utopian. Black conservatives acknowledge the hardships of the past —even as depicted by those proposing a radical restructuring of society— but tend to emphasize historic and contemporary accomplishments obtained in the face of obstacles. Indeed, since the early nineteenth century, black conservatives have insisted that a great deal of racial progress has been made in each succeeding generation, despite efforts by detractors to offer proof of black inferiority or argue the impossibility of black success in America. This unflinching optimism is perhaps best reflected by Booker T. Washington, who emphasized the magnificent progress of former slaves from 1877 to 1915—the same time period that most historians describe as the "nadir" of black history in the United States. Anti-utopianism and focus on present lived conditions leads black conservatives to fixate less upon the task of constructing an ideal society and more upon the struggle to make good within the society in which they find themselves. In this sense, many black conservatives choose to accept conditionally the present state of affairs with the conviction and hope that lived conditions will eventually improve. Others seek to operationalize plans to generate material improvement in lived conditions but accept the existing social and institutional limitations of American society.

For African Americans, this pragmatic optimism has usually entailed the acceptance of a subordinate and second-class status, coupled with the aspiration and, in some cases, a plan for improvement in lived conditions. Black conservatives are routinely criticized for this "accommodationist" posture, but it is important to understand that accommodationism stems from the black conservatives' understanding of the fragility of the status of blacks in American society and certain practical constraints, such as concerns about the way liberal arrangements will play out for all, including blacks themselves. Black conservatives appreciate that racial progress has come at a dear price and that genuine, tangible achievements ought not be sacrificed so readily in the idealistic pursuit of intangible, symbolic goals. Accommodationism represents a bargain in which black conservatives agree to play by the rules successfully in exchange for greater acceptance and inclusion in American society, or because it represents the best of available options. Black conservatives play the accommodationist role in good faith because, in the final analysis, they sincerely believe that attempts by white America to keep blacks from full participation in society will collapse under the weight of their proven worthiness of inclusion and the inherent universality of democratic principles.

In addition to a healthy respect for the transformative power of American and Western institutions, black conservatives tend to possess a deep appreciation for the virtues of capitalism. The ideology of business success has been one of the central themes of black conservative thought from James Forten and Booker T. Washington to such latter-day advocates of black entrepreneurship as Tony Brown and Earl Graves. Black conservatives are drawn to capitalism in part because capitalism, *as a theoretical matter,* is less exclusionary toward particular persons and traditions. Capitalist success is believed to rely not upon inherited position, but on what one can actually contribute to and benefit from others. Black conservatives may disagree on the relative importance of political and legal action, but they generally agree that the most effective and lasting strategy for collective self-advancement is through the large-scale multiplication of individual capitalist success stories.

Not surprisingly, the touchstone of black conservative discourse has been the African American Protestant ethic—a sort of middle-class morality. The foundations of success, in this view, are respectability, proper deportment, and a serious commitment to a healthy and productive lifestyle. The black conservative political philosophy tends to be highly moralistic and deferential to authority, both black and white. Indeed, as early as Richard Allen, conservative entrepreneurial moralism formed the basis of moral discourse within the black church. Allen, whose leadership rested upon his role as pastor and status as a successful businessman, repeatedly told his congregation that hard work and "middle-class propriety" were vital to free blacks and that blacks were morally and spiritually obliged to make good use of the privilege of freedom. This sentiment, rooted in Christianity, has proved far more ecumenical within black religion, evidenced by its central importance in the teachings of Louis Farrakhan and the Nation of Islam.

These conservative themes coalesce in what has become the dominant form of black conservative writing—the African American jeremiad. Although the black jeremiad acknowledges the pervasiveness of white racism, it is principally an exercise in self-critique. Directed at blacks, the jeremiad speaks to the failure of blacks to take full advantage of their opportunities, often blaming blacks for their laziness, parochialism, and fetish for panaceas. Perhaps the earliest example is David Walker's 1829 *Appeal,* in which he recounts the various forms of white and black "wretchedness." Recent works of Shelby Steele, Thomas Sowell, and comments by comedian Bill Cosby express similar sentiments. What each of these exponents of the genre share is a twofold conviction that problems and obstacles faced by blacks can be best mitigated or resolved by blacks themselves, and that white racism is just an irritant that lacks the determinant power to define African Americans individually or collectively.

## From Precepts to the Present

These precepts serve as the principal animating devices of black conservative thought past and present. In the chapters that follow, I will highlight the manner in which these precepts take shape and evolve within and against the prevailing social, political, and economic realities of American life—from its origins in antebellum Christian evangelism and petty entrepreneurialism to its contemporary expression in policy debates over affirmative action, law enforcement practices, and the effects of urban African American artistic and cultural expression. My hope is that the account of black conservative thought contained in these pages will signal the beginning of a new era of engagement with the black conservative tradition, past and present—a time in which liberals indulge the ideas and experiences of their conservative counterparts, and modern conservatives reflect critically upon the traditional source of their contemporary ideology. It is imperative that liberals and conservatives pursue this moment in the spirit of intellectual curiosity, reasoned debate, and a sincere interest in exploring the myriad pathways to racial empowerment—if not out of a deep respect for those who have struggled for racial justice in the past, then for the benefit of generations of African Americans to come.

# ONE

# The Origins of Black Conservative Thought

## Evangelicals, Entrepreneurs, and Booker T. Washington

Many liberals think of black conservatives, past and present, as willfully blinded by their ideological commitments. When it comes to matters of racial empowerment, liberals tend to believe that black conservatives either fail to appreciate or deliberately choose to ignore the prevailing social, political, and economic realities that affect, often quite negatively, the lives of black Americans. Liberals are thought to be particularly sensitive and responsive to lived conditions of everyday people. By contrast, black conservatives are frequently viewed as aloof and distant, if not supremely out of touch with members of the black community and the issues that prove most confounding to black people.

Like most stereotypes, the caricatured image of the black conservative and black conservative thought does not bear the weight of serious scrutiny. As surprising as it may seem, the origins of black conservative thought reveal a deep and sustained connection to the lived experiences of black Americans. Indeed, black conservative thought is sourced from the distinctly African American Christian evangelical tradition of antebellum northern black society. Black conservatism would later evolve from Christian evangelism to a more ecumenical conservative entrepreneurial moralism, which would serve as the touchstone for nineteenth-century black conservative thought in the North. Following the Civil War, a renewed commitment to reintegration of the South focused political attention on the unique circumstances of that region. It was during this period of energized politics within African American communities that a new and distinct form of black conservatism—one grounded in the "southern way of life"—emerged and eventually supplanted its northern counterpart as the dominant political philosophy in African American life in the early twentieth century.

This chapter reveals a distinctly *organic* quality to early black conservative thought. By this, I mean that the core insights of black conservatism are generated from within black communities and developed, nurtured, and sustained primarily by black thinkers. This idea that black conservative thought, properly understood, is an organic intellectual development sourced from black communities is one that I will return to in later chapters in discussing modern black conservatives, whose ideas arguably do not share this organic quality. From the outset, however, it is clear that black conservatives were organic leaders and enjoyed presumptive legitimacy within black communities by virtue of their communal ties.

## Black Conservatism and the
## Pursuit of American Exceptionalism

A second theme that plays out in the evolution of black conservative thought is the pursuit of American exceptionalism. To fully appreciate the early development of black conservative thought, one must appreciate that black conservative thought takes shape within and against the prevailing mythology of *American exceptionalism.* Americans have always thought of themselves and their country as special—an island of political and cultural distinctiveness set apart from the rest of the world. The United States is, like any other country, a geographic or political designation, but the dream of America, as conceived by the founders, was of a new land unconstrained by Old World cultural institutions and promises. Far more than a geographic or political marker, America represents an almost mythical space of unlimited human potential—a territory flush with unimaginable opportunity and promise. It comes as little surprise to learn that many Americans prefer to view themselves as a chosen people of sorts—a communal beacon of hope and living example of the richness that freedom and democracy have to offer.

This belief in American exceptionalism has created an odd relationship with history. Americans are quick to indulge in a moment of nostalgia to reflect upon America's greatness, but the attributes that made

America great were the twin commitments to break with its Old World past and, perhaps more important today, to focus intently upon improving present and future realities. Put differently, to reflect on America's past is to be reminded time and time again that the American vision of success is one thought to be achieved largely without reference to history. The grand lesson of American history is that our present state and future slate of possibilities are often influenced but rarely ever predetermined by our past. Our nation is relentlessly and unapologetically forward looking.

Of course, mythology, like stereotypes and caricatures, has a way of melting away under the sustained pressure of the real-world considerations. The belief in American exceptionalism—the shared set of myths, symbols, rituals, and practices—creates, at best, an illusion of a progressive and unified moral-spiritual community. Beneath this superficial gauze lies a host of critical and confrontational impulses and age-old conflicts rooted in race, ethnicity, class, religion, language, sex, and cultural differences.

Of all these conflicts, the problem of race has proven the most confounding for American society. Slavery, segregation, and modern vestiges of racial bias exemplify a reality very much in tension with the prevailing American cultural mythology of freedom, democracy, and human equality. Indeed, the central question animating much of the struggle for racial empowerment over the centuries has been how best to overcome racism and racial oppression so that racial minorities might enjoy the fruits of American exceptionalism on par with whites.

Liberals have self-consciously engaged this question for decades, but they were not alone in this endeavor. Indeed, the essential project of black conservatives, from the outset to the present, has been to reconcile this mythology of American exceptionalism with the pervading reality of racial suffering experienced by blacks. The reality of racial suffering—rooted in claims of native and cultural inferiority—strike a profoundly dissonant chord in a society in which one's past is not predictive of ones current status or future progress. In a manner strikingly consistent with the best of American mythology, black conservatives have sought to develop a body of thought, over time, to sustain the view that blacks, too, are among the chosen people with a historic mission to save and remake the world in the name of freedom and democracy. In this way, black conservative thought can be understood as a public assertion of the essential "Americanness" of blacks living in the United States.

## Christian Evangelism and the Origins
## of Black Conservative Thought

It is impossible to trace the organic pursuit of American exceptionalism by black conservatives without examining the contributions of Booker T. Washington. Indeed, Washington's famous exhortation that economic concerns should take precedence over civil rights and social and political concerns is perhaps the most popularly known expression of black conservatism. But although Washington may have been the most recognizable early exponent of black conservatism, his core insights were not entirely novel. Indeed, one can point to a number of historic actors who can arguably lay claim to being founding figures of black conservatism. And as it turns out, the first of these figures—the Reverend Jupiter Hammon—developed and advanced the precepts of black conservatism a full century before Washington.

Jupiter Hammon, a slave his entire life, was born in 1711 to the prominent Lloyd family of New York, a British clan whose substantial wealth was attained mainly through the slave trade and a variety of other transnational business transactions. As early as 1640, New York had the second largest slave population north of Maryland. By the 1780s, almost half of the slaves in the northern colonies lived in New York. Most of these slaves were concentrated near New York City. Hammon lived and died[1] at Lloyd Manor House, an estate located in Oyster Bay, a small Long Island cove. The 1728 census reported that "there were 41 men, 27 women, 17 boys, and 26 girls" counted as African slaves residing in the community. Slaves owned by Long Island members of the Anglican Church were schooled by a handful of British missionaries, initially through periodic sermons by missionary Robert Jenney but later in a formal schooling environment established by missionary Daniel Denton. Given the Lloyd family's British roots and connections with the Anglican Church, it is likely that Hammon received the bulk of his formal education at the hands of these two British missionaries.

Hammon was the first published African American writer.[2] Beginning in 1760, Hammon published four poems, two essays, and one sermon that addressed the full range of sociopolitical questions facing African Americans. Although Hammon's work has received remarkably little attention, even among historians of African American literature,[3] one finds within his work some of the earliest expressions of black conservative thought.

Hammon's conservatism, rooted in his strong religious convictions, is perhaps best exemplified by his ambiguous stance on the slavery issue. Hammon urged slaves not to resist their masters, and to focus on the more important task of living a proper life and seeking salvation from God. In "An Address to the Negroes in the State of New York," delivered in 1787, Hammon urged his audience

> to think very little of bondage in this life; for your thinking can do no good. If God designs to set us free, he will do it on his own time and way; but think of your bondage to sin and Satan, and do not rest until you are delivered from it.[4]

Political resistance and agitation was unimportant to Hammon, who asked rhetorically "What is forty, fifty or sixty years, compared to eternity?"

Hammon, of course, never defended slavery, yet throughout his writings, he expressed acceptance of slavery as one of the various worldly institutions that must be dealt with until God's return. Indeed, Hammon believed that it was the Christian duty of all slaves to not only lead chaste and temperate lives, but to heed the words of Paul in Ephesians 6:5 and remain obedient to their masters. Referencing Paul's pronouncement, "Servants, be obedient to them that are your masters according to the flesh, with fear and trembling, in singleness of your heart, as until Christ," Hammon declared:

> Here is God's plain command for us to obey our masters. It may seem hard for us, if we think our masters wrong in holding us as slaves, to obey in all things, but who of us dares to dispute with God! He has commanded us to obey, and we ought to do it cheerfully and freely.

Rebelliousness, according to Hammon, carried with it the risk of sinful self-pride.

Hammon's views on the role of free blacks was similarly infused with providentialism. Freedom, in Hammon's view, was as much a privilege as a right. Indeed, Hammon is perhaps the earliest known proponent of the distinctly African American Protestant ethic. According to Hammon, free blacks bore the responsibility to uphold moral standards and remain industrious in order to dispel prevailing notions about the natural inferiority of blacks and the concomitant inability to manage their personal affairs. As Hammon once preached:

> If you do not use your freedom to promote the salvation of your souls, it will not be of any lasting good to you.... If you are idle and take to the bad courses, you will hurt those of your brethren who are slaves and do all in your power to prevent their being free.

For Hammon, living an ethical and productive life was the surest path to exposing the hypocrisy of white America's disrespect for blacks and failure to live up to its own ethical and religious ideals. As Hammon remarked:

> One great reason that is given by some for not freeing us, I understand, is that we should not know how to take care of ourselves and should take to bad courses, that we should be lazy and idle, and get drunk and steal.... Let me beg of you then, for the sake of your own good and happiness in time and for eternity, and for the sake of your poor brethren who are still in bondage, to "lead a quiet and peaceable life in all goodness and honesty."

Hammon's views surely diverge from later exponents of black conservatism, who focused more on the present than the afterlife. However, in Hammon, and in much of black conservatism, one finds a preference for a slow, organic, and moralistic program of black improvement premised upon cooperation rather than confrontation and conflict with whites.

The idea that an intellectual movement—black conservatism—might locate its origins in the religious writings of a slave runs counter to conventional assumptions, attitudes, and beliefs about the social status and intellectual capacity of African slaves. Conventional wisdom regarding the profound intellectual inferiority of slaves and their deeply constrained human agency often reinforces the false impression of slaves as mere "draft animals" who lacked full humanity. The story of Jupiter Hammon offers, among other things, an important counternarrative. Hammon's writings highlight that slaves did not fundamentally question their humanity and understood that they possessed the full range of thoughts, emotions, and aspirations that all humans enjoy. Society and laws aspired to deny the essential humanity of slaves. But Hammon's writings aptly demonstrate that this was a failed enterprise. More important, rather than confirm the lack of humanity of slaves, the attitudes and laws—at least from the perspective of slaves themselves—revealed a crucial moral failing on the part of dominant society. Hammon's affirmation of his own humanity and that of his fellow slaves in the face of efforts to deny the same provides one the earliest and most dramatic examples of early African American intellectual and cultural resolve. This cultural resolve to proclaim the essential humanity of blacks would inform black conservative thought for many years to come.

### From Christian Evangelism to Conservative Entrepreneurial Moralism: The Lifework of Richard Allen

Hammon, of course, spoke little of the material world beyond preaching a strong work ethic. However, the black conservative tradition, rooted in Christian evangelism, would soon embrace ideas of economic determinism as early black conservatives came to realize that racial empowerment necessitated *material* as well as *spiritual* uplift. The earliest expression of this vital merger of spiritualism and materialism appears in the teachings and lifework of Richard Allen. Allen, cofounder of the Free African Society and founder and first bishop of the African Methodist Episcopal Church, was born into slavery in Philadelphia, Pennsylvania, on February 14, 1760. His master, Benjamin Chew, was a prominent Philadelphia lawyer and chief justice of the Commonwealth from 1774 to 1777. Early in his childhood, Allen, his parents, and his siblings were sold to Stokely Sturgis, a Delaware planter whom Allen described as "an unconverted man ... but ... what the world called a good master." Despite his master's "tenderhearted" ways, Richard longed to be free, "for slavery is a bitter pill, notwithstanding we had a good master." Allen had personally tasted the bitterness of slavery when his mother and three of his five siblings were sold to satisfy the debts of his master.

Like Hammon, Allen's conservatism was rooted in religious faith, albeit the teaching of the Methodist Church. His ascension within the Methodist Church began in 1777, when he was formally converted by Freeborn Garretson, a charismatic white itinerant preacher. Garretson also converted Allen's master and convinced him that on Judgment Day, slaveholders would be "weighted in the balance, and ... found wanting." His newly repentant master encouraged Allen to purchase his freedom and granted Allen permission to pursue gainful employment. Allen obtained work as a day laborer, sawing cordwood and driving a wagon during the Revolutionary War. He eventually earned enough money to purchase his freedom, and eventually took the surname "Allen" to signify his free status.

For the next six years, Allen worked as a "licensed exhorter," preaching Methodist teachings to blacks and whites from New York to South Carolina. In 1786, Allen was appointed as an assistant minister of the faith by Francis Ashbury, the first American bishop of the Methodist Church, and was asked to serve the African American members of the racially mixed congregation of St. George's Methodist Church in Philadelphia. The appointment proved a mixed blessing, as Allen was required to preach at 5 A.M. so that his services would not interfere with those reserved for white members of the congregation. At the same time, Allen grew particularly sensitive to the unique spiritual and material needs of black church members. It was at this moment that Allen "saw the necessity of erecting a place of worship for the colored people."

White church elders harshly condemned Allen's plan for the creation of a separate and, perhaps more important, self-directed black ministry within the church. Allen recounted that church elders "used very degrading and insulting language to us, to try and prevent us from going on. We all belonged to St. George's church. . . . We felt ourselves much cramped; but my dear Lord was with us, and we believed, if it was his will, the work would go on, and that we would be able to succeed in building the house of the Lord."

In an effort to reconcile his faith with his racial identity, Allen, within a year of his service at St. George's, joined ranks with the Reverend Absalom Jones, ex-slaves, and Quaker philanthropists to create the Free African Society, a nondenominational fellowship and mutual aid society to benefit "free Africans and their descendants." The Free African Society was arguably the first mutual aid society dedicated to the uplift of black Americans. The preamble, dated April 12, 1787, explains that the original intent of Allen and Jones was "to form some kind of religious society [for] the people of their complexion whom they beheld with sorrow, because of their irreligious and uncivilized state." The Articles of the Free

African Society, approved on May 17, 1787, called for members "to advance one shilling in silver Pennsylvania currency a month" for a year, after which they will aid "the needy of this Society ... provided, the necessity is not brought on them by their own imprudence." Membership in the Free African Society required adherence to a strict code of conduct: "no drunkard nor disorderly person [will] be admitted as a member, and if any should prove disorderly after having been received, the said disorderly person shall be disjointed from us if there is not amendment, by being informed by two of the members, without having any of his subscription money returned." Furthermore, in order to receive benefits, the widow of a deceased member was also required to "[comply] with the rules thereof."

The Free African Society, which reflected Allen's fundamental commitment to the principles of self-help, self-determination, and self-reliance, institutionalized many of the precepts of black conservative thought that would grow and evolve over the next 150 years. Indeed, the society became the prototype for hundreds of self-help and benevolent organizations in the North, and it served as an important historical antecedent to southern black conservative institutions such as Booker T. Washington's Tuskegee Institute and his network of black trade and professional associations. The Free African Society grew in stature and community prominence, eventually becoming the African Episcopal Church of Philadelphia.

Despite the success of the Free African Society, Allen continued with his Methodist ministry. He rejected an appointment as pastor of the African Episcopal Church, informing his supporters that "I could not be anything else but a Methodist, as I was born and awakened under them." Yet his deep commitment to racial empowerment did not square with prevailing white Methodist practices. Although most white Methodists in the 1790s supported the emancipation of Negro slaves, they did not treat free blacks as equals. They refused to allow African Americans to be buried in the congregation's cemetery and, in a famous incident in 1792, banished them to a newly built gallery of St. George's Methodist Church.

The increasing racial hostility of the white congregation, however, did not shake Allen's faith in the transformative power of Methodist teachings. Exuding the anti-utopian pragmatism that would come to define black conservative thought, Allen remained convinced of the essential goodness of the Western religious institution and its teachings and viewed these events as an opportunity to merge religious entrepreneurship with racial empowerment. In the spirit of conservative entrepreneurial moralism, Allen decided to form his own congregation consistent with his staunch belief in the principles of self-help, self-determination, and self-reliance. He gathered a group of ten black Methodists in a local blacksmith's shop in the increasingly black southern section of the city, converting it to the Bethel African Methodist Episcopal Church. Although the Bethel church opened in a ceremony led by Bishop Francis Asbury in July 1794, its tiny congregation worshiped "separate from our white brethren."

In the Bethel church, Allen institutionalized the growing desire among African Americans to control their religious lives—to exercise the power, in Allen's words, "to call any brother that appears to us adequate to the task to preach or exhort as a local preacher, without the interference of the [Methodist] Conference." By 1795, the congregation of Allen's church numbered 121; a decade later it had grown to 457, and by 1813 it had reached 1,272. When white Methodist ministers began to retreat from their antislavery principles and attempt to curb the autonomy of African American congregations, Allen responded by adding an "African Supplement" to his church's articles of incorporation. In 1816, Bethel won legal recognition as an independent church. In the same year, Allen and representatives from four other black Methodist congregations in the mid-Atlantic states met at the Bethel church to organize a new denomination—the African Methodist Episcopal Church. Allen was chosen as the first bishop of the church, the first fully independent black denomination in America.

In his capacity as bishop, Allen quickly became a leading religious and civic leader in black Philadelphian society. He had succeeded in charting a separate religious identity for African Americans grounded in the hybrid notion of conservative entrepreneurial moralism. However, Allen was not a political separatist. He possessed an abiding faith in the American institutions of church and government, and he was deeply skeptical of the radical idea that blacks should seek to colonize in Africa or remote parts of Canada. In a direct response to this suggestion, offered by William Thornton on behalf of the American Colonization Society, Allen openly declared his patriotism and desire to pursue racial empowerment on American soil:

Not doubting the sincerity of many friends who are engaged in that cause; yet we beg leave to say, that it does not meet with our approbation. However great the debt which these United States may owe to injured Africa, and however unjustly her sons have been made to bleed, and her daughters to drink of the cup of affliction, still we who have been born and nurtured on this soil, we, whose habits, manners, and customs are the same in common with other Americans, can never consent to take our lives in our hands, and be the bearers of the redress offered by that Society to that much afflicted country.

Rather than seek refuge from racism in foreign lands, blacks should pursue their future in America, Allen preached. He never ceased to remind his congregation that hard work and "middle-class propriety" were vital to the success of free blacks in America and, like Hammon, that blacks were morally and spiritually obliged to make good use of the privilege of freedom.

For Allen, however, the pathway to spiritual and economic empowerment was education. Allen's thoroughgoing support for the formal education of blacks would, in many ways, prefigure the emphasis upon increasing educational opportunities within black conservative thought in the decades that followed. In 1795 he opened a day school for sixty children, and in 1804 founded the "Society of Free People of Colour for Promoting the Instruction and School Education of Children of African Descent." By 1811 there were no fewer than eleven black schools in the city.

### Moral Deportment, Business Savvy, and Social Advancement: The Legacy of James Forten

If Hammon and Allen can be understood as preaching the basics of black conservatism, James Forten provided a living example of black conservative success through studious adherence to those precepts. Indeed, Forten, a Philadelphia abolitionist, entrepreneur, and civic leader, was a symbol of the possibility of African American moral deportment, business savvy and social advancement. Born free on September 2, 1766, to a working-class family, Forten received minimal formal education and acquired an apprenticeship to a local Philadelphia sail maker. Forten excelled, moving from apprentice to graduate to foreman and eventually to master in his own right. He eventually earned the status of Philadelphia's preeminent sail maker and, through judicious investment of his profits, became a leading moneylender in the region. Forten would convert his newfound wealth into political power, becoming one of the leading civic leaders in Philadelphia.

Like most black conservatives, Forten was deeply patriotic. As a child, he gathered with others in the Philadelphia State House Yard for the first reading of the Declaration of Independence. The struggle for independence left a strong impression on Forten, who was acutely aware that men of color had fought to establish the Republic. Indeed, Forten himself had served as a powder boy on a ship during the war. Forten's writings express dismay that the memory of blacks' contribution to the war effort had survived little more than a generation. In a letter to William Lloyd Garrison, Forten lamented that America was "the land that gave us birth, and which many of us fought for, during the war which established our Independence.... All this appears to be forgotten now."[5] Whereas African Americans were mired in slavery or second-class treatment, "emigrants from every other Country are permitted to seek asylum here from oppression," Forten noted. In an open letter to the Philadelphia Senate, Forten assailed what he believed to be deep-seated hypocrisy by whites who prohibited blacks from celebrating Independence Day:

> It is a well known fact that black people, on certain days of the publick jubilee, dare not be seen after twelve o'clock in the day, upon the field to enjoy the times; for no sooner do the fumes of that potent devil, Liquor, mount into the brain, than the poor black is assailed like the destroying Hyena or the avaricious Wolf! I allude particularly to the FOURTH OF JULY!—Is it not wonderful, that the day set apart for the festival of Liberty, should be abused by the advocates of Freedom, in endeavouring to sully what they profess to adore.

Unlike his good friend Paul Cuffe, a wealthy African American committed to resettling blacks in West Africa, Forten was thoroughly convinced that the future of black people was in America. He was a thoroughgoing integrationist who practiced what he preached, employing equal numbers of whites and blacks at his sail loft. When a visitor to the loft commented upon this fact, Forten responded, "Here, you see what may be done, and ought to be done in our country at large."

To that end, Forten remained a vocal advocate of the African American Protestant ethic—temperance, education, and social refinement—and steadfastly believed that, if given the chance, all blacks could compete as equals in American society. Forten steadfastly believed that the Constitution's framers believed in the equality of all men, regardless of color. Commenting upon the framers' intentions, Forten observed:

> It cannot be that [they] . . . intended to exclude us from its benefits, for just emerging from unjust and cruel emancipation, their souls were too much affected by their own deprivations to commence the reign of terrour over others. They knew we were deeper skinned than they were, but they acknowledged us as men, and found that many an honest heart beat beneath a dusky bosom. They felt that they had no more authority to enslave us, than England had to tyrannize over them. [They had declared "all men" free without reference to race] because they never supposed it would be made a question whether we were men or not.

However, Forten was not an egalitarian in the sense of believing that all people should be treated alike. Although committed to the revolutionary ideals of freedom and equality, Forten took social responsibilities seriously and thought that equal opportunity should be provided only to those who lived a temperate life.

In response to a rash of street crimes committed by blacks, Forten joined other black civic leaders in condemning lawlessness within the African American community. As Forten recounted, we are "deeply impressed with sorrow for the recent depredations . . . and burdened with shame that they should have been traced to that unfortunate portion of society to which we belong." For Forten, these events imposed a duty upon upstanding blacks "to vindicate our character as a community" because "the better sort" had "happiness, privileges, and reputation at stake." Speaking on behalf of the community leaders, Forten hoped that the public would not "withdraw their confidence [in us and] leave to ignominity and misery all that is honest or respectable among us."

To that end, Forten proposed that the "better sort" of blacks prevail upon the mayor of Philadelphia to provide assistance in closing down the "tippling-houses, gaming-houses, dance and eating-houses," and other dens of vice. As Forten explained,

> As lovers of order, friends of morality and religion, we detest vice; and while as Christians, our hearts bleed over the perpetrators of crime, we are determined, strenuously, to exert ourselves in bringing the guilty to justice.

Forten was well aware of the precarious position of blacks in Philadelphia. Not surprisingly, the promotion of racial harmony figured prominently in his civic reform efforts. As Philadelphia's racial climate began to decline with the rise in race riots in the 1830s, locals began to criticize the black elite for failing to mount an effective response. Nevertheless, Forten implored blacks not to meet violence with violence. Peaceful coexistence, he maintained, would occur only through self-control, moral reform, and a strong work ethic. The key, for Forten, was a sound education. "It is to the ... defective system of instruction, as it now exists among us, that we must in a great measure attribute the contemptible and degraded station which we occupy in society."

But Forten also advocated better education for white Americans, in large part because he believed that reason ultimately undermined prejudice. A crucial failing of white liberal education, according to Forten, was that whites remained largely ignorant of the cultural contributions of and successes within the African American community. Forten was convinced that if he could collect enough facts and figures to "prove" that blacks were industrious and law-abiding, properly educated whites would be convinced by such evidence and presumably would change their opinions about blacks. Over the years, Forten endeavored to collect stories of black successes and respectability in Philadelphia and across the nation for the explicit purpose of dispelling the myth of black inferiority.

For Forten, a sound education not only served to promote harmony but also worked as a unifying force and a basis for universal respectability. It provided a common ground for interaction and helped to dispel the conventional belief that intellect was determined by race. Not surprisingly, Forten's arguments went largely unheard. Indeed, his liberal contemporaries tended to view educated blacks, including Forten himself, as truly exceptional prodigies rather than merely educated persons. Forten resented "the well meant, though judicious, and sometimes really impolite notice that is taken, if any of us happen to do, or say anything like other people." At bottom, Forten simply wanted blacks to be viewed like every other person in America. As Forten himself pointed out, "If we have the same opportunity's [sic] of education, and improvement, what is there to prevent our being just like others, who have these advantages?"

## Lessons on Black Conservatism
## from Hammon, Forten, and Allen

The teachings and lifework of Hammon, Allen, and Forten provide an important window into the early development of black conservative thought in American race relations. From the outset, black conservatism was steeped in moral discourse. For Hammon and Allen, the guiding moral force of black conservatism was rooted in Christian evangelism and Methodist teachings, respectively. For Forten, the touchstone of black conservatism was strict adherence to an ethical and temperate lifestyle. At bottom, however, one can say quite confidently that all three men viewed the foundation of racial progress as resting upon a politics of respectability, proper deportment, and a serious commitment to a healthy and productive lifestyle.

The deep moralism within early black conservative thought reveals another important feature—a pronounced deference to authority, both black and white. Respectability and proper deportment, for early black conservatives, yielded a profound acceptance of current racial conditions. In the work of Hammon, Allen, and Forten, one finds the roots of accommodationism, famously expounded upon by Booker T. Washington after the Civil War. For Hammon, accommodationism in the real world was simply the price one paid for everlasting happiness in the afterlife. By contrast, Allen and Forten saw accommodationism as a necessary strategy to deescalate racial tension in service of a greater overarching aspiration of promoting black economic success and eventual inclusion in American society. For both men, however, their quintessential conservative outlook on American race relations was distinctly anti-utopian. They both understood the pathway to racial progress to entail the pursuit of pragmatic, incremental, but tangible gains.

Allen's and Forten's desire for greater inclusion in American society—particularly in the civic and economic arenas—highlights the deep respect for Western institutions of government and public education central to early black conservative thought. Unlike Hammon, who was perhaps at best agnostic on the question of patriotism, we see a deep commitment to American governance in the lifework of Allen and Forten. Indeed, the essential thrust of their conservatism was that reliance upon Western institutions—churches, local government, civil organizations, and the capitalist economy—provided all the means necessary to achieve racial progress. The roots of the black conservative credo of self-reliance are seen in Forten's insistence that blacks could learn to lead productive, self-directed lives if they were to embrace the best of what American society had to offer.

In Hammon, Allen, and Forten, one also bears witness to the creation of a distinctly black conservative agenda for American race relations. For early black conservatives, a fair opportunity to demonstrate worthiness of greater inclusion and to achieve economic success took precedence over the attainment of equal rights and substantive equality. Social worthiness necessitated not only the firm embrace of a politics of respectability, but a harsh condemnation of those who did not subscribe to conservative morality, reflected in strong endorsement of legal measures that criminalized "vice"—even when those measures were disproportionately applied to blacks. At the same time, however, black conservatives generally opposed government intervention in service of promoting black progress. For black conservatives, the surest and safest path to racial progress—be it economic success or greater inclusion in white society—was through one's own effort.

The black conservative agenda for American race relations proved appealing to local white leaders. However, it is important to realize that the conservative vision proved compelling to blacks as well. Hammon's views, though largely overlooked by historians, provided the basis for his moral and civil leadership among free blacks and slaves in Long Island. Likewise, the organic appeal of Richard Allen rested upon a belief, shared by his congregation and members of Philadelphia society, that blacks could live spiritually and materially productive and self-directed lives. Similarly, Forten's credibility as a civil and business leader in Philadelphia among blacks was unquestioned. Early black conservatives were indisputably organic leaders, chosen by their native constituencies, and enjoyed extensive backing within their communities. As black conservative thought grew in prominence, its leading proponents would enjoy substantial backing of an organic black constituency as well as growing support from the white establishment.

## Booker T. Washington and Post-Reconstruction Black Conservative Thought

Black conservative ideology, consigned mainly to the North prior to the Civil War, was powerfully shaped by prevailing views on federalism, Christian evangelism, and the full array of conservative forces in northern society. To be sure, northern black conservatives desired full civic and political equality. However, the preeminent focus was on obtaining the right to participate in the emerging industrial economy of the North. As a result, distinctly southern concerns, such as the agricultural basis of the southern economy, poverty, and lack of social, political, and economic advancement among the masses of black southerners, went largely unaddressed. This would change, however, as the Civil War and a renewed commitment to reintegration of the South focused political attention on the unique circumstances of southern American society.

Emancipation brought forth a flourishing of black political thought, ranging the entire ideological spectrum, although the hopes of African Americans would be frustrated by the turn of the twentieth century. It was during this period of energized politics within African American communities that a new and distinct form of black conservatism—one grounded in the "southern way of life"—emerged and eventually supplanted its northern counterpart as the dominant political philosophy in African American life in the early twentieth century.

The leading exponent of this new southern black conservatism was Booker T. Washington. Born a slave in Hale's Ford, Virginia, Washington worked in salt furnaces and coal mines as a child to help support his family after emancipation. At age sixteen, Washington left home and began formal schooling at the Hampton Institute in Virginia, where he supported himself by working as the school janitor.

As a child of Reconstruction, Washington was imbued with a deep skepticism of political and legal rights. The northern liberal agenda for the postbellum South emphasized a maximization of individual rights, legal equality, political participation, and the transformation of the mass of freed slaves from peasant plantation workers to free labors and petty entrepreneurs participating as equals in the southern economy. After 1877, it became increasingly clear to black southerners that this bestowal of rights was far more limited and, indeed, mutable than liberal proponents cared to admit. The gap between northern idealism and southern reality grew, with the erosion of newly acquired rights and the rise of racial terror and violence toward blacks.

For Washington, economic advancement seemed to be a surer, and less reversible, means for blacks to progress. But unlike his northern counterparts, Washington did not see black economic progress coming about through greater social integration with white southern society. Washington was convinced that the great masses of black southerners would remain in the South, and he therefore developed an approach to racial progress that would not unnecessarily provoke a hostile white response. Washington saw progress for blacks taking place within southern black institutions, which by definition were less reliant upon the favor of whites. At the same time, Washington eschewed the radical individualism of northern black conservatives and promoted the idea of collective racial enterprise. Blacks, he argued, must establish institutions and work within an institutional framework for the betterment of the "race" as a collective. By working within this framework of segregated southern institutions, blacks would demonstrate capacity that would eventually transform the racial status quo. As Washington was fond of saying, "The black man can sooner conquer Southern prejudice than Yankee competition."

Conquering southern prejudice, for Washington, began with the building of personal character. Like Forten, Washington believed education to be essential to building character. However, Washington was deeply skeptical of traditional liberal arts education. Indeed, Washington never ceased to remind listeners that "not all knowledge is power." Instead, he viewed education as a means of acquiring practical skills and strong work habits. Agricultural work and craft work were the prototypes of good education, according to Washington, precisely because they required attention to quality workmanship, routine, and detail—what Washington called "the value of little things." Education of this sort built character because it imbued students with common sense, practicality, and concrete experience rather than immerse them in an alien and elitist educational framework.

The idea of building character through industrial training, it turned out, was consistent with the needs of a growing industrial economy. Industrialism brought many workers onto commercial farms and into factories for the first time. Many had been used to working on their own schedules, at their own pace. Now they were working for employers who demanded accountability for time worked and staunchly regulated leisure time during business hours. Business owners shared the skepticism held by many intellectuals that not every person was capable of reading, writing, and abstract thinking. However, the owners understood that sound industrial education for working-class children might serve to enforce good behavior and classroom habits. This, in turn, might provide the groundwork for good factory discipline.

From the perspective of Washington and other proponents, industrial education for blacks presented a win-win situation. It not only served to build character; it prepared blacks for a practical life. Of course, it was equally true that support for industrial education for blacks was also motivated by contemporary views on the intellectual and professional capacities of blacks in particular. Practical trades, such as carpentry, were more immediately useful to working-class persons than was proficiency in Latin or Greek. But support for industrial education was also premised upon a belief that most blacks could not be expected to do anything more advanced than manual and semiskilled labor.

In any event, at the time of his death, Washington left behind a network of institutions that preserved his views on racial advancement. Of particular note were the Tuskegee Institute and the National Negro Business League. The Tuskegee Institute embodied Washington's pragmatic, anti-utopian philosophy of self-help, education, morality, entrepreneurship, and hard work. The National Negro Business League, founded in 1910, served as a coordinating center for his vast network of confidants, political operatives, and business leaders to spread black conservatism in both the North and the South. With the blessing of leading conservative white philanthropists, such as John D. Rockefeller, Collis P. Huntington, and Julius Rosenwald, Washington expanded his web of influence and power with the creation of the National Teachers Association, the National Negro Press Association, Negro Farmers Association, and the Negro Organization Society. The last organization, which he founded in 1913, epitomized Washington's commitment to self-help. Its motto, "Better homes, better schools, better health, and better farms" was particularly appealing to white leaders such as President Woodrow Wilson, Hampton Institute President H. B. Frissell, University of Virginia President Edwin Alderman, and Virginia Governor Henry C. Stuart.

Although Washington's pragmatism made him skeptical of the value of rights, he understood well the importance of obtaining political power. Like most southerners, Washington viewed politics as essentially a local affair in which one's civic authority was earned over time. The lessons of Reconstruction were clear to Washington: no blanket bestowal of rights, granted without reference to personal character or individual capacity, could provide lasting political clout. Political power, Washington maintained, came about only after one's authority was obtained and recognized in some other area. "The masses of Negroes were given the ballot without effort on their part and they soon lost it," observed Washington. "The masses of Negroes are gradually [re]gaining the ballot *through their own efforts,* and are likely to keep it when so gained."

Washington was criticized for his inability to take note—at least publicly—that black disenfranchisement functioned as a brake on educational opportunities and entrepreneurship, and that the lack of formal political empowerment not only exposed blacks to Klan violence but worked to entrench Jim Crow laws. For Washington, however, elected representation guaranteed little by way of political influence, let alone racial progress. Political power was a byproduct of economic power, moral authority, and character—perhaps in that order. As Washington once remarked to a Chicago audience, "There are other ways of getting into politics than by holding public office."

It would be a mistake to conclude, however, that Washington's eschewal of an open civil rights agenda and promotion of industrial education marked him as a "sellout." To some degree, it was simply a matter of emphasis. For instance, although Washington encouraged blacks to stay out of politics, he strongly opposed black disenfranchisement behind the scenes and privately financed "test cases" in many southern states to challenge the constitutionality of restrictive voting laws. Though Washington supported literacy tests for voters, he publicly urged that such tests be applied fairly, and he signed petitions to state legislatures to oppose bills that would disenfranchise blacks unfairly.

The same is true regarding Washington's stance on industrial education. For instance, Washington argued that industrial education should come first so that southern blacks could gain basic schooling and useful skills to become productive members of society. Yet, he also acknowledged that some blacks should pursue more formal higher education. Indeed, Washington sent his own daughter to Wellesley College and later to an institute in Berlin, Germany, to study music. Furthermore, Tuskegee, at the time, was one of the largest employers of black college graduates. Thus, while Washington envisioned blacks rising up from the bottom, he also understood the importance of having sound black leadership, and he recruited superbly educated members of the black community—what W.E.B. DuBois might refer to as members of the "Talented Tenth"—to lead his various institutions.

## Second-Generation Washingtonians and Post-Reconstruction Black Conservative Thought

Most historians contend that Washingtonian black conservatism faded with his death in 1915 and the later Great Migration to the North. Indeed, much of the historical focus on black political thought shifts from the southern accommodationism of Washington to the National Association for the Advancement of Colored People (NAACP) in the North and the rise of the civil rights movement. But the prevailing narrative fails to account for the extended legacy of Washington southern political life. Although second-generation Washingtonians would move black conservatism in new and interesting directions, their underlying commitment to black distinctiveness in southern life remained fundamentally intact.

Throughout the early twentieth century, black conservatives remained power brokers in the South, dominating the major institutions of black society—churches, schools, newspapers, and businesses. From newspaper editors such as P. B. Young in Norfolk, Virginia, to businessmen such as C. C. Spaulding in Durham, North Carolina, black conservatives functioned as organic leaders within the black community and exercised powerful roles as black opinion makers. Whereas northern black intellectuals asserted outsider status as a badge of authenticity and authority to mount a movement for racial progress, southern black conservatives held fast to the tenets of negotiation, compromise, and conciliation and remained comfortable with their positions of authority within southern black institutional life.

But second-generation Washingtonians did depart from their founder's precepts in important ways. Robert Russa Moton, Washington's successor at Tuskegee, provides an important window into the transformations of black conservatism during the interwar years. Like Washington, Moton believed that education was crucial to black advancement. However, Moton disagreed with Washington that primacy should be given to vocational education. Under Moton's tenure, Tuskegee became a degree-granting institution. Moton also disagreed with Washington's famous opposition to NAACP efforts to secure formal equality of rights and legal redress, and he would later cooperate with NAACP initiatives to a degree that Washington would not have countenanced. That said, Moton remained committed to the basic precept of southern black conservatism, which held that the proper place for blacks was in the South, within black-run institutions.

Perhaps the greatest departure, however, was Moton's openness to challenging southern white authority and in confronting racism. Washington's commitment to accommodationism made him unwilling to confront the ugliness of southern race relations head on. Indeed, his most straightforward attack on segregation laws was published after his death in "My View of Segregation Laws," in which he argued that mandated segregation in housing did little to promote good relations between whites and blacks. But Washington preferred to protest behind the scenes, secretly supporting a variety of progressive racial efforts in the North and in the South, including lawsuits against discrimination in housing, voting, and jury selection.

By contrast, Moton offered a more direct challenge to black subordination. In his most extended discussion of race, *What the Negro Thinks,* Moton argued that all forms of state-imposed segregation in housing and public accommodations were "undemocratic and unchristian, as unfair in principle as in practice." Like Washington, Moton pointed to segregation on common carriers, in schools and housing, in voting, and in jury selection as particularly worthy of condemnation. Yet Moton's criticism evinces an anger and resentment not seen in Washington's work. Moton suggested that the grand injustices of segregation were quite palpable, and that if most southern blacks, for prudent reasons, reacted calmly to such indignities, it was only to mask the anger that burned deep within. Indeed, Moton spoke admiringly of blacks who responded with uncontrolled rage—race martyrs who turned violently if not suicidally on whites. As Moton explained, blacks generally stand in awe of such martyrs and "the defiant spirit that burned itself out in violent protest." Though he never explicitly endorsed such actions, he clearly understood the frustrated dignity beneath the rage that fueled them.

But Moton's outrage at segregation did not necessarily lead him to support the NAACP's liberal agenda of pursuing formal equality and legal rights. Moton shared Washington's deep sense of racial pride, and he steadfastly maintained that blacks, much like whites, preferred to associate with their own. The problem, according to Moton, was that in the United States, all forms of black association, "voluntary or otherwise," carried with it "persistent, insidious implications of inferiority." In a world unready to accept blacks on equal terms, Moton held firm to the idea that separate black institutions were invaluable to black racial progress: "Other things being equal, the Negro prefers to retain his self-esteem in a restricted sphere rather than accepting a larger freedom of movement under the implication of being tolerated." Like Washington, Moton focused on the progress made by blacks through the institutional framework, despite many obstacles, as a testament to their importance as a means of enhancing participation in southern civil society. Unlike integrated settings, in which blacks were forced to deal with matters of personal prejudice on an individual basis without collective assistance, separate institutions enabled blacks to gain strength from the racial collective and become better equipped to do battle if and when competition with whites became both possible and fruitful.

Second-generation Washingtonians such as Moton were vital to keeping black conservatism alive during the interwar period, and they drew a number of unlikely converts, including W.E.B. DuBois. DuBois found Moton's insistence on the centrality of black institutional life particularly compelling, and he cited this as one of his reasons for leaving the NAACP, an institution he helped found. In 1934, DuBois announced that he was severing his relationship with the NAACP because it so strongly opposed segregation in all its forms. Drawing upon the insights of Moton and his old nemesis Washington, DuBois argued that the failure to recognize the importance of black institutions in a world hostile to blacks was tantamount to "race suicide." The pragmatic gains achieved through black institutional life and the sense of pride and accomplishment in fashioning a self-directed black life, in DuBois's view, should not be so readily sacrificed in service of achieving more abstract legal concessions of formal equality.

In the post-Reconstruction era, black conservatism evolved into a remarkably robust and uniquely African American strategy to achieve racial progress. Like Hammon and Forten, Washington and his followers made explicit their normative commitment to accommodationism, with a strong preference for negotiated peaceful resolutions to racial conflict. But accommodationism in the South was very different from its counterpart in the North; it entailed an unprecedented commitment to racial separation in social, political, and economic life. So in the South, black conservatism transformed from a modest integrationist philosophy to one focused on the virtues of black community life and the promotion of black self-pride. These features of black conservatism would remain important components of black politics throughout the twentieth century, embraced by a number of prominent militant black nationalist movements, including Marcus Garvey's exhortation of black pride and his repatriation efforts of the 1920s, the midcentury rise of the Nation of Islam, and the Black Power movement of the 1970s.

These aspects of Washingtonian conservatism were not simply promulgated as a set of beliefs, however; they were reified and concretized within southern black institutional life. This is not to suggest that black conservatism had not been institutionalized in any meaningful sense before Washington. Black conservatism was certainly an institutional feature in northern black churches and civic organizations. However, with Washington's Tuskegee machine, black conservatism was instantiated in southern institutional life on an unprecedented scale. In this way, the creation of infrastructure for blacks to lead self-directed lives became an important touchstone of the emerging black conservative agenda for American race relations.

At the same time, black conservatism began to embrace more fully the anti-utopian pragmatism that would become a hallmark of twentieth-century black conservative thought. Whereas Hammon, Allen, and Forten trumpeted the virtues of a conventional liberal arts education as a means of achieving greater integration in northern white society, Washington and his followers endorsed a vocational education and practical skills that could be put to immediate use to achieve economic gains. However, it is important to understand that both the Washingtonians and their northern counterparts shared the same basic belief that the surest pathway to political empowerment was through the creation of a stable mode of economic empowerment.

The post-Reconstruction black conservative focus on economic empowerment signaled a partial retreat from the moralism that defined early black conservative thought. Staunch adherence to the precepts of Christian evangelism and temperance gave way to a more expansive conception of what it meant to live a life with character and dignity. Traditional emphasis on respectability and deportment remained essential components of black conservative thought, though funneled into an aspirational norm of middle-class morality, one centered on promoting a healthy and economically productive lifestyle.

Post-Reconstruction black conservatism proved remarkably appealing to great masses of black Americans. Like antebellum black conservatives, Washingtonians were organic leaders who enjoyed substantial backing by a largely southern black constituency throughout the early part of the twentieth century. The ascension of the NAACP to national prominence and the robust expansion of the civil rights movement would soon compete with and quickly overshadow the conservative political tradition within black communities. Although the interwar years marked a moment of decline in black conservative thought, it nevertheless remained a relevant part of the black political landscape. Indeed, black conservative thought would influence the full range of black political and social expression throughout the early twentieth century, including the Harlem Renaissance and burgeoning Black Nationalist Movement—both watershed cultural moments in black history not commonly associated with black conservatism.

# TWO

# The Dawn of the Twentieth Century

Black Conservatism's Peak and
W.E.B. DuBois's Dramatic Assault against It

The dawn of the twentieth century proved to be the high-water mark of conservatism in black American political expression. The precepts of black conservative thought—pragmatic optimism, accommodationism, respect for Western institutions, and middle- class morality—had been validated in the lived experience of black leaders and businessmen in the North and South for nearly a century. These precepts not only served as the central animating principles of black political discourse but defined the structure and character of leading black social, political, and economic institutions. The black American vision of social progress and engagement had begun to crystallize, and its predominant trait was conservatism.

From a modern vantage point, it is difficult to imagine a world in which black Americans, often viewed as an unflinchingly liberal and progressive community, were by and large proponents of conservatism. This is especially true of liberals, who typically interpret the epic struggle for black racial empowerment as one characterized by flagrant opposition to the American status quo, relentless agitation and protest, and as sustained challenge to the racial orthodoxy etched in American public and private institutions. From this perspective, the freedom struggle was and is a progressive movement, with a decisively liberal posture. Conservatism, by contrast, is generally understood as marginally, if at all, relevant to the task of racial empowerment. Indeed, for many liberals, the mere invocation of conservatism in connection with strategic discussions about racial empowerment is enough to raise questions about the legitimacy and sincerity of such a strategy, and cast doubt upon the credibility of the speaker.

Yet as the previous chapter makes clear, black conservatism once enjoyed a widespread presumption of credibility as a viable mode of racial empowerment. To be sure, there was substantial disagreement as to whether an empowerment agenda shaped by black conservative precepts that placed a premium on local economic gains at the expense of social and political equality would achieve ideal levels of freedom and equality. This disagreement, of course, would foment and lead to the undoing of black conservatism as the dominant voice in black political thought by the middle of the twentieth century. But there is little doubt that many, if not most, turn-of-the-century blacks viewed conservatism as the most attractive means of securing racial progress in America.

Why did conservatism prove compelling for so many blacks of this era? Did its seductiveness derive from the perceived charisma and importance of its major proponents? Was it the intuitive or intellectual appeal of the ideas themselves? Or might other reasons have aided its ascension to dominance?

Though charisma, intuition, and logic certainly contributed to conservatism's mass appeal, there is little doubt that the harsh reality of black life in the early twentieth century made it painfully clear to blacks that their realistic political choices were tragically constrained. It may very well be the case that conservatism presented a compelling case for racial progress not because it was ideal, but because it was, for better or worse, the most viable mode of racial empowerment available to blacks.

## Black Conservatism: A Politics of Necessity

In the wake of the Civil War and ratification of the Thirteenth Amendment, legal and political elites were faced with the daunting task of delineating a path of transition for blacks from slavery to freedom. Although it was clear that blacks would no longer be enslaved, the status they would assume was far less certain. For the remainder of the nineteenth century and much of the early twentieth century, the struggle for racial progress centered on defining the status of the Negro as an American citizen, securing the full range of political rights accorded to all citizens, and demarcating a pathway to social equality for blacks. Each step was undertaken in the face of deep and sustained white resistance.

The early-twentieth-century portion of this struggle to secure racial progress in the face of staunch and often violent opposition is commonly referred to as the nadir of American race relations. It was during this period that American blacks were most vulnerable to widespread oppression at the hands of state officials and white individuals. Opposition to African American advancement took many forms. Among the intellectual elite, it found expression in the eugenics movement, the scholarly appeal of which lay in part in the hope of securing scientific proof of blacks' genetic inferiority. Opposition among the masses was manifested in cruder forms—widespread lynchings throughout the South and the West and race riots in urban areas, and an extreme elaboration of de jure segregation throughout the nation. Though the lynchings were brought to a halt, many of the laws and customs evincing anti-Negro sentiment survived into the mid-twentieth century, including de jure and de facto segregation, denial of equal citizenship, and wholesale rejection of political equality.

Modern American culture creates ample space for political dissent within black communities regarding how best to counteract newer forms of racial bias and develop strategies and empowering responses. But it is important to appreciate that this is a late development, and one that is itself a product of racial progress. In the early twentieth century, racial hostility—some of it institutionalized—severely restricted African Americans' political options. Though they had been guaranteed social and political equality by law following the Civil War, these guarantees were never effected practically. The courts, in a dramatic dereliction of duty, turned a deaf ear to legitimate legal claims of racial injustice. By severely curtailing legal recourse for violations of civil rights, the courts effectively signaled that such rights, in practice, were of little value. With no refuge in the law, blacks essentially had no option but to adopt inwardly focused strategies of racial empowerment premised upon self-help and minimal assistance of white public institutions.

## The Limits of Law

Today, we like to think of civil rights laws as providing a bulwark against racial oppression by the majority. Following the Civil War, Congress enacted the Thirteenth, Fourteenth, and Fifteenth Amendments to abolish slavery, provide for equal citizenship and protection of the laws, and secure the right of blacks to vote, respectively. In addition, Congress passed civil rights legislation to strengthen these protections. Congress's clear purpose in passing these laws was to provide newly emancipated blacks with rights roughly on par with whites *and* with the means to enforce those rights in American courts.

By the turn of the twentieth century, the Supreme Court had struck down a handful of these provisions and had narrowly interpreted the remaining ones. The effect was threefold. First, the rights bestowed upon blacks were construed so narrowly that, as a practical matter, a great deal of racial discrimination was allowed to persist. Second, in narrowly construing these rights, the Court made clear that it would be hostile to protecting what rights remained whenever blacks attempted to seek enforcement. Third, in emphasizing the limits of what law could do to remedy racial injustice, the Court had signaled to both blacks and whites that the law would not provide a refuge for blacks suffering from racial discrimination.

The Supreme Court's notorious opinion in *Plessy v. Ferguson* (1896) exemplified the Court's approach during this period, and struck a decisive legal blow against black empowerment. In *Plessy*, the Court declared that racial segregation was not only lawful, but undertaken in accordance with the "established usages, customs, and traditions of the people" and "with a view to the promotion of their comfort and the preservation of the public peace and good order." Racial segregation was not discrimination, according to the court, but simply a "reasonable race distinction."

By defining segregation as "reasonable," consistent with prevailing customs, and crucial to securing "pubic peace" and "good order," the Court simultaneously denounced efforts to secure the social benefits of equal citizenship as presumptively unreasonable, inconsistent with prevailing custom, and destructive of domestic tranquility. Blacks had no "right" to the social equality that the Court was legally obliged to protect. Indeed, the pendulum had swung completely in the opposite direction. The Court's decision announced its intention to protect the "rights" of whites to remain separate from blacks.

The Court's opinion reverberated through the American cultural consciousness. As an initial matter, *Plessy* cleared the pathway for the most virulent form of social and governmental oppression against blacks since slavery. It sanctioned Jim Crow legislation, which criminalized the mixing of races in virtually all aspects of public life—in public transportation and accommodations, meeting houses, churches, schools, work sites, and so on. At the same time, it simultaneously declared law "powerless" to overcome racial prejudices.

The decision also effectively split any developing alliances between poor whites and blacks by legislating separation and reinforcing core perceptions of black inferiority. By conferring "reasonableness" upon racial segregation, the Court perpetuated profoundly negative stereotypes of blacks as socially inferior and thus justifiably exiled them to the margins of society. At the same time, the Court steadfastly refused to acknowledge the obvious implication of its decision. In response to the argument that racial segregation stigmatized blacks, the Court responded that if there is a badge of inferiority that arises from segregation policy, "it is solely because the colored race chooses to put that construction upon it."

Six years later, in *Giles v. Harris,* the Supreme Court would declare its hostility to protecting the political rights of blacks as well. In *Giles,* a group of five thousand eligible black voters in Alabama mounted a legal challenge to a variety of laws that had the effect of excluding them from the voter registration rolls. At the time, Alabama had instituted the full range of mechanisms to disenfranchise blacks—poll taxes, residency requirements, literacy tests, and grandfather clauses. The plaintiffs argued that applying these provisions to exclude black voters violated the U.S. Constitution, and they petitioned the Court to add their names to the list of registered voters so that they might vote in the coming election.

In a remarkable opinion, the Supreme Court acknowledged and accepted the allegations of the plaintiff, but declared itself powerless to provide a remedy. According to Justice Oliver Wendell Holmes, if the voter list is compiled in an unconstitutional way, simply adding the names of these five thousand black voters would not cure the constitutional defect. Rather, he argued, the list would need to be compiled in a manner consistent with the Constitution. The Court also maintained that it did not have the authority to compel the state of Alabama to compile the list in a constitutional manner. According to Holmes, the plaintiffs alleged that "the great mass of the white population intends to keep blacks from voting," and if true, a declaration by the Court to cease this practice would not accomplish much at all. Instead, Justice Holmes recommended that the group of would-be voters appeal to the "political branches of government"—the same local Alabama legislators who had enacted the provisions that were challenged in the case.

Law provided no safe harbor for blacks seeking protection against racial discrimination. Civil and political rights bestowed by Congress had been largely eviscerated. In the wake of *Plessy* and *Giles*, American society returned to the sort of pigmentocracy that existed prior to Reconstruction. Blacks were radically segregated in nearly all forms of social life—from railroad cars to restaurants to water fountains to cemeteries. African Americans were also stripped of a great deal of political power. In 1880, the majority of black men voted in local, state, and national elections. By 1890, this number was reduced dramatically, and by 1900, blacks were almost completely disenfranchised.

At the same time, there was a dramatic increase in racial terror in black communities. Lynching was, in many ways, the power offstage that terrorized blacks into political submission and forced many blacks to vacate public office. During the late nineteenth and early twentieth centuries, the NAACP documented more than forty-seven hundred lynchings, and the victims were black in 75 percent of the cases. The phenomenon of lynching persisted throughout the early twentieth century, despite the efforts of Ida B. Wells-Barnett to publicize the horror and absurdity of lynching in the cradle of American democracy and of liberal law professors such as Robert Hale, of Columbia Law School, to get federal antilynching laws passed. Because lynching was technically murder, federal officials agreed that state and local officials retained primary authority to investigate and prosecute these crimes—a notion that rested uncomfortably with many blacks who viewed local law enforcement as particularly unsympathetic.

The technical features of lynching and the lack of legal response tell only part of the story. The larger point is that lynching proved to be a cultural phenomenon. It provided a loud and clear signal to blacks that racial empowerment through civil rights law was fleeting, and that legal concepts such as freedom, equality, and democracy—at least for blacks—were extremely fragile and easily subverted. Greater protection would be needed, and blacks saw clearly that this protection had to be secured by blacks themselves.

## The Midcentury Decline of Black Conservatism

Understood within its proper context, the rise of black conservatism at the dawn of the twentieth century is not difficult to understand. Black conservatism had grown out of the lived experience of northern and southern blacks and was then embodied in leading African American institutions. Equally clear, however, was that America was not ready for a more progressive alternative. The pathway of black conservatism, though compromised, represented the obvious and perhaps inevitable choice.

By the middle of the twentieth century, however, this was no longer the case. By the 1950s, black conservatism as an intellectual movement had withered to the point that it had become a mere shadow of its former self. African Americans, who largely closed ranks and embraced strategies of racial empowerment that did not rely upon law and the goodwill of white society, would come to embrace civil rights and integration as the primary mechanisms to secure racial empowerment. What accounts for this groundswell of liberal thinking in the midst of black conservative political dominance?

This is a question that has never been fully answered. However, one can identify a number of phenomena that provide some insight. As an initial matter, one can point to major cultural and demographic shifts in American society. Massive immigration from 1880 to 1924 fundamentally altered American culture. In 1850, white America was comprised mainly of Protestants of Anglo-Saxon and Northern European origins, with small pockets of Irish Catholics. The racial minority population consisted mainly of slaves of African origin, Native Americans, and Asian American laborers in the Midwest and West. By World War I, the nation looked and sounded like a different place. The influx of millions of Catholics and Jews destroyed the Protestant hegemony. Immigrants from eastern and southern Europe and the Far East similarly undermined the dominance of Northern European culture.

Migration also played an important role in refashioning American culture. In the early twentieth century, race relations were profoundly regional. Issues arising between whites and Asians largely were confined to central and western United States. Conflicts between whites and Indians were located primarily in the Southeast, Midwest, and West. The most pressing issues between whites and blacks were generally understood to be confined to the South.

However, in the early twentieth century, blacks began to migrate from rural areas to cities, and from the South to the North. Some sought higher wages. Others sought a life outside of the southern pigmentocracy and racial terror. The concept of state's rights and state identity—so critical in the years immediately following the Civil War—gradually crumbled as the borders between states became increasingly artificial.

Pluralism through immigration and migration presented a fundamental challenge to the prevailing social and economic order of American life. Differences in culture, family structure, and background presented a rich diversity of opportunity to brush conventional understandings of race and place against the grain. The transformation was most pronounced in major American cities. It is here, in these rising industrial communities, that one can locate the origins of radical challenges to American racial and economic orthodoxy—the rise of the NAACP, the American Communist Party, and the American Civil Liberties Union.

Global warfare also contributed to changes in American thinking that created space for liberal political alternatives. In World War I, one finds the origins of international protection of civic equality, as the United States wages war in the name of preserving democracy. For many blacks, and black veterans in particular, World War I highlighted a stark contradiction in American democracy. Blacks were being asked to fight and sacrifice to make the world free and safe for democracy, and yet life in America remained profoundly undemocratic. The contradiction became all the more apparent when returning black veterans, who sought to live the spirit of freedom they secured for others, met with acts of overt racial violence and even lynchings—often euphemistically referred to as "race riots."

Following World War II, in which the United States waged war against the profoundly racist Nazi regime, it became clear to a great many Americans that the cognitive dissonance created by persistent racial oppression within a purportedly democratic society needed to be addressed. This tension would reach a crescendo during the Cold War, as the American superpower sought to persuade nations around the world, including Second and Third World nations populated mainly by people of color, of the virtues of democracy and the folly of communism. America, seeking to act as the post–World War II global leader and proponent of democracy, faced tremendous foreign policy difficulties, in part because many nations viewed the racial oppression of African Americans as fundamentally antithetical to democracy.

Changes in American culture and demography created space for intellectual struggle and the ascension of liberal thought that would eventually supplant conservatism as the dominant mode of racial empowerment for blacks. One of the principle architects of this shift was William Edward Burghardt DuBois.

## DuBois, the NAACP, and the
## Liberal Assault on Black Conservatism

DuBois, the self-described "master propagandist" and a founder of the NAACP, was the first African American intellectual to openly challenge Washingtonian conservatism. Born in Great Barrington, Massachusetts, in 1868, DuBois was an academic prodigy who graduated from Fisk University at the age of twenty and in 1895 became the first African American to receive a Ph.D. from Harvard University. A sociologist by training, DuBois published *The Philadelphia Negro* in 1899, the first in-depth case study of a black community in the United States.

In his early years, DuBois was a supporter of Washingtonian conservatism. However, his sociological investigations of living conditions of blacks revealed that the status of blacks during Washington's ascendancy was in decline. DuBois concluded that social change would not come about through conservatism and that racial progress would come about only when whites were informed about the harms produced by racial discrimination and when leading white institutions made changes.

In 1903, DuBois published his most influential book, *The Souls of Black Folk*, which offered a direct challenge to Washington's program and effectively divided the black community into "conservative" Washington supporters and "radical" critics of his approach. Washington's legacy proved particularly troubling to DuBois's vision of social progress for several reasons. As an initial matter, Washington was the preeminent advocate of industrial education. DuBois, by contrast, viewed higher education as essential to equip black youth with the knowledge and wisdom to serve the race. The creation of a cadre of college-trained leaders charged with the task of elevating blacks economically and socially—what he referred to as the "Talented Tenth"—required that scarce resources be directed toward black colleges. Washington's influence among leading white philanthropists effectually cut off DuBois's access to sources of funding—a diversion of resources that DuBois viewed as counterproductive to racial progress.

DuBois also objected to what he viewed as self-aggrandizing behavior on Washington's part. Of particular concern to DuBois was Washington's use of connections to expand his Tuskegee machine while apparently doing little to challenge caste barriers that produced social and economic devastation within black communities. For DuBois, Washington's influence and popularity came at the expense of flattering racist whites, voluntarily relinquishing the pursuit of equal rights, and belittling blacks. In 1903, DuBois publicly denounced Washington, declaring that Washington had "practically accepted the alleged inferiority of the Negro."

Two years later, DuBois convened twenty-nine delegates for a conference on the Canadian side of Niagara Falls. The delegates, all white men drawn from elite colleges and universities in the North, created the Niagara Movement and met annually over the next five years to develop strategies of racial protest. The 1905 mission statement declared:

> We repudiate the monstrous doctrine that the oppressor should be the sole authority as to the rights of the oppressed.... The negro race in America is stolen, ravished, and degraded, struggling up through difficulties and oppression, needs sympathy and receives criticism, needs help and given hindrance, needs protection and is given mob violence, need justice and is given charity, needs leadership and is given cowardice and apology, needs bread and is given stone.... We do not hesitate to complain and to complain loudly and insistently. To ignore, overlook, or apologize for these wrongs is to prove ourselves unworthy of freedom. Persistent agitation is the way to liberty.

The spirit of unrest embodied in the Niagara Movement soon captured the attention of prominent whites who had become disillusioned with Washington's accommodationist platform. With support for the Niagara Movement declining, DuBois joined with this new group of whites to create a new, interracial protest organization that would embody the same beliefs and aspirations of the Niagara Movement. This new organization, founded in 1908, was the NAACP.

Although the membership of the NAACP was overwhelmingly black, the organization was largely funded and administered by whites. Indeed,

DuBois was the only black within the leadership, serving as director of publicity and research and editor of *The Crisis,* the official organ of the NAACP. With the passing of Washington in 1915, DuBois and the NAACP assumed a more centrist and less radical role in the black community. Protest and agitation remained essential elements of the NAACP project. Increasingly important, however, were the litigation and lobbying efforts that would yield important legal victories and attract increasing support.

Perhaps the most important NAACP victory that solidified the organization's role within the black community and black politics was *Buchanan v. Warley.* In 1908, wealthy black businessmen and professionals in Louisville, Kentucky, began to buy homes in white residential neighborhoods. Apparently, this caused a great deal of alarm and consternation among whites. To avoid the possibility of being "trapped" next to black neighbors, many whites decided to rent homes rather than buy. Public agitation for a segregation ordinance began in November 1913. W. D. Binford, the editor of the Louisville *Courier-Journal and Times,* advocated a segregation ordinance in a speech to the Louisville Real Estate Exchange. He argued that such an ordinance would protect "the property owners of Louisville who have sacrificed so much in the past from the effects of the negro's presence."

In January of 1914, a councilman introduced such a bill. The bill expressly forbade "any colored person to move into and occupy as a residence ... any house upon any block upon which a greater number of houses are occupied ... by white people than are occupied ... by colored people." The bill contained a similar restriction that applied to whites. Anyone violating the ordinance was subject to a fine of no less than $5 nor more than $50 per day of violation. A group of prominent blacks, meanwhile, formed a branch of the NAACP to fight the proposed ordinance. Despite the best efforts of the NAACP, the City Council voted 21-0 in favor of the ordinance in March.

The local opposition organized a test case. William Warley, an active member of the Louisville NAACP, signed an agreement to purchase a lot on a majority-white block from Charles Buchanan, a white real estate agent who opposed the segregation ordinance. The contract between the two parties specified that the transaction would not be consummated unless Warley had "the right under the laws of the state of Kentucky and the city of Louisville to occupy said Property as residence." Warley refused to complete the transaction when he "discovered" that the Louisville segregation law would prohibit his residing in a house on the lot he was to purchase. Buchanan, represented by NAACP lawyer Clayton Blakley, then sued Warley in local court.

The NAACP argued that the ordinance interfered with the property rights of homeowners. The Fourteenth Amendment states that "no state shall deprive any person of life, liberty, or property without due process of law." Property rights were generally understood to include the right to purchase, convey, sell, and dispose of property. By restricting who may occupy a particular house, the ordinance effectively prohibited sale and disposition of property, thereby depriving potential sellers due process of law.

In its initial 121-page brief to the court, the state of Kentucky, defending the ordinance, countered that law "only seeks to regulate that natural and normal segregation which has always existed and to prevent a few of each race from overstepping the racial barriers which Providence and not human law has erected." "Can it be," asked the state rhetorically, "that a negro has the constitutional right ... to move into a block occupied by white families," even though this would lower the value of property owned by whites and create racial tension "simply to gratify his inordinate social aspirations to live with his family on a basis of social equality with white people?"

The state claimed that "philosophy, experience and legal decision, to say nothing of Divine Writ" show that the races should live apart to "preserve their racial integrity." According to the state, the average person finds such race-mixing "repugnant." Those who do not share this prevailing view and choose to live in proximity to members of the other race threaten "the peace and good order of society." The State concluded that it is neither a natural nor a constitutional right to live in "social intimacy" with members of a different race.

In a landmark decision, the *Buchanan* court rejected the state's arguments and decided the case in favor of the NAACP. The court reasoned that although the statute purported to regulate only "occupancy," the effect was to restrict the ability of the white property owner to sell that property to an African American purchaser. The court distinguished this case from previous cases challenging segregation. Whereas those cases sought to vindicate a social right to associate with members of another race, the court viewed property rights as far more important. Limiting access to railroad cars was one thing, but restricting economic transactions and infringing upon property rights—protected by the Constitution since the nation's founding—was quite another. The argument was perhaps all the more compelling in this case because it was the property rights of white sellers that were being restricted.

Civil rights advocates were overjoyed with the result in *Buchanan*. Moorfield Storey wrote to NAACP cofounder Oswald Garrison Villard that *Buchanan* was "the most important decision that has been made since the Dred Scott case, and happily this time it is the right way." *Buchanan* also received an enthusiastic reception in the African American media and in journals sympathetic to civil rights, such as the *New Republic* and the *Nation*. As it turned out, *Buchanan* did not end residential segregation in America. It eliminated de jure residential segregation, but that practice was simply replaced with de facto residential segregation through the rise of privately entered racially restrictive covenants that did not, at the time, run afoul of the Fourteenth Amendment's prohibition on state deprivation of property. But the case ensured that whites bore far more of the burden of their discriminatory attitudes than they would have if *Buchanan* had been decided in Kentucky's favor, and effectively prevented state governments from passing harsher antiblack measures than the one at issue in Buchanan.

The legal victory in *Buchanan* spurred the growth of the NAACP and signaled a turning point in the U.S. Supreme Court's jurisprudence on racial issues. The Supreme Court heard twenty-eight cases involving African Americans and the Fourteenth Amendment between 1868 and 1910. Of these, African Americans lost twenty-two. However, between 1920 and 1943, African Americans won twenty-five of twenty-seven cases before the Court.

In the wake of *Buchanan,* law had become a viable means of protecting black interests. The Court, it seemed, had grown some teeth, and civil rights, reduced to a mere slogan just a generation before, now had bite. Blacks, previously resigned to an independent, albeit exilic, life of self-help and self-direction, yearned to have their rights as equal citizens protected in the ordinary course of things, much as other Americans did. The liberal legal alternative of racial empowerment through vigorous enforcement of civil rights had proved its worthiness as an ideological competitor of black conservatism. Mounting legal victories by the NAACP would test the depth of old-line conservatives' commitment to the pathway of racial empowerment set forth by Washington.

## The Conservative Side of NAACP Litigation

If the NAACP victory in *Buchanan* signaled the arrival of a liberal legal approach to racial empowerment, it also emphasized the importance that conservative ideas would have on the trajectory of civil rights litigation. Although *Buchanan* was a civil rights victory, it also made clear that the civil rights worthy of protection by the court were not the social rights often associated with integration but those that possessed an economic character—the right to contract without government interference, the right to own private property, and the right to enjoy the fruits of one's own labor.

The significance of this was not lost on racial justice advocates. The NAACP, responding to the urgent demands from working-class blacks, began the daunting task of incorporating a strategy of economic justice into its limited repertoire of conventional civil rights litigation. The salary equalization cases, in which the NAACP litigated on behalf of African American teachers who received lower salaries than white teachers, were its initial foray into the sphere of economic justice. Although the NAACP publicly described these cases as part of its overall education strategy, the focus on wage differentials emphasized the prevailing view that racial justice carried with it a distinctly economic component.

The NAACP's tentative embrace of economic justice strengthened during and after World War II, as blacks struggled to find and hold on to jobs in highly segregated and often demeaning and harassing workplaces. It was during this time that the NAACP achieved significant labor-related victories, the most prominent of which involved the protection of African American workers from discrimination and inequality in shipyards across the country, the protection of black union workers in New York, and the protection of African American workers from employer and union discrimination on the railroads. Although the mixing of labor issues with traditional civil rights issues posed unique political and doctrinal challenges for the NAACP, the combination was, in some ways, inevitable because of the very nature of racial subordination during the Jim Crow era. As Charles Hamilton Houston explained, "In the United

States, the Negro is economically exploited, politically ignored and so-cially ostr[a]cized."[1] Given the holistic nature of African American re-pression, it is unsurprising that the pursuit of freedom would entail a civil as well as distinctly economic response.

The NAACP, however, would soon abandon this approach, which merged the best of liberal legalism and conservative aspirations for eco-nomic empowerment, in favor of one that focused almost exclusively on civil rights. The reasons for the abandonment of the economic component of civil rights litigation are varied and complex. Some commentators ar-gue that the rise of domestic anticommunist repression put the NAACP and labor activists on the defensive and forced a retreat from labor-related cases to classic civil rights cases that sought to protect minority rights un-der the U.S. Constitution and the American concept of democracy. Oth-ers point to politics within the NAACP and the institutional privileging of middle-class interests at the expense of the interests of poor and work-ing-class blacks. One might also argue that the Supreme Court's apparent willingness to breathe new life into the Fourteenth Amendment and en-force equal protection of the laws, and its explicit endorsement of the idea that stigma and psychological injury were the essence of racial harm, made it increasingly difficult for NAACP lawyers to articulate legally cog-nizable claims that addressed both racial oppression and economic sub-ordination.

Whatever the reasons for the switch away from an economic focus, the outcome was clear. The liberal NAACP strategy for racial empower-ment yielded an egalitarian constitutional view that has successfully es-tablished liberal legal principles without securing meaningful economic progress. For many blacks, protection of civil rights had symbolically secured the prospect of a better future but had not secured meaningful changes in their everyday lives. Conservatism had promised far more than liberal legal solutions had delivered up to this point. A self-directed and economically productive life worth of pride and respect—one that rose or fell based upon individual effort and did not rely upon the goodwill of white society—remained the core aspiration of many blacks. The NAACP victories had created space for a liberal alternative mode of racial empowerment, but for many blacks, conservatism remained the best available strategy.

# THREE

# Shades of Black Conservatism

## The Interwar Years, from the Harlem Renaissance to Mary McLeod Bethune and Marcus Garvey

The NAACP's failure to produce meaningful economic changes in the lives of everyday people in the early twentieth century ironically ensured that conservatism, though in decline, would not disappear entirely. Conservatism, as an overt political movement, had largely disbanded, but the basic thrust of conservative ideas remained an important part of the black American ideological landscape. The political, cultural, and intellectual vibrancy that began to develop in the early twentieth century blossomed during the interwar years, and many blacks were eager to indulge in the expanded sense of freedom and opportunity occasioned by an increasingly liberal society. The reality, of course, was that freedom and opportunity remained highly constrained for blacks. Rampant unemployment in the rural South and industrialized North, widespread racial segregation, limited educational opportunity, and poverty were facts of life for most blacks. Yet changes in American life wrought by war, migration, and a burgeoning culture of democratic dissent created space for human flourishing.

The interwar years would mark an important moment in radical black self-expression and political engagement. African American artists, eager to give voice to the black experience and share their unique perspective with the world, would give us jazz, cabaret culture, and the Harlem

Renaissance. Political activists, disenchanted with American democracy, would provide us with socialist and militant nationalist movements. Others would find space to advocate for blacks within American democratic structures, ensuring that governmental largess in the form of New Deal patronage and programs would flow to blacks as well as whites. Even quiet, middle-class blacks who typically avoided drawing attention to themselves filled the ranks of progressive black organizations such as the NAACP and the Urban League, and they developed social networks of fraternities, sororities, and social clubs.

The spirit of liberalism and radicalism that defined much of black American political and cultural life during this period, however, did not completely obliterate the spirit of conservatism that was so prominent just a few years earlier. Conservative ideas and instincts that are born from people's own experiences—ideas, generations in the making, that galvanized a people and ensured their survival during times of social crisis— are not quickly abandoned. Even in the most liberal and radical spheres of public life during this period, one finds shades of black conservatism.

## Black Conservatives and the Harlem Renaissance

The Harlem Renaissance, one of the great African American cultural movements of the twentieth century, was one of these places. Also commonly referred to as the New Negro Movement, the New Negro Renaissance, and the Negro Renaissance, the movement was centered in the Harlem neighborhood of New York City. Although it was primarily a literary movement, the Harlem Renaissance influenced the full range of African American music, theater, arts, and politics. The movement emerged near the end of World War I in 1918, on the heels of the great African American migration to the North and the opening up of new educational and employment opportunities. As educated and socially conscious blacks began to settle in New York City, Harlem became the new intellectual and cultural center of black America.

In the early 1920s, three works signaled the arrival of this new creative and energetic moment in African American culture. Claude McKay's volume of poetry *Harlem Shadows* (1922) became one of the first works by a black writer to be published by a mainstream, national publisher, Harcourt, Brace. *Cane,* the acclaimed 1923 experimental novel that combined poetry and prose by Jean Toomer, presented a moving depiction of black life in the rural South and urban North. Finally, *There Is Confusion* (1924), the first novel by writer and editor Jessie Fausset, presented a stunning portrait of middle-class life among black Americans from a woman's perspective.

The fledgling movement would soon capture the attention of major sponsors and publishers. On March 21, 1924, Charles S. Johnson of the National Urban League hosted a dinner to recognize the new literary talent in the black community and to introduce the young writers to New York's white literary establishment. On the heels of this dinner, the *Survey Graphic*, a magazine of social analysis and criticism that was interested in promoting intellectual diversity and cultural pluralism, produced a Harlem issue. Featuring the works of black writers and edited by black literary scholar Alain Locke, the March 1925 issue of the *Survey Graphic* announced and defined the aesthetic of black literature and art. However, it was the publication of *Nigger Heaven* in 1926 by white novelist Carl Van Vechten that solidified the movement. The book, presented as a sympathetic exposé of Harlem life, proved immensely popular, particularly among whites eager to gain a glimpse of "Negro life." Although the book offended some members of the black community, its coverage of both the elite and the baser side of Harlem helped create a "Negro vogue" that drew thousands of sophisticated New Yorkers, black and white, to Harlem's exotic and exciting nightlife and stimulated a national market for African American literature and music. Finally, in the autumn of 1926 a group of young black writers produced *Fire!!*, their own literary magazine. With *Fire!!* a new generation of young writers and artists, including Langston Hughes, Wallace Thurman, and Zora Neale Hurston, assumed stewardship of the literary renaissance.

The diverse literary expression of the Harlem Renaissance ranged from Langston Hughes's explicit incorporation of the syncopated rhythms of African American popular music into his poems of ghetto life, as in "The Weary Blues" (1926), to McKay's use of "traditional" poetic forms such as the sonnet to structure decidedly nontraditional poetic assaults on racial violence, as in "If We Must Die" (1919). McKay also presented glimpses of the "glamour and the grit" of Harlem life in *Harlem Shadows*. Others, such as Countee Cullen, used both African and European images to explore the African roots of black American life. For example, in the poem "Heritage" (1925), Cullen discusses being both a Christian and an African, yet not belonging fully to either tradition. Women artists, like their male counterparts, also sought to assert their perspective on black life. *Quicksand,* a 1928 novel by novelist Nella Larsen, offered a powerful psychological examination of an African American woman's loss of identity, whereas Hurston's *Their Eyes Were Watching God,* published nearly a decade later, used folk life of the black rural South to drive a remarkable narrative of race and gender in which a woman finds her true identity.

Diversity and experimentation also flourished in the other arts. The influence of the era was reflected in the marriage of blues and ragtime by pianist Jelly Roll Morton, the instrumentation of bandleader Louis Armstrong, and the orchestration of composer Duke Ellington. "Primitive" style and references common to Negro culture appeared in the blues singing of Bessie Smith as well as in the paintings and illustrations of artist Aaron Douglas.

The Harlem Renaissance represented the first serious attempt by artists to bring the lived experiences of black people to the forefront of American cultural consciousness. Their work collectively shined a spotlight on the vibrant racial tradition that had largely been ignored by the great masses of Americans. Despite their relatively small numbers, the Harlem Renaissance artists served a primary role in reshaping prevailing attitudes, assumptions, and beliefs about blacks in American life. As cultural critic Rudolph Fisher exclaimed in 1927, "The Negro's stock is going up, and everybody is buying."

Given the liberal and often confrontational approaches embodied in the work of Harlem Renaissance artists, one might be inclined to think that black conservatives did not support the movement. But this assumption proves incorrect. Indeed, black conservatives not only supported the Harlem Renaissance—at least initially—but actively participated in its development. They supported the cultural movement, in large part, because it appeared to embrace important features of conservative thought. One of the principle aspirations of the Harlem Renaissance was to acknowledge and validate the distinctive cultural heritage of African Americans. Many artists, including Claude McKay and Langston Hughes, drew their inspiration from poor blacks, and they were often derided by cultural elites as "sewer dwellers" and "members of the debauched tenth," a play on DuBois's Talented Tenth. Yet the idea that one can and should draw inspiration from the bottom resonated with Washingtonian conservatives, whose embrace of accommodationism and pursuit of an independent and self-directed black community life was premised upon the twin beliefs that there was nothing shameful about the lives of ordinary black people and that African American culture was a reservoir of rich, transformative possibilities.

The Harlem Renaissance also sought to promote the idea that blacks should take pride in their contributions to American culture. This basic view is perhaps best exemplified by the work of James Weldon Johnson, whose works included "O Black and Unknown Bards" (1908), which identified and praised largely unknown creators of black folk music; *Fifty Years* (1913), which chronicled black history during the fifty years following Emancipation; and *Black Manhattan* (1930), which presented a history of black cultural life in New York City. A passage from Johnson's "O Black and Unknown Bards" captures this sentiment most effectively:

> There is a wide wonder in it all,
> That from degraded rest and servile toil
> The fiery spirit of the seer should call
> These simple children of the sun and soil.
> O black slave signers, gone, forgot, unfamed,
> You—you, alone, of all the long, long line
> Of those who've sung untaught, unknown, unnamed,
> Have stretched out, upward, seeking the divine.

Johnson's work reflects the inward focus of black conservatism and shares the same impulse to focus upon and validate contributions made by blacks. Johnson's work also highlights a second and related aspect of black conservatism: namely, the attitude of pragmatic optimism and focus on gains rather than setbacks. Much like the generations of conservatives that came before him, Johnson self-consciously elected to celebrate the growth and accomplishments of black society rather than dwell on the extended legacy of racial oppression and relative deprivations of black society.

Another feature of the Harlem Renaissance that proved attractive to conservatives was the spirit of self-determination and racial solidarity exuded by the artists. Despite substantial patronage from whites, the artists remained focused on presenting black life as they saw it, sourced from the lives of the black masses and not the thin stratum of the black cultural elites. Their depiction of ordinary black life implicated not only white racial oppression but exploitation by black elites as well. They had, in many ways, carved out cultural space for themselves, and they worked to define and control this space for themselves and future artists. In this sense, the approach of Harlem Renaissance artists was not altogether different from that undertaken by Washington's Tuskegee machine, which viewed the creation of an infrastructure for blacks to lead self-directed lives as the touchstone of racial empowerment in American life. For Washington, the creation of black-operated institutions ensured that blacks would retain both control over and accountability to its members. Harlem Renaissance artists were of like mind, for they too sought to create a movement of their own in order to maintain creative control of their art and to ensure that they remained accountable, first and foremost, to other affiliated artists.

Despite sharing these important ideological commitments, black conservative support for the Harlem Renaissance was far from unconditional. Though the movement embodied crucial conservative precepts, there were a number of important divergences that proved to be sources of consternation for conservatives. Perhaps the strongest set of criticisms were levied upon the images of the "New Negro" projected by Alain Locke and other artists. Black conservatives conceded that the image of blacks could be profitably transformed through the arts, but they were particularly wary of the risks of stereotyping. It was one thing to elevate underrepresented aspects of black life; it was quite another to valorize and depict elements of the "lowly life" to appeal to the fetishes and exotic stereotypes held by white America. Some critics maintained that Harlem Renaissance art did little to transform white public opinion about blacks and simply "exchanged a cabin for a cabaret." Indeed, Sterling Brown, himself a Harlem Renaissance artist, was particularly appalled by what he viewed as the exploitation of black culture and the trafficking in "caricatured stereotype."

Conservative Kelly Miller, a leading black intellectual and dean of Howard University, amplified Brown's argument. Miller himself has spent a substantial portion of his career working to discount prevailing stereotypes of blacks as lazy, irresponsible, and dishonest. He initially extolled the transformative possibilities of popular culture to improve race relations, noting that it proved "an exceptional way . . . to explore the mass mind." Yet he also criticized Harlem Renaissance artists for, in the words of Howard Suggs, "perpetuating the image of the Negro as a comic figure through their use of vaudeville and jazz."

Langston Hughes offered an impassioned defense of the images used by Harlem artists in his famous essay "The Negro and the Racial Mountain":

We young Negro artists, who create now intend to express our individual dark-skinned selves without fear or shame. If white people are pleased, we are glad. If they are not, it doesn't matter. We know we are beautiful. And ugly too. The tom-tom cries and the tom-tom laughs. If colored people are pleased we are glad. If they are not, their displeasure doesn't matter either. We build our temple for tomorrow, strong as we know how, and we stand on the tope of the mountain, free within ourselves.

Hughes's vivid assertion of Negro artistic autonomy provided dramatic validation for the movement, and the spirit of independence in which it was written arguably should have appealed to the critics' conservative sensibilities.

For many conservative critics, however, Hughes's strategic invocation of race pride and self-expression rang hollow. The problem was not that Hughes was a Negro artist, but that his art was too Negro expressive. To paraphrase conservative Countee Cullen, Hughes's mistake was to throw open "every door of the racial entourage, to the wholesale gaze of the world at large," in violation of the black middle-class code of propriety. The thrust of Cullen's criticism was amplified by Allison Davis, who lamented that "our 'intellectuals' . . . have capitalized the sensational aspects of Negro life, at the expense of general truth and sound judgment. . . . Our poets and writers of fiction have failed to interpret [the] broader human nature in Negroes, and found it relatively easy to disguise their lack of higher imagination by concentrating upon immediate and crude emotion." Negro self-expression, at least for some critics, ran afoul of the basic conservative precepts of middle-class morality, respectability, and proper deportment that had been in place for more than a century.

Conservatives were equally skeptical of the Harlem artists' claim that art produced by Negroes was racially distinctive in any meaningful sense. This argument was put most forcefully by conservative George S. Schuyler, a man who would become the dominant voice of black conservatism in the middle of the twentieth century. In an article titled "The Negro Art Hokum," Schuyler argued that the category of Negro art was, at bottom, an act of self-deception. According to Schuyler, there is nothing "expressive of the Negro soul" in the work of black artists whose way of life was not so different from that of other Americans. Schuyler argued:

> He is not living in a different world as some whites and few Negroes would have us believe. When the jangling of his Connecticut alarm clock gets him out of his Grand Rapids bed to a breakfast similar to that eaten by his white brother across the street ... it is sheer nonsense to talk about "racial differences" between the American black and the American white man.

Negro art, he maintained, may very well exist, but not in America. "[It] has been, is, and will be among the numerous black nations of Africa; but to suggest the possibility of any such development among the ten million colored people of this republic is self-evident foolishness."

Jazz music was subject to similar criticism. Black conservative elites, such as educator Carter G. Woodson, summarily declared that "jazz is not real music," but merely another example of the low and frivolous creations of the new Negro.[1] The association of jazz with cabaret life and alcohol and drug consumption stigmatized the music in the eyes of conservatives. As conservative playwright Benjamin Brawley pointed out, jazz could not be understood as "art" precisely because it "annihilated form" and emphasized a "low and 'exotic' life."[2] To be sure, black conservatives were not alone in their criticism of jazz. Indeed, the ascension of jazz drew fire from music traditionalists more broadly, regardless of ideological affiliation. The significance of the black conservative critique, however, lies not so much in the critique of the form, but of the larger culture that nurtured and sustained jazz. Put differently, jazz was objectionable to black conservatives not simply because it ran afoul of traditional musical structure and convention, but because it derogated from conservative norms of morality, civility, and human decency. Validation of jazz necessarily entailed acknowledgment of inspirations of jazz, inspirations that many conservatives viewed as "inauthentic" and improper representations of black life and, perhaps more pointedly, a serious threat to the project of black racial empowerment.

## Prefiguring Modern Conservative
## Critiques of Black Culture

The conservative cultural critique of the Harlem Renaissance in some ways foreshadowed modern conservative criticism of gangsta rap and other forms of urban artistic and cultural expression. Much like the conservative critics of Harlem Renaissance artists, contemporary conservatives are often torn when it comes to modern black popular cultural expression. Juan Williams, in his recent book *Enough: The Phony Leaders, Dead End Movements, and Culture of Failure That Are Undermining America—And What We Can Do about It,* exemplifies this attitude. Williams glorifies early forms of underground hip-hop, likening it to innovators of jazz and blues who "with little music education and few instruments ... found a way to create a new sound [and] used their voices, hands, and feet to make a joyful noise and tell their story." However, Williams laments that "like all beauty and new creations, rap and hip-hop were open to corruption," and that "gritty street reporting gave way to nihilistic glorifications of the "thug life." Hip-hop today, according to Williams, is "unthinking social commentary," and the rap business does little more than "satisfy white America's desire to see Jim Crow jump in blackface minstrel shows."

Perhaps most troubling for Williams is the thought that black popular culture destroys the hard work undertaken by previous generations to secure civil rights and promote an image of blacks as dignified and of equal worth to whites. As Williams explains:

> Totally lost on the hip-hop crowd is the idea that this generation of black people having an identity far deeper than the latest overpriced T-shirt from a hip-hop clothing company. That deeper identity for this generation of black Americans is a part of the arc of struggle for equal rights, education, and opportunity in America. But the current hip-hop identity does not allow for any hint that doors have opened to black America since the *Brown* decision. The crucial idea that this generation has an unprecedented opportunity to rise up in America and establish itself through education, discipline and even sacrifice is totally absent. And when it appears, it is dismissed as stupid. Why? The only real black man or woman in rap is a victim, whose street credibility comes

from being a victim, disrespected, and on the way to jail. That is why the wisdom offered in contemporary rap is paean to the virtue of being a mindless, vacant soul intent on short term gratification.

Williams is not alone. Bill Cosby, C. Delores Tucker, and the editors of *Essence* magazine have all called for marches and protests against hateful and hurtful depictions of blacks by hip-hop artists while reserving faint support for aspects of the medium that do not promote these images. Others, however, tend to be more uniformly opposed. For example, Thomas Sowell, in *Black Rednecks and White Liberals,* dismisses hip-hop expression as "thuggish gutter words" spoken by artists who valorize a "brutal hoodlum lifestyle" that echoes "violence, arrogance, lose sexuality, and self-dramatization." The deeper problem for Sowell is that these artists project an image of the "ghetto black" that is, in turn, used as an identity litmus test. This effectively confines the identity of blacks to a stereotype, and creates strong disincentives for individual blacks to deviate from the racial script. Those blacks confined to the stereotype, according to Sowell, are cut off from those who had advanced beyond it, and are thereby deprived of "examples, knowledge, and experience that could have been useful to those less fortunate." At the same time, those blacks that had moved beyond the stereotype feel the need to emulate "ghetto" cultural practices, "perhaps using ghetto language, in order to prove their 'identity' within their own race." John McWhorter, a conservative black social critic whose criticisms are similar to Sowell's, observes that rap's core message seems to encourage a young black man to nurture "a sense of himself as an embattled alien in his own land. It is difficult to see how this can lead to anything but dissention and anomie."[3] Or as critic Nick Crowe would write in a 2004 essay that appeared in *Prospect* magazine, rap has "an endless appetite for self-gratification, its self-destructive nature [contributing] nothing to the community."

Much like their conservative counterparts of the 1920s and 1930s, modern critics of popular black artistic expression reveal much about their own politics in their criticism. Juan Williams's sour observation that "behind the thumping beat is a message that building a family, a community, and political coalitions are all bad bets" and that rap also projects the idea that "parents nurturing children and believing in education as a long-term investment is also for suckers" reveals a normative commitment to racial empowerment that is strongly rooted in black conservative values—values championed by traditional black conservatives nearly a century ago, under strikingly similar circumstances, and for remarkably similar reasons. The modern critique of rap music and urban artistic expression is but one example of the longevity and transhistorical appeal of the black conservative tradition.

## Black Conservatism and Social Welfare

By the mid-1930s, the Harlem Renaissance had faded considerably as a result of the Great Depression. Organizations such as the NAACP and Urban League, which had actively promoted the Harlem Renaissance in the 1920s, shifted their interests to economic and social issues. Many influential black writers and literary promoters, including Hughes, James Weldon Johnson, Charles S. Johnson, and DuBois, left New York City. Finally, a riot in Harlem in 1935—set off in part by the hardships of the Depression and mounting tension between the black community and the white shop owners—shattered the notion of Harlem as the Mecca of the New Negro.

The Great Depression also had a profound influence on the trajectory of black conservatism. The southern textile plants and northern industries were struck hardest by the economic downturn, and blacks, disproportionately employed in these sectors, suffered the most. Hard times engendered harsh responses among blacks, as desperation drove many law-abiding black employees into criminality. Conservative P. B. Young, who preferred the sobriquet "militant independent," observed that the economic crisis in the South was "making thieves of servants." Blacks who had once stood shoulder-to-shoulder with the conservative Washingtonian elites began to question whether staunch adherence to prevailing conservative philosophy was really the best available strategy for racial empowerment.

But although the Depression blunted the influence of Washingtonian-style conservatism in the South, it also provided a source for the reaffirmation of black conservative philosophy. Hard times reinforced the invaluable lessons of self-help, and these lessons informed the possibility of social welfare policy in the early twentieth century. The Great Depression, much like the Civil War and the period following Reconstruction, produced rampant poverty and an orphaned community of children. In the absence of local, state, and federal welfare policy, black women, building upon the legacy of mutual aid societies of the nineteenth century, organized and expanded volunteer and philanthropic organizations to meet needs. One of the earliest of these groups was the National Association of Colored Women (NACW), founded in 1896. Its first president, Mary Church Terrell, described the mission of the group in terms that reflected the prevailing conservative philosophy of the times:

> Through the children ... we must build a rock of integrity, morality, and strength, both of body and mind, that floods of proscriptions ... prejudice, and persecution ... may not move.... The real solution to the race problem ... lies in the children.[4]

Terrell was not alone in this endeavor. Some ten years earlier, Carrie Steele founded an orphanage in Atlanta, Georgia, to care for abandoned black children. A similar home for "colored girls" was opened near Richmond, Virginia, in 1915, providing care for some five hundred young girls. In 1934, Frederick Perry opened the Colored Big Sisters Home for Girls in Kansas City, Missouri.

The NACW and similar organizations all shared an abiding philosophy that emphasized morality, self-control, religious teaching, and domesticity. The prevailing Washingtonian emphasis on industrial education was translated into a focus on "home-life skills," in which young girls were taught to appreciate the importance of housework (such as laundry and sewing) and communal ties with neighbors. The ascension of Mary McLeod Bethune to the presidency of the NACW solidified the conservative tenor of these groups. Like Washington, she championed the conservative values of patriotism, good citizenship, and racial solidarity. She also emphasized the importance of self-help and self-sacrifice as the proper pathway to racial empowerment. Unlike Washington, however, she was not a self-proclaimed accommodationist. Although an effective power broker behind the scenes, Bethune preferred a "strong ... direct voice" to initiate and shape policy that would benefit blacks. Yet in true conservative fashion, Bethune viewed the transformations wrought by the Depression in optimistic terms—as an opportunity to shape a new democracy and a new place for blacks in the years to come.

Bethune's vision was shaped, in part, by Theodore Roosevelt's 1910 declaration of a "new nationalism," which promised an expansion of democracy and responsibility of government to citizens lacking political power and economic capital. Bethune had rejected the Hoover administration's claim that the Depression would be over quickly and that, in the meantime, "federal aid would be a disservice to the unemployed." Whereas Washington might have held fast to notions of self-sacrifice, business entrepreneurship, and racial solidarity, Bethune remained open to the possibility that a touch of federal paternalism would not prove catastrophic and could possibly enhance the realization of racial empowerment for blacks.

Bethune soon joined Robert Weaver, H. A. Hunt, William Hastie, Lawrence Oxley, Frank Horne, and others to serve as advisors to newly elected president Franklin Delano Roosevelt and shape New Deal policy as it applied to blacks. As a member of the president's so-called black cabinet, Bethune's vision of a new, post-Depression Negro gave way to political realities. In her public appearances, particularly among mixed audiences, Bethune adopted a surprisingly accommodationist posture. Bethune had been named by Roosevelt in 1936 to head the Division of Negro Affairs of the National Youth Agency (NYA), a welfare program designed to train people for skilled and semiskilled jobs. Despite Bethune's pleading to integrate the program, it remained starkly segregated, and blacks and whites were considered separately, and in theory equally, for admission. Because the program was administered by state and local officials, however, there was more than a passing suspicion that blacks were being trained exclusively for traditional "Negro jobs" as maids and janitors or were denied access outright to the program on the basis of race.

During her tenure as director of the agency, Bethune often couched her appeals for racial equality in the admissions and administration of the program in terms flattering to whites. Her demeanor was often that of a supplicant whose primary approach lay in appeals to white people's consciences and sense of fair play. In a 1946 address to the NYA National Advisory Committee, Bethune argued that more blacks should be appointed to state and local posts within the organization by saying that she would "like to see more of those darkies doting around here." She closed her remarks by saying: "After being down in Harlem, I'm glad to have the opportunity of being up here in the Waldorf-Astoria with you white folks. I wish more of my people could share this opportunity."

But if her public persona proved troubling, her private interactions offered some degree of atonement. Although the Roosevelt administration declined to deal with segregation head-on, Bethune continued to advocate for desegregation behind the scenes. She continued to back black state appointees to the NYA, and she frequently demanded that white national NYA officials overrule the segregative hiring practices of state and local officials. "It's about time," she told the NYA national director in 1937, "that white folks recognize that Negroes are human too, and will not much longer stand to be the dregs of the work force."

Bethune never achieved her vision of racial equality in the administration of the NYA. She eventually embraced the pragmatic view that segregation was an unfortunate reality, and that while it remained a reality, Negroes such as herself must seek to ensure equal, though separate, consideration. Speaking to the National Advisory Committee in 1936, Bethune remarked:

> In places where there is no need for a separate program, for Negro and white groups, we most heartily recommend the one program. And in fields where it is necessary for us to have a separate program, we most heartily recommend a separate program, taking, of course, under advisement, the necessity of proper leadership and guidance.[5]

This was certainly the case for the NYA, but Bethune understood that it may also be true for other aspects of American life.

Although Bethune's tenure as an NYA official and member of Roosevelt's black cabinet produced less than ideal results, it would be a mistake to characterize her role in national public life as a failure brought about by conservatism. It is worth remembering that Bethune faced real constraints not only as a black woman in a predominately white administration, but also as a result of Roosevelt's policy on race. The administration had simply refused to take on southern opposition to racial integration, leaving Bethune little choice but to embrace shades of conservatism and demand equal support for black trainees and administrators. One can criticize the accommodationist public persona, but one must also acknowledge that Bethune's complex advocacy ensured that blacks in the rural South received some benefit from the New Deal. Bethune understood, perhaps better than anyone, that in the midst of clamoring for more, sometimes it is best to take what is offered. As she famously stated to a conference of Southern whites, "You white folks have your swimming pool if you think that best. Just give us one to enjoy too."

## The Conservatism of Marcus Garvey

Another place that one might locate the continuing influence of conservative ideas is in the lifework of Marcus Garvey. A native of Jamaica, Garvey arrived in the United States in 1916 with little money and almost no American contacts. Within a decade, he had constructed one of the largest and most influential African American mass movements in American history. Although his movement was short-lived—it had all but ceased to exist by 1935—Garveyism and the uncompromising ideology of militant black nationalism that it came to represent left an indelible imprint on American black politics.

What often goes unappreciated, however, is the extent to which Garveyism reflected shades of black conservative thought that had existed within black politics for over a century. With its emphasis on black pride and heritage, self-help, and the creation and maintenance of black-run institutions, Garveyism is perhaps best understood as an urban, international variation on the conservative philosophy advanced by Washington in the rural South.

Marcus Mosiah Garvey was born in 1887 in St. Ann's Bay, a rural town on the northern coast of Jamaica. The circumstances of his upbringing both shed light on the conservative values he would hold as an adult and foreshadow the demise of his movement. As Garvey recounted:

> My parents were black negroes. My father was a man of brilliant intellect and dashing courage. He was unafraid of consequences. He took human chances in the course of life, as most bold men do, and he failed at the close of his career. He once had a fortune; he died poor. My mother was a sober and conscientious Christian, too soft and good for the time in which she lived. She was the direct opposite of my father. He was severe, firm, determined, bold and strong, refusing to yield even to superior forces if he believed he was right. My mother, on the other hand, was always willing to return a smile for a blow, and ever ready to bestow charity upon her enemy. Of this strange combination I was born.[6]

Equally intriguing is the fact that Garvey grew up in a racially integrated community despite the fact that, at the time, Jamaica operated under an explicit racial hierarchy that placed the islands 650,000 blacks beneath the 168,000 "coloureds" (a catchall category for anyone not "pure" white or black), who themselves ranked beneath the 15,000 white inhabitants. His closest friend and playmate as a child was a white girl, the daughter of one of two white families that lived on adjoining land. As Garvey explained, "To me, at home in my early days, there was no difference between white and black." Later his best friend was sent away to be schooled in Scotland and, according to Garvey, was instructed by her parents "never to write or try to get in touch with me, for I was a 'nigger.'" He remained friends with the boys in the family, although those friendships would cease as the boys reached adolescence. It was at this time that Garvey grew "to see the difference between the races more and more" and realized that he "had to make a fight for a place in this world."

At age fourteen, Garvey left school to become a printer's apprentice. Working among men strengthened Garvey's character, and he would later claim that it was his experience in the printing trade that confirmed in his own mind that he was "strong and manly" and worthy of respect. Two years later, he left home to take a position as a printer with his uncle in the city of Kingston. There Garvey advanced his knowledge of the printing and newspaper business, and his career in printing advanced quickly. He spent his free time, however, as someone consumed with the power of oratory; he carefully observed preachers as they delivered church sermons, studying and adopting their various styles. Advocacy and influence became an obsession of sorts, and Garvey soon was organizing elocution contests for Kingston's underprivileged youth.

Politics also became an obsession as Garvey grew increasingly sensitive to societal injustice. During the printer's strike of 1907, Garvey was the only foreman who sided with the workers. He was blacklisted from the printing industry and turned to a career in political influence. In 1910, Garvey helped found the fledgling National Club, a political activist organization in Kingston, and he created the *Watchman*, the first of his many newspapers. Both ventures collapsed because of insufficient funding, but Garvey realized that his future lay in politics and not printing. He left Jamaica for Costa Rica, where a relative had secured a job for him at a banana plantation. Appalled by the working conditions of black West Indian migrants, Garvey traveled to Limon to lead a protest at the British consul's office. The indifference of British officials convinced Garvey that black lives were of no consequence to white officials, and he founded his second newspaper, *La Nacionale*, hoping that negative publicity would secure a response. Garvey traveled throughout Central and South America, only to find similar exploitative conditions. He returned to Jamaica in 1911 and demanded that the governor take steps to protect Jamaicans working overseas. When British officials in Jamaica declined to take action, Garvey, with the assistance of his sister Indiana, who worked as a child's nurse in London, set out to make his case to officials in England.

Garvey arrived in London in 1912, and it was there that he developed a clearer understanding of the political role that he would assume. Garvey, always sensitive to the power of words, again encountered words that had the power to shape his ideas—and in this case transform his life. It was the words not of a white British official but of a black man from the U.S. South that would set his course. As Garvey explained:

> I read "Up From Slavery" by Booker T. Washington, and then my doom—if I may so call it—of being a race leader dawned upon me in London.... I asked, "Where is the black man's Government? Where is his King and kingdom? Where is his President, his country, and his ambassador, his army, his navy, his men of big affairs?" I could not find them, and then I declared, "I will help to make them."

Before leaving England, Garvey articulated a vision that would unite his Jamaican upbringing with the cause of the entire black race. He declared, "The people who inhabit that portion of the Western Hemisphere will be the instruments of uniting a scattered race who, before the close of many centuries, will found an Empire on which the sun shall shine as ceaselessly as it shines on the Empire of the North today."

Upon his return to Jamaica on August 1, 1914—the anniversary of the emancipation of the British West Indies—Garvey established the Universal Negro Improvement and Conservation Association and African Communities League, later shortened to the UNIA. The association's aims seem patterned after those that Washington espoused. The local goals of the UNIA involved the establishment of educational and industrial colleges for blacks, the elevation of the degraded to "a state of good citizenship," the promotion of commerce and industry among blacks, and the strengthening of "the bonds of brotherhood and unity among the races." The UNIA's general objectives elaborated on this basic theme, including the establishment of "a Universal Confraternity among the race," "to promote the spirit of race pride and love," and "to conduct a worldwide commercial and industrial intercourse."

Much of Garvey's early rhetoric was strongly derivative of Washington's ideas. In his first annual address to the UNIA in 1915, Garvey summarily declared that "the bulk of our people are in darkness and are really unfit for good society." In a subsequent address, again echoing Washington, Garvey counseled his fellow Jamaicans that Europeans were "longing to see the Negro do something for himself," and that upon showing such an initiative, "all other races would be glad to meet [the Negro] on the plane of equality and comradeship." But Garvey cautioned that "it is indeed unfair to demand equality when one of himself has done nothing to establish the right to equality."

Thus, like Washington, Garvey argued that pride in oneself and one's own accomplishments are the touchstone for racial progress. This proved particularly troubling in Jamaica, where mixed-race people did not want to self-identify as Negro. Although Garvey often found support among white government officials and clergy, he was often opposed by affluent members of his own race. "I was openly hated and persecuted by some of these colored men," recounts Garvey. "They hated me worse than poison. They opposed me at every step." It was not simply his organization, but his very pretensions to leadership that they opposed. As Garvey explained, "I was a black man and therefore had absolutely no right to lead; in the opinion of the colored element, leadership should have been in the hands of a yellow or a very light man." Before leaving Jamaica, Garvey wrote a final appeal for racial solidarity to his fellow Jamaicans:

> For God's sake, you men and women who have been keeping yourselves away from your own African race, cease this ignorance; unite your hands and ears with the people of Africa.... Sons and daughters of Africa, I say to you arise, take on the toga of race pride, and throw off the brand of ignominy which has kept you back for so many centuries.... Be a Negro in the light of the Pharaohs of Egypt, Simons of Cyrene, Hannibals of Carthage, L'Ouvertures and Dessalines of Haiti, Blydens, Barclays and Johnsons of Liberia, Lewises of Sierra Leone, and Douglasses and DuBoises of America, who have made and are making history.

Garvey's arrival in the United States in 1916 was inauspicious, but his movement quickly gained momentum as he combined the best of anticolonial protest and political militancy with traditional conservative ideas of racial awareness and cultural pride, social conservatism, and black capitalism. He established the New York Division of the UNIA in 1917 and began to centralize his efforts in America. Garvey said that American blacks were superior to their West Indian counterparts in "the spirit of self consciousness and [self-]reliance," and that "the Negroes of both hemispheres have to defer to the American brother."

By 1920, the UNIA was one of the largest and wealthiest black organizations in the North. Like Washington, Garvey created a network of institutions that embodied his core nationalist philosophy. His commitment to economic conservatism and black capitalism was reflected in the creation of a cooperative network of grocery stores, laundries, restaurants, and large-scale enterprises such as the Negro Factories Corporation, the Black Star Line, the Black Cross Navigation and Trading Company, doll factories, printing plants, and a fleet of moving vans. His commitment to educational uplift was reflected in the proliferation of UNIA-sponsored elementary schools, scholarships for students wishing to attend New York's Booker T. Washington University or Liberty University in Claremont, Virginia, and training fellowships at UNIA auxiliary organizations such as the Universal African Black Cross Nurses. His commitment to promoting race pride was reflected in UNIA organs such as the *Negro World* and *Daily Negro Times*, which regularly published historical and poetic works about the status of Negro life; in the promotion of concerts and cultural events at UNIA's Liberty Hall auditoriums; in demonstrations of Negro pageantry in parades; and in the honoring of "race champions" with induction into the order of the Knights of the Nile.

To become a Garveyite was, in a sense, to undergo a critical moment of cultural transformation. Like his conservative predecessors, Garvey was himself a self-conscious exercise in the promotion of the self-esteem of a race of people. As sociologist E. Franklin Frazier explained:

[Garvey] not only promised the despised Negro a paradise on earth, but he made the Negro an important person in his immediate environment. He invented honors and social distinctions and converted every social invention to his use in his effort to make his followers feel important. While everyone was not a "knight or sir," all his followers were fellow-men of the Negro race.[7]

At the same time, Garvey's ambition, racial chauvinism, and political militancy often extended well beyond his conservative roots. His relentless pursuit of Pan-Africanism—exemplified by periodic International Conventions of the Negro Peoples of The World; his "Back to Africa," "Africa for Africans," and "Princes Shall Come Out of Egypt" sloganeering; and his self-proclaimed title of "provisional president" of the "Republic of Africa"—directly contradicted the conservative mantras of American patriotism and the anti-utopian orientation to making America, with all its flaws, a "home" for the Negro. Similarly, the creation of an assortment of UNIA paramilitary units—the African Legion, Garvey Militia, Ladies Brigade, Black Eagle Flying Corps, and the Universal African Motor Corps—though reflecting a conservative respect for Western military institutions, pushed the conservative ideas of self-help and self-reliance into new and uncharted territory.

Indeed, one can argue that it was Garvey's political militancy and excessive racial chauvinism that paved the way for his ultimate downfall. As historian Manning Marable observed in *Black Leadership*:

> In practical terms, Garvey's version of racial solidarity required an explicit rejection of black intellectuals such as W.E.B. Du Bois and reformist organizations like the NAACP. Black elites who favored racial integration, from this perspective, were clearly working against the best interests of Negroes. Blacks should not "beg" whites for social equality and acceptance, but should establish their own racial standards and values.

But in flamboyant Garvey fashion, the rejection produced a spate of intraracial ideological feuds. Garvey relentlessly attacked DuBois, deriding the NAACP as standing for "Nothing Accomplished After Considerable Pretense," while referring to the UNIA as an acronym for "United, Nothing can Impede your Aspirations." Personal attacks ensued. DuBois described Garvey as "a little, fat black man, ugly, but with intelligent eyes and a big head" who was either "a lunatic or a traitor." Garvey, in turn, described DuBois as a "lazy, dependent mulatto" and a "monstrosity" who "bewails every day the drop of Negro blood in his veins." Labor organizer A. Philip Randolph referred to Garvey in his *Messenger* magazine as "the supreme negro Jamaican Jackass," a "monumental monkey," and an "unquestioned fool and ignoramus." Not surprisingly, the intraracial name-calling and general rancor alienated many potential allies and crucial lines of support.[8]

Such rejection by leading American blacks and institutions prompted Garvey to seek allies in strange places. Frustrated by black elites and liberal whites, Garvey became convinced that aside from other blacks of the same mind as him, the only persons who were capable of honest and sincere dialogue with blacks were overt racists and white supremacists. In a strategic blunder that would further alienate his core constituents, Garvey met with representatives of the Anglo-Saxon Club and the White American Society—two auxiliary groups of the resurgent Ku Klux Klan. Despite Garvey's claim that the Klan's separatist ideology was similar to that of the UNIA, it was clear that Garvey had underestimated the deep-seated hatred that many American blacks reserved for the Klan and its legacy of racial terror. Not surprisingly, Garvey lost significant credibility within black communities as a result of these dealings.

Garvey's credibility was further eroded when a number of black leaders and journalists with whom he had been feuding alerted government officials about possible improprieties regarding his management of Black Star Lines—a fledgling shipping unit of UNIA designed to promote international commerce among blacks. Financial and legal difficulties ensued, and Garvey was eventually convicted of mail fraud. In November 1927, after serving two years of a five-year prison term, Garvey was deported as an undesirable alien. He remained active in Jamaica, Toronto, and London, publishing his final magazine (*Black Man*), holding regional conferences of the UNIA, promoting the Pan-African ideal, and eventually establishing a School of African Philosophy to recruit and train prospective leaders for the UNIA.

Beset by financial troubles, Garvey died in isolation in London in 1940, nine weeks short of his fifty-third birthday. The words he had once written of his father seemed now to apply to him: "He took human chances in the course of life, as most bold men do, and he failed at the close of his career. He once had a fortune; he died poor." But just as Washington's death had not stopped the spread of his ideas, so Garvey's death did not entail the death of the ideas that made him great. Reverberations of his conservative contribution to racial empowerment continued to resonate deep within American politics, and would serve as the building blocks for future militant black nationalist movements, such as the Nation of Islam and the Black Power movement. In the interim, however, the mantle of black conservatism would be carried by an important, but rarely discussed, midcentury black cultural critic—the irascible and enigmatic George Schuyler.

# FOUR

# The Agonistic Voice of Midcentury Black Conservatism

## The Strange Career of George Samuel Schuyler

In *The Souls of Black Folk* (1903), DuBois described the condition of the Negro in American life in terms of double consciousness: "One ever feels his twoness—an American, a Negro; two souls, two thoughts, two unreconciled strivings; two warring ideals in one dark body, whose dogged strength alone keeps it from being torn asunder." DuBois, of course, was speaking of the inner struggle of blacks to join mainstream American life without sacrificing racial identity. Yet DuBois's grand metaphor also pointed to the larger struggle within American society to remedy the dissonance created by its commitment to fundamental ideals of freedom and equality and prevailing practices of devastating modes of racial oppression. In this sense, the reconciliation of blackness and Americanness might be understood as both a personal quest to achieve an inner racial peace for blacks and an American quest to nurture and sustain a racially inclusive and empowering democracy.

As the foregoing chapters make clear, the dilemma of "twoness" eloquently described by DuBois was not an artifact of liberal politics but a feature that defined black American life, regardless of ideology. Black conservatives, from James Forten to Booker T. Washington to Mary McLeod Bethune to Marcus Garvey, deployed the principled insights of black conservative thought in an effort to broker peace between these "two warring ideals." Although their approach differed markedly from the likes of DuBois and other mainstream liberals of that era, black conservatives similarly understood their challenge as race advocates to be the vital task of locating social, political, and economic space within American life for blacks to flourish and prosper.

The critical divergence between liberals and conservatives on this issue concerned the manner in which the balance between Americanness and blackness was to be struck. Early-twentieth-century liberals tended to place a premium of importance on racial identity, just as liberals today do. Early-twentieth-century conservatives generally agreed that racial identity was important in its own right, but they preferred to emphasize patriotism and American identity over race. Over the years, however, black conservatives struck the balance decisively in favor of a more robust conception of American identity. Put simply, black conservatives chose to view themselves as Americans first, blacks second.

This is not to suggest that midcentury black conservatives sought to evade or deny their racial heritage. To the contrary, black conservatives were intimately aware of their race and its larger implications in American society. Black conservatives were not immune to racial slights, insults, or segregation. Rather, they tended to believe that the African American identity could not be reduced to "Negro-ness," and that after centuries of living in America, blacks were as American as anyone else.

The struggle between liberals and conservatives over the identity of blacks powerfully informed their competing strategies for racial empowerment, and during the interwar years and well into the civil rights movement of the 1960s, no conservative spoke more loudly and forcefully on this issue than the enigmatic journalist and cultural critic George Samuel Schuyler. Echoing DuBois, Schuyler opened his autobiography, *Black and Conservative:*

> A black person learns very early that his color is a disadvantage in a world of white folk. This being an unalterable circumstance, one also learns very early to make the best of it. So, the lifetime endeavor of the intelligent Negro is how to best be reasonably happy though colored.

Unlike DuBois, however, Schuyler adopted a far more conservative approach to reconciling his pervading sense of double consciousness:

> I learned very early in life that I was colored but from the beginning this fact did not distress, restrain, or overburden me. One takes things as they are, lives with them, and tries to turn them to one's advantage or seeks another locale where the opportunities are more favorable. This was the conservative viewpoint of my parents and family. It has been mine throughout life, not consistently but most of the time.

For Schuyler, race was but one of the many obstacles that a person potentially faced in the ordinary course of life. Much like class, education, or social ties, race was something that one adapted to; the point was to make the most of the hand that one was dealt.

Schuyler advanced his conservative ideas throughout a prolific and controversial career that spanned more than fifty-four years. Although his lifework has received scant attention in the historical literature, it is here that one discovers the important evolutionary link between nineteenth-century and modern black conservatism. Indeed, Schuyler's sustained critique of liberal race policy—including the civil rights movement—ensured the continued relevance of the conservative intellectual tradition within midcentury black political thought and provides much of the grist of modern conservative critiques of liberal race policy.

## The Making of a Conservative

George Samuel Schuyler was born February 25, 1895, in Providence, Rhode Island, but was raised in Syracuse, New York, where he enjoyed a middle-class upbringing in an integrated community. The Schuylers were the only black family living on a vibrant city block that included a bicycle factory, a German butcher shop, and an Irish pub. Their racial isolation, however, was not unusual in Syracuse, according to Schuyler, because "there were fewer than one thousand Negroes in the total population of about 100,000, and they were scattered over the south and east sides of town."

The Schuyler family boasted of having been "free" as far back as anyone could remember, and like many northern blacks, they looked down upon blacks—especially southern blacks—who could trace their lineage to slavery. The family did not identify with slave songs and spirituals, and Schuyler's parents viewed southern migrants as "illiterate, ignorant, ill-bred, and amoral; as people with whom they neither had nor wanted anything to do." Schuyler's mother was particularly fervent in this regard, declaring an open preference for the company of white northerners because they were "her kind of people." The Schuyler family embraced the habits and dispositions of the northern whites for whom they worked, including disdain for European immigrants. As Schuyler recalled, the family "regarded poor European immigrants, who were culturally on par with the people from Dixie, as in the same class."

The haughty disposition of the Schuyler family was reflected in its household surroundings. The "Holy of Holies" in the Schuyler home was the rarely used parlor, replete with "stiffly starched laced curtains, gleaming black square piano with a zither atop it, rose upholstered French chairs and sofa, a whatnot with curios from the Columbian Centennial Exposition of 1893 in Chicago, and a large green rug with a Saint Bernard dog depicted upon it." The room was accented by "two large potted palms almost reaching the ceiling," to lend elegance to the scene, "and between them on a small table was a large kerosene lamp with a hand-painted globe."

The room was reserved for "special occasions," and its double doors remained closed and window shade drawn most days. Yet in many ways, it embodied the tone established by Schuyler's father, a chef at a local hotel. As Schuyler recounts, a head chef was "an aristocrat in the colored community." Accordingly, his father wore a "stately mustache" and "affected baronial living" by insisting upon fine furnishings and proper attire and deportment. The tradition continued after his father's death, when his mother married Joseph E. Brown, an ambitious and industrious "light colored man with wavy hair parted in the middle" who belonged to "a couple of Negro fraternal organizations and cut quite a figure in his lodge uniform with plumed hat and gleaming sword."

A similar theme pervaded ritual family moments. Adjoining the parlor room was a sitting room where the family gathered for evening Bible readings by George's grandmother, a "sage, crusty and industrious matriarch, the repository of knowledge, it seemed, and a mine of folklore. Any youthful dereliction was rewarded with a sharply pinched ear or the thumping of a bony knuckle against the side of the head."

Cleanliness and proper representation were important features of the Schuyler household:

There was a rigid schedule of dusting, sweeping, mopping, scrubbing, laundering, ironing, soap-making, cooking and baking.... There were a dozen kerosene lamps to be filled and cleaned, and have their wicks trimmed. There was kindling wood to be chopped and fetched. There was a front and back stoop to be swept or washed down. There were windows to be cleaned, and a dozen other chores to do. Order and discipline prevailed, and it was all very impressive.

Cleanliness and proper representation were viewed not as onerous tasks but as part of how the family defined itself. As Schuyler explained, "I was delighted to participate in maintaining our home. Here was something admirable to be preserved and improved. People are conservative when they feel they have something to conserve."

Conservatism and industriousness were not peculiar to the Schuyler home. These were community-wide ethics. "All these people were workers," according to Schuyler. "They went to their jobs at seven or eight o'clock in the morning and returned around six o'clock in the evening.... Many workers came home for lunch as did the children. There was no such thing as a school lunch."

Despite being a strong student ("I never experienced that aversion to school which so many children have"), Schuyler dropped out of high school to join the U.S. Army in 1912. The reason, according to Schuyler, was that it had become "increasingly clear to me that the Negro had his place in Syracuse, and it was nowhere near the top, nor would it be, no matter what his schooling." He elaborated:

The colored people seemed to be in a rut, and I did not want to stay down there with them. So what should I do? Where should I go? The United States Army seemed to be the best choice.... Opportunities were very slim, not only in Syracuse, but just about everywhere. In the Army, I could see the world I wanted to see and have a chance to advance myself.

Schuyler's six-year stint in the military was, on the whole, successful. He served with distinction in the famous black First Battalion, Twenty-fifth Infantry. During World War I, he was selected to attend the Army officer training camp in Fort Des Moines, Iowa, and received a commission

as a first lieutenant. After serving in Seattle and Hawaii, Schuyler was dis-
charged in 1919 and worked as a civil servant in New York, processing
military prisoners shipped in from abroad. Eventually, the pool of prisoners began to dry up, and Schuyler received notice that his civil service
employment would soon end. Although he was eager to remain in New
York, the lack of permanent employment proved too great a burden to
bear. Reflecting on his decision to leave New York City and return to Syracuse, Schuyler remarked, "I quit the fetid world of steam, odors, dirty
dishes, and twelve-hour days, went back to the familiar streets and faces
of nine years before, to try to start all over."

## From Left to Right—
## A Socialist's Journey to Conservatism

Once he was back in Syracuse, Schuyler began a new life as a socialist.
"The most active group around town, intellectually, was the Socialists,
and it was not long before I began meeting with them in their forum and
discussing the momentous happenings of the day," Schuyler recalled. In
1921, he became an official member of the Socialist Party of America and
was elected its educational director. Tasked with creating intellectual fer-
ment for socialism in Syracuse, Schuyler advertised for and coordinated
his first meeting, in which he delivered a lecture titled "An Intelligent Program for Intelligent Negro Workers" to an audience of about ten people.

The tepid reception did not surprise the naturally skeptical Schuyler,
who observed that meetings of socialists "were quite dull, [although] I attended them regularly." Later, he began to question socialist claims, arguments, and predictions. He soon struck up a friendship with Rollen
Bolton, a union painter and fellow skeptic, and the two began to wonder
aloud about virtues of socialism:

> We questioned that every occurrence could be explained on the
> basis of class struggle; that the poor were getting worse off all
> the time; that capitalism would destroy civilization; that a swarm
> of bureaucrats in Washington could run the country better than
> the decentralized free enterprise power structure. We noted that
> the results of socialism in the Soviet Union had been chaos and
> famine, compelling a return to capitalism under the name of

New Economic Policy. Worse, we both began to question Marxist Holy Writ in party meetings, thus quickly isolating ourselves. This was treason but we both enjoyed it and had fun twitting the orthodox.

Disenchanted with his role within the Socialist Party and with socialism itself, Schuyler quit the party and left Syracuse for new horizons in New York City.

In 1922 in New York, Schuyler met A. Philip Randolph, cofounder and editor of the *Messenger,* at a meeting of the Friends of Negro Freedom, a socialist organization. Despite his misgivings about socialism, Schuyler quickly established a good rapport with Randolph, and he began submitting articles for the *Messenger* the following year. Soon, Schuyler was a regularly featured columnist, publishing under the heading "Shafts and Darts: A Page of Calumny and Satire." The column focused on issues of race, religion, politics, and culture, and it skewered mainstream African American society and race movements. As Schuyler would recount, "To me, nothing was above a snicker, a chuckle, a smile or guffaw."

One of his early targets was Marcus Garvey. Randolph, who despised Garvey, had no quarrels with Schuyler's desire to humiliate the Pan-African head of the UNIA. Following Garvey's arrest on charges of mail fraud in connection with his Black Star Line shipping corporation, Randolph encouraged Schuyler to use his column to criticize Garvey. In July 1924, Schuyler delivered a scathing portrayal of Garvey as a fraudulent opportunist. He satirized Garvey as skillful enough to convince UNIA members to support a failing shipping line that had "the finest rat trap [the S.S. Shadyside] in the Harlem River." He went on to lampoon Garvey as a flagrant opportunist, saying, "Like Brother Marcus, my motto is: One God, One Aim, One Destiny—The Almighty Dollar."

Schuyler was developing into a critic and satirist of African American culture, but his own ideological commitments remained obscure until he directed his satirical gaze at the Harlem Renaissance. In 1926, the *Nation* published Schuyler's most famous critique of the Harlem Renaissance, "The Negro Art Hokum." Schuyler declared that the idea of "Negro art" existing in America was foolishness, and that "the Aframerican is merely a lampblacked Anglo-Saxon." He continued:

> If the European immigrant after two or three generations of exposure to our schools, politics, advertising, moral crusades, and restaurants becomes indistinguishable from the mass of Americans of the older stock, how much truer it must be for the sons of Ham who have been subjected to what the uplifters call Americanism for the last three hundred years. Aside from color, . . . your American Negro is just plain American.

Unlike his persona in previous moments of satire, Schuyler here reveals his own belief that national identity, rather than racial identity, deserves primary status.

> Consider Coleridge Taylor, Edward Wilmot, Blyden, and Claude McKay, the Englishmen; Pushkin, the Russian; Bridgewater, the Pole; Antar, the Arabian; Latino, the Spaniard; Dumas, *pere* and *fils*, the Frenchmen; and Paul Laurence Dunbar, Charles W. Chestnut [sic], and James Weldon Johnson, the Americans. All Negroes; yet, their work shows the impress of nationality rather than race. . . . Why should Negro artists in America vary from the national artistic norm when Negro artists in other countries have not done so? The only explanation for the popularity of the Negro-art hokum [is the misguided belief in] fundamental, eternal and inescapable differences between white and black Americans.

Schuyler laments that too many Negro artists are willing to "lend this myth a helping hand."

As touched on in the previous chapter, Langston Hughes's response, the article "The Negro Artist and the Racial Mountain," offered an impassioned defense of the authenticity of Negro art as a distinctive cultural expression that takes place within and against prevailing notions of American nationality. As Hughes famously declared, "The mountain standing in the way of any true Negro art in America [is the] urge within the race toward whiteness, the desire to pour racial individuality into the mold of American standardization, and to be as little Negro and as much American as possible."

The interchange between Schuyler and Hughes highlighted the distinction between conservative and liberal positions on the New Negro movement and the existence of a distinctive Negro culture within the American framework. But it also provided Schuyler with an issue from which to launch a more expansive discussion on competing modes of racial empowerment. In a follow-up letter to the editor, Schuyler equated Hughes's emphasis on Negro distinctiveness to "primitivism," and described such work as mere "protest against a feeling of inferiority." He would later amplify this point in his January 1926 "Shafts and Darts" column in the *Messenger,* when he offered "advice" to aspiring black authors:

> Success depends, however, on the ability of the striving writer to do the Charleston, sing the spirituals, and chatter amiably with the abandon supposed to be characteristic of members of a race with a primitive background. . . . [Depictions of blacks] should always without exception be bizarre, fantastical and outlandish, with a suggestion of the jungle, the plantation or the slum. Otherwise, it will not be *Negro* literature, and hence unacceptable. The predominant characteristic of the writings offered should be naiveté, as befits simple children just a century or two removed from the so-called uncivilized expanses of the Dark Continent.

For Schuyler, the writings of Harlem Renaissance authors were not simply crabbed and contrived; they damaged the fragile reputation of blacks.

Schuyler would later expand his critique of primitivism in black literature in "Negro Authors Must Eat" (written under the pen name George W. Jacobs), arguing that the popularity of "Africanisms" in literature was doing a disservice to blacks. Unlike his previous column, Schuyler pursued a more optimistic path, acknowledging artists whose work presented a fuller, more respectable image of blacks. Schuyler identified the works of Nella Larsen and Jessie Fausset as proof that "granted the same environmental conditions, the Harlem black and Broadway white fit not dissimilarly into the mode of our mechanized American culture." Schuyler was particularly fond of Fausset's fiction, praising her portrayal of the "best" Negroes who were largely unknown to whites, but provided "the inspiration of a rising generation." In a prior review of Fausset's *There Is Confusion,* Schuyler described the book as "the first novel, not obviously propaganda, by an American Negro woman about American Negroes (who are more truly American than the loud mouth 'Nordics' and Kluxers who must try the patience of the gods with their ignorant gibberish."

Although some may view Schuyler's critique of the Harlem Renaissance as unduly harsh, it is important to realize that Schuyler was not condemning the movement as a whole. His critique, much like that of Harlem Renaissance artists Countee Cullen and Sterling Brown, was directed at those elements of the movement that undermined a vision of racial empowerment powerfully informed by a strong sense of middle-class morality and conservative politics of respectability.

## Schuyler's Americanism
## and the Critique of Dr. King

By the end of the early 1930s, Schuyler had established himself not only as a leading cultural critic but as an author in his own right, publishing two critically acclaimed novels: *Black No More,* a satire on the Harlem Renaissance, and *Slaves Today,* a fictionalized account of slavery in Liberia based upon events he personally witnessed during his travels in the country. He had begun to write regularly for the *Pittsburgh Courier,* the leading African American newspaper of the period, and his work was gaining increasing recognition among both blacks and whites.

Schuyler was also becoming increasingly conservative. In 1931, nine black youths were unjustly convicted of raping two white women in Scottsboro, Alabama. The International Labor Defense, which served as the legal arm of the Communist Party came to their defense, ultimately securing their release. In the face of this legal success, Schuyler nevertheless accused the organization and the Communist Party of using the case as a means of manipulating poor and working-class blacks into abandoning capitalism as the primary means of racial empowerment. As Schuyler wrote in his autobiography:

> The most fantastic programs appeal to some elements of any population, and the inroads to Negro society by the Communists utilizing the Scottsboro case became very great in a short time. Volunteers to aid the International Labor Defense arose on every side. At least twice the number of Scottsboro mothers as there actually existed were sent about the country to appear in Negro churches.... Ordinary Negroes were won over because they did not see that the speakers sent to their churches were communists

bent on destroying a way of life which they approved, but saw them simply as advocates of justice for nine black boys caught in the toils of southern justice.

Schuyler's response to the Scottsboro Boys case immediately cast him in an unfavorable light among liberal blacks, who interpreted his comments as critical of the trial's outcome. Some commentators, such as E. Franklin Frazier, condemned Schuyler as being singularly unhelpful to the cause of racial justice.

For Schuyler, however, the essential problem was not the outcome of the case but the extent to which liberal blacks, in the pursuit of racial justice, were willing to sacrifice their fidelity to the larger American democratic ideal. Whereas liberal blacks viewed Scottsboro as a battleground for racial justice, Schuyler viewed it as a battleground for American democracy. Schuyler was simply warning blacks that although they might feel victimized in American democratic society, their fate could be far worse under a totalitarian communist regime. Not surprisingly, Schuyler would recall the decade of the 1940s as "one of great importance" in his career as a cultural critic because he had "devoted at least fifty full-length columns to the subject in the *Pittsburgh Courier* alone."

By the 1950s, Schuyler had evolved into the consummate African American patriot and, drawing upon his skepticism of socialism, presented himself to the world as the foremost African American anticommunist during the Cold War era. He joined the American Committee for Cultural Freedom and delivered a scathing rebuke of communism in its first meeting in Berlin. He developed open associations with right-wing conservatives and used his "Shafts and Darts" column to amplify Senator Joseph McCarthy's campaign against the communist threat.

Schuyler's unwavering belief in gradualism, patriotism, and economic empowerment would soon put him at greater odds with the burgeoning civil rights establishment. Not one to be easily intimidated into editorial silence, Schuyler turned his critical attention upon liberal civil rights leaders and advocates. In response to racial terror spawned by the Supreme Court's 1954 decision in *Brown v. Board of Education*, Schuyler condemned civil rights advocates for failing to plan for potential backlash. "Due to our misleadership which has mistaken legal shadow for economic substance and oration for organization, we have not used the weapons and resources we possess for warfare which was implicit in the prematurely accelerated drive for integration." Schuyler, like Washington, believed that economic security for blacks was far more important to securing social rights to integration. Schuyler elaborated,

> Were we possessed of as many cooperative societies, credit unions, business enterprises, factories, and banks in Hog and Hominy Land and North, East and West as we have social clubs, fraternities, churches and NAACP branches, we could laugh at the crackers' threats. As it is, we can't and there's no point in pretending that we can. You can't bring about equality ... not even from the Supreme Court.

Schuyler was equally critical of the 1956 Montgomery, Alabama, bus boycott. Boycotts of white-owned businesses and white-operated public services missed the point, according to Schuyler. The more urgent problem was that blacks often failed to patronize black-owned business and lead self-directed economic lives. Rather than ask why whites refused to serve blacks on equal terms, Schuyler demanded to know why blacks "discriminate against their own professional and business folk who live in the community, are identified with the community, rear families in the community and whose success aids the community." Although the boycott ultimately proved successful in securing integration of the city's buses, Schuyler remained unfazed: "Now that it has been 'won' ... so what? Montgomery Negroes could have owned the bus company without doing all that walking if they had used their heads instead of their feet and tonsils."

Schuyler believed that Martin Luther King Jr. and his organization, the Southern Christian Leadership Conference, were largely responsible for leading black society astray. When, in 1959, King suggested a march in Mississippi to protest lynching, Schuyler immediately criticized the plan, suggesting that it was not only irrational but would serve to "enrich the undertakers in this volatile region." Demonstrating strong fidelity to Western institutions—including their laws—he would later condemn King for suggesting that unjust laws should not be obeyed. "Obviously," he wrote, "if citizens are to choose the laws they want to obey, the result will be anarchy and chaos, with the Negroes the worst sufferers." Schuyler further cautioned, "[Negroes] have reached their present state of development because the majority of white people were tolerant and helpful, and willing to obey most of the laws enacted in the Negro's behalf and supported by the Courts."

In "King: No Help to Peace," Schuyler continued to assail King and what he perceived to be the folly of the civil rights movement. He argued that King was neither worthy of the Nobel Prize nor had made any meaningful contribution to domestic or world peace:

> Dr. King's principal contribution to world peace has been to roam the country like some sable Typhoid Mary, infecting the mentally disturbed with perversions of Christian doctrine, and grabbing fat lecture fees from the shallow pated.... His incitement has packed jails with Negroes and some whites, getting them beaten, bitten, and firehosed, thereby bankrupting communities raising bail and fines, to the vast enrichment of Southern "law 'n' order." ... Alfred Bernard Nobel will probably whirl in his tomb on Dec. 10 when Dr. King receives the bauble and bankroll.

If "King: No Help to Peace" confirmed Schuyler as a political outcast to African American communities, his article titled "He Reaped the Whirlwind: A Cool and Critical Appraisal of Martin Luther King's Works," published shortly after the leader's death, confirmed his exile. He began the essay with a declaration that nonviolent resistance only served to inflame racial passions and violence. He wrote, "Countless mass demonstrations which started to advance a good cause have ended in clashes with police, looting, vandalism, and killing rather than the good will and understanding originally intended."

In contrast, Schuyler presented the conservative alternative of gradualism and economic empowerment as the superior mode of engagement: "Wherever the Negro lives in the United States, he prospers only to the extent that he has the good will, tolerance, and acceptance of his white neighbors and fellow workers." King's mistake, in his view, was that of moving too quickly. Racial progress, explained Schuyler, "cannot be speeded by the razzle-dazzle tactics which arouse suspicion and lend support to the propaganda of Negrophobes." He further assailed supporters of the civil rights movement as "retarded, half-witted" and "criminally inclined people" who, like King, failed to appreciate that nonviolent protests served only to further racial violence. "Dr. King tragically never learned this," remarked Schuyler. "His followers had better."

## Schuyler's Critique of the Nation of Islam and Malcolm X

Given Schuyler's skepticism of the agitative posture of the civil rights movement and his lingering disdain for black nationalist militancy, which began with his virulent opposition to Marcus Garvey, his opposition to the Nation of Islam came as little surprise to anyone. In a remarkable 1961 radio discussion[1] with religious scholar C. Eric Lincoln, novelist James Baldwin, and Malcolm X, Schuyler offered a scathing critique of black nationalism and a staunch defense of his conservative vision of black empowerment. In his opening comment, Schuyler attacked the foundational Nation of Islam position that white Christians were responsible for slavery in the world and thus responsible for the sorry state of American race relations. "The Moslem carried on slavery for something like twelve or thirteen hundred years before the White European Christians started it," Schuyler said, and he further observed that "one of the outstanding slave traders in Africa ... is Tip Bu Tip, who devastated all central and east Africa.[2] ... This is one of the many falsehoods upon which this movement [Nation of Islam] is founded."

Consistent with his conservative critiques of Garvey and the Harlem Renaissance, Schuyler proved sensitive to "falsehoods" and "misrepresentations" about black life. Of particular concern to Schuyler was the view proffered by Elijah Muhammad and Malcolm X that blacks were shut out of capitalist opportunities in America. Schuyler disagreed vehemently, and in a moment of exasperation, declared, "I want to get back to the field of reality":

> There's something like two hundred thousand individual Negro farmers in the United States. They raise cotton, corn. They sell milk and all of that, but they are selling it to white people, and the white people would be very hard put if they didn't have this cotton, corn, meat and other things that Negro farmers raise to buy from them. ... Nobody's stopping Negroes from either buy-

ing or selling in the United States. Many of them are doing it all the time, and I think it's a perversion of the fact to say the Negro has no part in the economy—that's ridiculous.

More generally, Schuyler was exasperated by the Nation of Islam's consistent focus on obstacles to black success rather than achievements and opportunities secured by blacks in the face of such obstacles. Responding to James Baldwin's suggestion that the Nation of Islam was correct in calling upon white people to "pay for the history written in the color of my skin," Schuyler commented:

I marvel sometimes. If, as is said by the Muslim speakers, the white man has hated the Negro since he has been on earth, why has the white man done so much to help the Negro? For example, I notice they abolished the slave trade in Africa, and from here to Africa, and I don't know whether any Moslem states have done that. They've set up schools and clinics and hospitals and asylums and colleges throughout all black Africa.... Now, these things have been done, and it doesn't seem to me that this is the action of people that hate a whole people. Of course there are white people who hate Negroes, but I don't see any reason or justification for exaggerating the situation.

For Schuyler, falsehood, misrepresentation, and exaggeration by the Nation of Islam proved particularly troubling because it served as the foundation for a separatist ideology that ran afoul of the conservative sense of patriotism, national identity, and respect for Western institutions of government. Malcolm X's articulation of the Nation of Islam's religious goal of racial separatism from white America led to this interesting exchange, in which Schuyler's patriotic nationalism is placed in stark relief with black nationalist ideology:

Schuyler: Just wait a minute, now. At the risk of going into politics, I would like to know how any group in the United States is going to separate part of the United States for them to live in without having something to do with politics. Do you plan to do this through warfare?

Malcolm X: Sir, I don't think that it's necessary to bring about any warfare. If the ex-slave in America has to go to war with his former slave master to get what is his by right, then that itself is a condemnation of the former slave master. If Lincoln issued the Emancipation Proclamation a hundred years ago ... and yet at the same time today the so-called Negro is knocking at the White House door, still begging his master to pass legislation that will give him recognition or protection by the constitution that is supposed to represent him, I think sir that the man who is depriving him of these rights cannot open his mouth and say that it would be war.

Schuyler, not to be outdone, would respond to Malcolm X's comments later in the conversation, observing that "these 18 million some-odd Negroes that you're talking about in the United States are some of the healthiest, wealthiest, have the most property, [are] the best educated, and [are] best informed group of Negroes in the world, and that includes all those in the Muslim countries." Responding directly to Malcolm X's invocation of Lincoln and the Emancipation Proclamation, Schuyler asked rhetorically, "Where is there anything in the Constitution or anything that Lincoln said or wrote that says that a group has a right to part of the United States to take it off by itself? I thought that issue was settled a hundred years ago."

Although Schuyler was deeply skeptical of the separatist ideology of the black nationalist movement, he was willing to praise the Nation of Islam's embrace of capitalism and the politics of respectability. In a 1959 *Pittsburgh Courier* article, Schuyler offered this backhanded compliment:

Mr. Muhammad may be a rogue and a charlatan, but when anybody can get tens of thousands of Negroes to practice economic solidarity, respect their women, alter their atrocious diet, give up liquor, stop crime, juvenile delinquency and adultery, he is doing more for the Negroes' welfare than any current Negro leader I know.

Schuyler would reiterate his approval of Nation of Islam policies of self-improvement in the 1961 radio-broadcast debate. After stating his emphatic opposition to black nationalism as the solution to problems faced by blacks, Schuyler conceded:

I am in complete agreement [with the Muslim movement regarding] the greater interest in Negroes acquiring an economic stake in this civilization. Also, in the fine work of rehabilitation they've done in some young members who have been juvenile delinquents and criminals—and they have come out, and by virtue of the teaching they receive, have changed their way of life. Now, that's been done by other movements; the Moslem movement has no monopoly on it, but they have done it, and you have to give credit for that.

When the radio host suggested to Schuyler that the Nation of Islam's insistence upon a separate, black economy was inconsistent with "economic uplift of the Negro," Schuyler reiterated his compliment, noting that "they may want two separate economies, but they are interested in economic uplift of the Negro, and I think they deserve great credit for that."

His 1973 article "Malcolm X—Better to Memorialize Benedict Arnold," which appeared in the ultraconservative *American Opinion*, exemplifies the simmering hostility he felt toward the slain leader and the Nation of Islam. Here, Schuyler goes to great lengths to downplay the cultural significance of Malcolm X, observing that "no important Negro leader eulogized the 'martyr' and that "the black masses did not mourn his passing, but were largely indifferent." He characterized the modest support and sympathy expressed following Malcolm X's assassination as "mass madness," all the more confounding, according to Schuyler, because "like most of the loudmouthed black leaders, he had but a tiny following, perhaps not more than a couple of hundred ... and all equally ignorant, if not more so."

He also directed a personal assault on the character of Malcolm X that recalled his critique of Martin Luther King from the previous decade He maligned Malcolm X as "a bold, outspoken, ignorant man of no occupation after he gave up pimping, gambling, and dope selling to follow Mr. Muhammad." He characterized Malcolm X as a traitor—to black people and perhaps to America itself—suggesting that efforts to honor him were tantamount to celebrating the birthdays of infamous traitors Benedict Arnold and Alger Hiss. Lumping Malcolm X in with a group of black leaders summarily described as "mediocrities, criminals, plotters, and poseurs," Schuyler wondered aloud, "How is it then that so many black charlatans have been able to get a following gullible enough to believe them?"

The answer offered by Schuyler, however, revealed more about his own conservative politics and aspirations to be a cultural icon than it did about Malcolm X's followers. "There are those in the black community who want to get something for nothing," he wrote, those "who are allergic to honest toil and thus susceptible to the bamboozlement of sharpers who prey upon their fears, weaknesses, frustrations, and misfortunes." These "sharpers," according to Schuyler, included nearly "every black movement started this past century," from Garveyism and the NAACP to the Black Panthers and the Nation of Islam. Individual thinkers such as Schuyler, "who have questioned these movements and their self-anointed leaders, have been bulldozed into silence or acquiescence."

## Schuyler and the Future
## of Black Conservatism

Schuyler lamented that "the Eldridge Cleavers, the Hubert 'Rap' Browns and the Malcolm Xs will continue their madness and bedevil society just as long as they can find encouragement to do so." Clearly Schuyler, by then the dominant voice of black conservatism, had grown increasingly frustrated and isolated. His campaign against the Civil Rights Bill in 1963 had eroded what little support he received from his iconoclastic black conservative base. His open support for right-wing Republican Barry Goldwater in the presidential race against Democratic candidate Lyndon B. Johnson ultimately led to Schuyler's demotion at the *Pittsburgh Courier*, which had publicly endorsed Johnson for president. After leaving the *Courier*, Schuyler would veer even further to the right, joining the ultraconservative John Birch Society. For the remainder of his career, his voice would be heard primarily in *American Opinion* and *Review of the News*, two Birch Society publications.

In "The Reds and I," an autobiographical essay first published in the *American Opinion* in 1968, Schuyler asks himself, "How is it ... that an American who is colored can be simultaneously a 'Conservative' and unalterably opposed to the Communist rumble-bumble?" The answer, for Schuyler, was obvious: American blacks had benefited the most from conservatism and capitalism. As Schuyler explained:

> Homo Aframericanus is fundamentally "Conservative" because, as Bert Williams used to sing, "I May Be Crazy, But I Ain't No Fool"—knowing that he has more to conserve in America than

elsewhere on the globe. To this the million or more colored who have been abroad to the far corners will readily agree, having noted that welfare recipients in Dayton are living more expansively than the sable aristocracy in Dahomey, and without fear of a Leopard Society or the local Liberation Front. Thus, I can claim no uniqueness in being black and "Conservative." In truth, I would be unique if I were not.

Though plainly a unique figure in America politics for the first half of the twentieth century, Schuyler understood that his novelty was in the mode of expression and not substance. The conservative ideas he advanced had circulated within black politics for more than a century—a point that Schuyler was quick to emphasize:

> What the average colored person feels [today] was no better expressed than at the conclusion of the New York City convention of the American Society of Free Persons of Color in 1831, when the forty-odd delegates unanimously resolved that: "This is our home, and this is our country. Beneath its sod lies the bones of our fathers; for it some of them fought, bled and died. Here we were born, and here we will die.

Reflecting upon Schuyler's lifework proves useful in understanding the trajectory of black conservatism in the modern era. By the end of his career, Schuyler had moved from the center of black life to the margins of white society. His conservative mantra of capitalism, respectability, and self-critique fell on increasingly deaf ears. The darling of mainstream media in his early years, by midcentury Schuyler had become a political pariah—an author whose views forced him in to obscurity.

Unlike early-twentieth-century conservatives, who enjoyed mass support from the black community, Schuyler's strongest allies, late in his career, were ultraconservative whites. This proved a most devastating consolation prize for a man who had dedicated his entire life to empowering the black community though conservative philosophy. George Schuyler lived and died believing that blackness and conservatism were not antithetical, yet he ultimately failed to persuade the masses of black people as to the "correctness" of his position. Although Schuyler would lose the ideological battle within his lifetime, his contributions, which provided legitimate warning that liberal approaches to racial empowerment imposed messy and unrealistic expectations on American society, ensured that the legacy of black conservative thought would remain available for resuscitation within black political discourse by future generations of conservatives. But much like Schuyler, modern blacks who chose the path of conservatism would find support within the black community fleeting. They too would find themselves at the margins of society, and they too would seek refuge in the company of ultraconservative whites and their institutions.

# FIVE

# Black Conservatism in the Civil Rights Era

## Why the Nation of Islam, Elijah Muhammad, Malcolm X, and Stokely Carmichael's Black Power Movement Are Part of the Black Conservative Tradition

The civil rights era and the decade that followed thrust black conservatism and conservatism more generally into a period of deep and sustained crisis. Conservatism had remained a viable alternative throughout the interwar years in large part because of the Roosevelt administration's failure to engage in a full frontal assault on the civil rights issue and economic oppression sourced from racial animosity. Welfare initiatives in unemployment, housing, and agriculture did lead many blacks to question their faith in a conservative philosophy of racial empowerment, but for many blacks, it remained far from clear that the liberal ideology of the New Deal, which left segregation and racial hostility largely untouched, provided a better mode of racial empowerment. Black voters, skeptical of the liberal promise, offered their cautious support to New Deal Democrats and their liberalism in deliberate and gradual fashion.

The conversion of conservative blacks to liberalism would increase precipitously, however, in the 1960s, as the liberal Democratic administrations under Presidents John F. Kennedy and Lyndon B. Johnson delivered more forthrightly on those features of black empowerment left untouched by the New Deal. Liberal Democrats secured the passage of major civil rights legislation, including the landmark Civil Rights Act of 1964 and the Voting Rights Act of 1965. The new civil rights legislation provided for sweeping federal intervention in the southern states to secure civil and political rights for blacks. Unlike previous efforts, this new legislation focused on the race problem in the economic and social spheres of American life, securing nondiscriminatory access to education, employment, and housing. The liberal legal strategy had, in short, delivered on the promise of civic and social equality championed almost a century before by progressives during Reconstruction.

At the same time, liberal Democrats launched the "War on Poverty." Building upon the liberal insights of the New Deal, Johnson's promotion of "The Great Society" involved a classically liberal array of programs that not only improved access to education, housing, heath care, and education, but generally increased the capacity of blacks to enjoy the fruits of American citizenship and participate in the political process. Most commentators agree that the War on Poverty lifted a great many blacks out of a life of poverty, and spurred the growth and development of the black middle class. Civil rights legislation, combined with sustained economic relief, had solidified the appeal of liberalism in the hearts and minds of everyday black people.

White conservatives, by contrast, appeared anachronistic and largely out of touch with changes in society. They proved hostile not only to the challenges delivered by the twentieth century but to new ideas and approaches to deal with those challenges. Senator and presidential candidate Barry Goldwater, in *The Conscience of a Conservative,* exemplified this increasingly conservative philosophy, observing that the "conservative approach" was best understood as "an attempt to apply the wisdom and experience and the revealed truths *of the past* to the problems of today." For Goldwater, conservative ideology did not need to adapt to meet new challenges. It was, in his view, not an ideology, but a set of principles "derived from the nature of man, and from the truths that God has revealed about His creation" that "have no dateline." Conservative principles, wrote Goldwater, are "ancient and tested truths that guided our Republic through its early days [and] will do equally well for us." "The challenge to Conservatives," opined Goldwater, was "to demonstrate the bearing of a proven philosophy on the problems of our own time."

White conservatives discovered a new hero in Barry Goldwater—one who would articulate an "enlightened" view on conservatism that lay claim to both spiritual and material positions of the founding fathers and "our sacred political heritage." In practice, however, Goldwater-style conservatism translated into vigorous opposition to liberal programmatic change. Goldwater conservatives opposed civil rights, Social Security, rural electrification, Medicare, urban renewal—all measures that Americans were beginning to appreciate as essential to their individual well-being—on the ground that such programs were, at bottom, un-American and violative of the "ancient and tested truths" of our national forefathers.

Goldwater's views proved particularly troubling to blacks. His vote against the Civil Rights Act of 1964, his defense of "state's rights," and his vocal opposition to "forced integration" in the name of preserving "individual freedom" were largely interpreted as minimally disguised endorsements of segregation and retrograde customs of racial hostility. It was becoming clear to many blacks that conservatism, at least as practiced by the white establishment, was standing in the way of racial progress. White conservatism, in the words of black conservative and Massachusetts senator Edward W. Brooke, had come to mean "Stop! Thou shall progress no further. What you cannot do for yourselves does not deserve to be done." According to Brooke, "This [was] a perversion of authentic conservatism and an invitation to electoral defeat."

Not surprisingly, in the years that followed, liberalism became the consensus ideology for blacks. Liberalism became the dominant voice of black leadership, and was reflected in the attitudes and voting behavior of ordinary blacks. Liberals had opened the door for progress, and blacks were not inclined to live in the past. The blind and stubborn allegiance by white conservatives to outmoded ideas, paired with clear opposition to efforts to improve their daily lives, made clear to many blacks that the liberal strategy for racial empowerment was, in many ways, now superior to its conservative counterpart.

Given these events, one would expect black conservatism to have died a lonely death. Surprisingly, this did not happen. How could this be? Why would some blacks continue to hold fast to conservatism, which provided for modest gains, in the face of dramatic racial progress occasioned by implementation of liberal philosophy?

The answer may very well have been provided by Goldwater himself. According to Goldwater,

The root difference between Conservatives and Liberals today is that Conservatives take account of the *whole* man, while Liberals tend to look only at the material side of man's nature. The Conservative believes that man is, in part, an economic, an animal creature; but that he is also a spiritual creature with spiritual needs and spiritual desires. What is more, these needs and desires reflect the *superior* side of man's nature.... The first obligation of a political thinker is to understand the nature of man. The Conservative does not claim special powers of perception on this point, but he does claim a familiarity with the accumulated wisdom and experience of history, and he is not too proud to learn from the great minds of the past.

For many blacks, certain precepts of black conservative thought—pragmatic optimism, self-help and autonomy, respect for Western institutions, and middle-class morality—represented their "accumulated wisdom and experience of history" as blacks living in white America. Furthermore, like Goldwater, blacks were not "too proud" to live by principles that had been validated in the lived experience of *their* "founding fathers"—black leaders and businessmen—for more than one hundred years. In a manner not unlike members of the previous generation, some civil rights and post–civil rights blacks would draw upon this black conservative tradition when advancing new strategies for racial empowerment. And like *their* forbears, not all fit the conventional model of a "conservative."

## Senator Edward Brooke and the Repositioning of Black Conservatism

Perhaps the most important moderating voice of black conservatism in the 1960s was Sen. Edward W. Brooke III. Brooke, whose father, Edward William Brooke Jr., was an attorney for the Veterans Administration for more than fifty years, was born in 1919 and raised in largely segregated neighborhoods in Washington, D.C. Despite the divisiveness embodied in the Jim Crow laws of the day, Brooke said that his worldview was not profoundly shaped by racism. "I was a happy child," he was quoted as saying in John Henry Cutler's *Ed Brooke: Biography of a Senator*. "It would make a better story if some white man had kicked me or yelled 'nigger,' but it just never happened. I grew up segregated, but there was not much feeling of being shut out of anything." Having been spared this victimization, Brooke would always refuse to define himself in terms of his race, and he thus viewed politics through a much broader ideological lens.

Brooke attended public schools in Washington, and at the age of sixteen he enrolled at Howard University, where he earned his B.S. in sociology in 1941. Upon graduation, Brooke entered the Army, and served in the all-black 366th Combat Infantry Regiment. In charge of discipline and recreation at Fort Devens, in Massachusetts, Brooke's primary duty was to defend enlisted men in military court cases. During the Italian campaign, Brooke was sent overseas, where he crossed enemy lines to fight with the Italian Partisans against German and Italian troops. For his leadership during 195 days in combat in Italy, Brooke was awarded the Bronze Star and a Distinguished Service Award, and he was promoted to the rank of captain. When he returned from the war, Brooke enrolled in Boston University School of Law, earning an LL.B. in 1948 and an LL.M. a year later, as well as serving as editor of the school's Law Review. Brooke began his private law practice in the Boston neighborhood of Roxbury after declining offers to join other firms, including an offer from his father to open a father-and-son practice in Washington, D.C.

In 1950 and 1952, Brooke ran two strong but unsuccessful campaigns to secure a Republican seat in the Massachusetts House of Representatives. In 1960, he became the first African American to be nominated by a major party for a statewide office in Massachusetts, running as the Republican candidate for secretary of state—in itself widely considered to be a substantial accomplishment because there were fewer than a hundred thousand black residents in the entire state. Though he lost the election, he received more than one million votes.

Brooke's perseverance paid off in 1962 when he was elected attorney general of the Commonwealth of Massachusetts—the first African American in the entire country ever to hold that post. Brooke cut an unusual figure for statewide office in Massachusetts. In a state that was 98 percent white, two-thirds Democrat, and overwhelmingly Catholic, Brooke was black, Republican, and Protestant. He was, as he said, an American first, a Republican second, and a black incidentally. "I'm not running as a Negro," he once said. "I never have. I'm trying to show that people can be elected on the basis of their qualifications and not their race." Much as John F. Kennedy had reassured the nation by saying that his Catholicism would be irrelevant to his duty as president, so did Brooke pacify Massachusetts voters by repeatedly assuring that race and religion would play no part in his plans to strengthen law enforcement in the state. He won reelection in 1964, and during his tenure as attorney general, Brooke developed the reputation of being a vigorous prosecutor of organized crime. His successful investigation of the "Boston Strangler" case, advocacy of consumer protection, and opposition to housing discrimination made him popular among whites and blacks.

Brooke also proved that he was independent of mainstream black organizations. In 1963, he fought the NAACP and other civil rights groups that had called for students to boycott their schools to protest segregation in Boston. Brooke withstood the militant black leaders' charges that he had sold out to the white establishment, reiterating that his job was to enforce the state's laws, which required children to attend school. Brooke quickly established a reputation as an independent man of principle.

Brooke remained attorney general until 1966, when he won election to the U.S. Senate, the first African American to do so since 1881, by defeating Democratic former governor Endicott Peabody by almost half a million votes. Brooke was reelected to the Senate in 1972, soundly defeating Democratic challenger John Droney. One of the most respected senators in Congress when he began his campaign for a third term in 1978, Brooke soon found himself caught in a storm of allegations of financial impropriety fueled by acrimonious divorce proceedings with his wife. Brooke faced several charges: misrepresenting his assets to shelter money in a divorce settlement, improperly transferring funds from his mother-in-law's account so that Medicaid would pay her nursing home bills, and failing to report loans to the Senate Ethics Committee. Though he was never convicted of any crime, the stain on his reputation cost him dearly at the polls. Brooke would be unseated in 1978 by Democrat Paul Tsongas, securing only 41 percent of the vote. Since Brooke's tenure as senator, only two other African Americans—Carol Mosley Braun and Barack Obama—have served in the Senate, and he remains the sole African American to have won a second term.

Brooke proved to be a voice of moderation in the Republican Party. During his first term in the Senate, Brooke spent a great deal of time on issues relating to Vietnam, traveling to Asia on fact-finding missions. As a result of his investigations, he urged that the U.S. military cease bombing and dropping napalm, a flammable gel used to clear vegetation that destroyed both the environment and countless human lives. Later, he called for an end to trade with South Africa because of its apartheid policies. In 1967, President Lyndon B. Johnson appointed him to the President's Commission on Civil Disorders, which made recommendations that ultimately took shape as the 1968 Civil Rights Act. Brooke also challenged Richard Nixon's Supreme Court nominees Clemon Hainsworth and B. Harold Carswell—two known anti–civil rights judges—even though he had supported Nixon's bid for the presidency. Brooke later became the first senator to call for Nixon's resignation over the Watergate scandal.

## Brooke's "Genuine Conservatism" and the Reclamation of Conservative Philosophy

Senator Brooke was, in many ways, the anti-Goldwater Republican. If Goldwater's *The Conscience of a Conservative* served as the guiding light of ultra-right-wing white conservatives of the era, Brooke's *The Challenge of Change,* published on the eve of his first Senate victory, is perhaps best understood as an attempt to reclaim the tradition of conservatism—a tradition that, in his view, embraced the possibility of black empowerment.

As an initial matter, Brooke harshly condemned his party's "southern strategy" of 1964 to win the votes of white southerners and, in the words of historian Kevin Phillips, construct "a winning coalition without Negro votes." The results proved disastrous, as nonwhite Republican votes slipped below 7 percent and mainstream whites defected from the party for fear of being perceived as racist. Brooke described the "1964 catastrophe" as a tragic example of ultraconservative excess unbecoming of the conservative tradition:

> The strategy of the 1964 campaign rested to a large extent on two bizarre gambles which have been called Operations "Dixie" and "Backlash." It was hoped that large numbers of Southerners motivated by anti–civil rights (or anti-Negro) sentiment would flock to the "new" Republican Party, and that a huge "backlash" movement in normally Democratic cities containing heavy concentrations of Negroes would top off the electoral bonanza.

These gambles, Brooke said, "reflected shamefully on the party's moral stature" and were inconsistent with the principles that the party had once stood for:

Here was the party of Abraham Lincoln, as we are proud to call it, fighting for wrong on an absolutely clear-cut ethical issue—the issue of human dignity on which the Republican Party was founded. At best, Operations "Dixie" and "Backlash" were repudiations of the Lincoln tradition. At worse, they were appeals to naked racism.

For Brooke, pandering to white racial hostility was not only morally problematic, but ran afoul of the Republican tradition. Brooke acknowledged that he would be "deeply discouraged were the Republican Party to alter its position in order to accommodate itself to the attitudes of the traditional deep South," observing that "Republicanism oriented toward segregation and racism would have nothing in common with the origins of the party."

Brooke further discounted the argument that such a strategy would provide Republicans with a permanent base of political support, noting that such a position "ignores the inevitable changes about to overtake Southern politics." As Brooke explained:

The 1964 campaign swelled Republican support in rural areas of the deep South—in just those areas where white citizens are straining to pull away from the rest of the nation on racial issues. But in the "modern" South of new industry, growing cities, and a developing tendency to accommodate itself to the rest of the nation, the 1964 campaign undermined the development of a new Republican Party.

Brooke went on to point out that Republican electoral gains occurred in "one hundred counties where Negroes outnumber whites but cannot yet exercise their right to vote." When blacks eventually were permitted to vote in these counties, there would be little doubt that the political balance would swing against "those Republican candidates who base their appeal on a promise to outdo Democratic white segregationists." Thus, Brooke concluded that "Republicanism based on segregation is anything but a permanent source of national and local party support."

What troubled Brooke most about Goldwater's conservatism was that it was a deviant form of ultraconservatism masquerading as "genuine conservatism." In an effort to restore "genuine conservatism" to its rightful place, Brooke countered Goldwater's description of conservatism with one of his own—a more moderate conservatism that embraced both the precepts of black conservative thought and the possibility of progressive social change. He agreed with Goldwater that "conservatism is indeed a mood or an instinctive belief that the work of past generations should not be discarded without careful thought." But conservatism, according to Brooke, did not demand reflexive repudiation of change:

> Something quite different is being passed for conservatism in America. That something tries to do precisely what genuine conservatism does not. It tries to substitute as a policy for coping with specific economic and political problems a justification for opposing changes in political institutions and economic methods. It destroys the delicate balance between stability and flexibility, permanence and change—and destroys the appeal of genuine conservatism.

Genuine conservatives, according to Brooke, understand that it is one thing to respect the past and quite another to be captured by it. Genuine conservatives "treasure the past not as a Utopia, but for insights into the problems of the present and the future." In contrast to Goldwater conservatives, who categorically rejected the possibility of government-sponsored reform, genuine conservatives "are skeptical about reforms, but willing to accept them—indeed, to propose and engineer them—when they are required."

Brooke's recasting of the conservative tradition as one guided by the past, but not beholden to it, represented an important affirmation of the black conservative tradition. After all, black conservatives embraced conservatism precisely because they viewed it as providing the best means of securing present and future empowerment—not because they wanted to preserve the status quo or return to the days of white supremacy. By defining the "genuine conservative" tradition in this manner, Brooke created space for black conservatives to maintain their fidelity to conservative principles. For Brooke, black conservatives were core members of the group of "genuine" conservatives who "want to profit from the past, not live in it."

Brooke's "genuine conservative" tradition also emphasized the anti-utopian pragmatism and overriding sense of optimism that characterized black conservative thought from its inception. Much as Booker T. Washington, Mary McLeod Bethune, and George Schuyler had, Brooke understood that it is better to focus one's energy and adapt to accommodate the possibility of progress rather than dwell on obstacles. Genuine conservatives, in his view, believed that new problems required new solutions. Furthermore, genuine conservatives understood that social progress was necessary to ensure societal stability, and that "unless changes are made in the superstructure of society, the pressures for change will undermine the foundation of that society." Genuine conservatives, he said, "look forward to the future as a time of opportunity, not a time of trouble."

By contrast, the "new" conservatism advanced by Goldwater and others was unduly pessimistic and out of touch with social reality, in Brooke's view. "Senator Goldwater's conservatism," he argued, "sacrifices the opportunity to guide the nation through periods of change. It leaves the nature of the changes to be determined by drift or by Democratic leadership—and therefore, in the long run, leaves us less to conserve." This, according to Brooke, left conservatives in a position of relative powerlessness in a changing American society. He argued that conservatives must come into the present and deal with all its myriad changes if they were to take control of America's future. "The task is not to oppose change," he pointed out, "but to help accomplish it in keeping with conservative traditions—to direct it as *we* believe it should be directed."

But what direction did Brooke believe reform should take? For Brooke, conservatism remained the lodestar of political and economic empowerment, and he firmly believed that the strategy must focus on individual self-development. "Conservatism must be founded on deep respect and the interests of individual men—in their freedom, their security, their opportunity for development, their overall wellbeing." But a focus on individualism did not mean that conservatives were unconcerned about larger issues of social welfare. To the contrary, Brooke believed that a concern for individual well-being necessarily entailed attention to larger social problems. As Brooke commented, "It is absurd to believe that conservatives are uninterested in such problems as water pollution or medical care for the aged or the fate of America's underprivileged minorities."

When it came to the fate of these "underprivileged minorities," however, Brooke preached a sermon of individual self-reliance. Much as his black conservative forbears had, Brooke maintained that racial empowerment could be brought about only when blacks developed the skills necessary to compete effectively with whites. "Unless a program is specifically designed to encourage the outcasts to engage in individual competition," argued Brooke, "it cannot be successful." Brooke also chastised liberals for ignoring the importance of individual self-development and focusing instead on group-based relief. Focusing on individual self-development, according to Brooke, was essential to get at the core aspiration of most blacks: that they be able to compete effectively against whites and live a self-directed life with dignity and respect. Liberals "have never offered the nation a conscious, analytical approach to the problems of poverty, race, and urban decay ... that would marshal the energies of government toward the goal of self-improvement," argued Brooke. "In fact they do not even talk about self-improvement; they do not seem to value it." Liberals, he maintained, "have always been suspicious of individual enterprise" and were "ill equipped to reach the heart of our current problems—they prefer to deal with categories, groups, 'general welfare' programs, rather than the individual."

Whatever appeal conservatism had with blacks prior to 1964, Brooke conceded that most minorities had switched to voting Democratic. But Brooke believed that racial minorities tended to vote Democratic largely by default. "Democrats have not won them so much as we have lost them," he lamented. "In fact, we all but exiled them, including those minority groups such as the Negroes, who were once staunch Republicans."

Nevertheless, he argued that liberal approaches to racial empowerment harmed blacks precisely because they ran afoul of the black conservative precepts of self-development and self-reliance. According to Brooke, liberal welfare policy eased the suffering of blacks but ignored "the primary need for individual self development." Using a medical analogy, Brooke argued that such policy worked to "alleviate the misery of the patient," but failed to cure the "disease" because it dealt with "the symptoms of our national problems instead of the causes." This approach, in Brooke's view, was destined to fail "no matter how frenzied the attempts to deal with the ever-growing problems—no matter how grandiose the programs planned and how huge the sums spent."

This flawed approach, according to Brooke, was also reflected in the liberal pursuit of civil rights. Although a vigorous supporter of civil rights legislation, Brooke, in true Washingtonian fashion, nevertheless took issue with liberals who put the attainment of civil rights before acquisition of basic skills of self-reliance. Brooke conceded that racism remained rampant, and that "we cannot call ourselves a free country until the restrictions are removed and equality of opportunity is established in fact as well as in theory." But he maintained that the removal of restrictions alone would not solve the "Negro problem" because the underlying problems concerned "people more than laws or customs." The essential task, in his view, was to "provide Negroes with the physical and psychological, intellectual and cultural equipment to compete with whites." Brooke believed that government funds and energies must be directed to overcoming these deficiencies, not to simply making inequality more bearable, which is how he characterized liberal policies. Without effort to overcome these deficiencies, such palliatives "can only help the Negro tread water."

Brooke directed a similar criticism toward liberal housing policy, which at the time centered on providing public housing to poor and minority constituents. He firmly believed that the provision of public housing, with a corresponding effort to rehabilitate and develop the residents, was a waste of valuable government resources. As Brooke explained, "The ultimate cause of blighted neighborhoods is human shortcomings, not solely shabby housing." He acknowledged that deteriorating housing impoverishes the quality of people's lives, but he put responsibility squarely in the inhabitants' court: "Surely people determine the quality of the housing more than the other way around." The misdirection of money and energy on housing, Brooke argued, "is characteristic of almost all Democratic programs," and he found it hard to imagine that such an approach, though perhaps desirable, could provide a permanent solution.

But if Brooke took issue with liberal approaches to civil rights and housing, his deepest criticism was reserved for liberal programs that provided for unemployment benefits that, in practice, had no effective termination point. Again, Brooke emphasized that unemployment compensation failed to address the root of the problem—chronic unemployment. Providing unemployment compensation, he said, "does nothing to develop useful skills and a sense of self-confidence on the part of millions of our people who are more or less permanently unemployed and virtually unemployable." As a consequence, temporary unemployment compensation was tantamount to permanent relief because these "economic outcasts" could theoretically be "paid forever" without ever being equipped "to participate actively in the give and take of our economy." The idea of permanent relief was particularly offensive to Brooke. "There is something about relief—permanent relief—that cripples the spirit and violates the recipient's sense of honor and self-respect," he said. "It is a negation of the American Dream." More important, according to Brooke, it allowed the government to skirt the root problem by addressing one of its effects; liberals, he said, "have ... largely ignore[ed] the real causes of modern unemployment, and avoid[ed] its real challenges."

However, Brooke also bristled at the idea of temporary relief. "Giving a man temporary unemployment compensation," he maintained, "with no concern about his ability to secure permanent employment is a grave injustice." The injustice, in Brooke's view, was that temporary relief, more often than not, simply prolonged suffering. He described temporary unemployment relief as "an act of mercy, a kind of charity which demonstrates compassion for those in distress, but gives them little of what they most need: the means to end the conditions that cause distress." Quoting sociologist Thomas Merton, Brooke declared, "This kind of charity has no real effect of helping the poor; all it does is tacitly condone social injustice and to help to keep conditions as they are—to help to keep people poor."

According to Brooke, "it is fair to say that Democrats have done little to help dependent people to become self-supporting because they seem to have thought little about it. It is simply not in the tradition of the Democratic Party." But if genuine conservatism was so obviously correct, and liberal strategies so tragically flawed, why hadn't liberals come to embrace conservative strategies of empowerment? Brooke offered two important reasons. First, political inertia was largely to blame. Brooke believed that Democrats were "crippled by their old dogmas." They understood that during the Depression, something had gone drastically wrong with the nation's economy—that "the pump needed to be primed, and New Deal measures were designed to do it." Rather than devise new and innovative workable solutions to address midcentury problems, Democrats chose the path of least resistance, Brooke argued—they embraced the "old solutions" of the New Deal.

Brooke also suggested that liberals were simply exploiting the misfortune of poor and minority communities for political advantage—a point that many modern black conservatives continue to argue today. Brooke opined, "People existing on unemployment ... are usually beholden to the Democratic party because it is invariably the Democratic party that provides them these supports." But Brooke warned that in the long run, such exploitation only served to hurt minorities and the poor, and he chastised liberals for promoting policy "most injurious to the self-respect and the ability for self-support of the very people who are temporarily helped."

Senator Brooke exemplified the best of the black conservative tradition in the 1960s and 1970s. He successfully merged the modern conservative impulse toward individualism with the evolving themes of black conservative thought—anti-utopian pragmatism, a relentless disposition of optimism, self-help, economic independence, and the desire to lead a self-directed life worthy of dignity and respect. Despite Brooke's best efforts, however, the majority of blacks were not moved by his reclamation effort. For better or worse, conservatism, as political ideology, had come to be associated with the protection of whites and their institutions. It no longer resonated as a philosophy designed to protect people's rights, and it certainly lost its appeal as a guiding philosophy for black racial empowerment. Genuine black conservatives such as Senator Brooke were a dying breed, but the conservative precepts that animated their belief system would outlive them and would influence modern proponents of black nationalism and black power.

## Black Conservatism and the Nation of Islam

In 1959, conservative cultural critic George Schuyler praised the self-improvement programs instituted by the leader of the Nation of Islam, Elijah Muhammad, observing that "when anybody can get tens of thousands of Negroes to practice economic solidarity, respect their women, alter their atrocious diet, give up liquor, stop crime, juvenile delinquency and adultery, he is doing more for the Negro's welfare than any current Negro leader I know." Schuyler extended this praise even though he vehemently opposed black nationalism and perceived Elijah Muhammad to be a "rogue and a charlatan."

Praise from Schuyler, always difficult to come by, was reserved for those aspects of the Nation of Islam that he believed were consistent with his own views on conservative racial empowerment. When one thinks of proponents of black conservatism, rarely does one consider the Nation of Islam. Yet throughout its history, the Nation of Islam has embodied much of the tradition of black conservatism. In a manner not unlike Garveyism of the 1920s, the Nation of Islam sought to combine the best of black conservative thought with a radical, albeit religious, doctrine of black, separatist empowerment.

The Nation of Islam claims to have originated on July 4, 1930, in a Detroit ghetto with the arrival of a mysterious silk trader, Wallace D. Fard. In addition to peddling silks and other exotic items, Fard purportedly preached to locals a version of Islam in which black Americans were the Lost-Found Nation of Islam. According to Fard's teachings, blacks were the first and only humans, and whites were genetically mutated "devils" who had collectively denied blacks their place as rulers of the world. On Judgment Day, however, God would overthrow white supremacy and restore blacks to their rightful station atop the hierarchy of humanity. In the meantime, blacks were to prepare for this day by renouncing their present lives as Christian "Negroes" and live an Islamic lifestyle in accordance with the teachings of the Koran.

One of the recipients of Fard's teachings was Elijah Poole, a Georgia native who, like many others, had come to Detroit seeking better employment opportunities only to have those opportunities destroyed under the crushing weight of the Depression. Fard's message resonated with Poole, and he later joined Fard's growing following. Poole would be "reborn" under Fard's tutelage, and he would eventually change his surname to "Muhammad" to mark that rebirth. Fard's popularity grew during the early 1930s, and he eventually established a mosque and a school, the University of Islam, in Detroit. In 1934, Fard mysteriously disappeared, and Elijah Muhammad assumed control of Fard's institutions.

Muhammad would later claim that Fard was God himself in human form, and that he was God's messenger. Perhaps taking his cue from Garveyism, Muhammad established within the Nation of Islam a vast array of institutions, ranging from small businesses to schools for the children of Nation of Islam members to the Fruit of Islam, a paramilitary group trained in martial arts that provided security for Muslim temples and its leaders and provided community policing in areas where Muslims lived. Unlike Garveyism, however, membership was not open to everyone. Prospective members had to write a short essay, setting forth their reasons for wanting to join, and subscribe to a variety of Nation of Islam customs, including abstaining from pork, alcohol, and tobacco. Membership, however, did have its privileges. In exchange for physical and cultural withdrawal from mainstream black (and white) society, Muslims were embraced in a community that promoted both religious and economic solidarity.

The Nation of Islam quickly gained small but loyal followings in major northern cities, including Detroit, Chicago, and Washington, D.C. At the same time, most blacks—particularly Christians, the well educated, and the social elite—viewed the Nation of Islam's rigid lifestyle and rejection of American culture with a great deal of suspicion. This would change with the arrival of Malcolm X.

## Malcolm X's Fierce Denunciations

Malcolm Little was born in Omaha, Nebraska, in 1925. His father, Earl Little, was a farmer, local preacher, and a Garveyite. His mother, Louise Little, was a Grenadian immigrant. Orphaned at an early age, Malcolm grew up in foster homes. Despite a modicum of academic success, Malcolm's aspiration to become a lawyer was crushed by an insensitive teacher. He turned to a life of juvenile crime and was eventually sent to live with a relative in Boston, where he fell into an even deeper life of criminality. His involvement with a life of drug dealing, pimping, and burglary eventually landed him in prison, where he served six years for burglary.

While in prison, Malcolm's younger brother Reginald introduced him to the teachings of Elijah Muhammad. Malcolm converted to the Nation of Islam, and spent the remainder of his time in prison devouring books and preparing himself for a reconditioned life outside prison. In 1952, Malcolm X was paroled and, shortly thereafter, he traveled to Detroit to live with his brother Wilfred, who had also joined the Nation of Islam. Malcolm quickly impressed the Detroit Muslim community and soon became a full-time Nation of Islam minister and evangelist.

Malcolm X can be credited with dramatically expanding the Nation of Islam across the nation. He organized temples in New York, Boston, Philadelphia, and Los Angeles. As a traveling minister, Malcolm X was instrumental in drawing converts as well as sustained media attention. As the national spokesman of the Nation of Islam, Malcolm X lashed out at white supremacy and encouraged blacks to declare their independence from white oppression. In Malcolm X's view, four hundred years of racism suggested that whites were not inclined to view blacks as equals, and he criticized black establishment leaders for proposing that blacks "integrate" into a society that despised them. Just as Garvey had suggested some thirty years earlier, Malcolm X argued that blacks should withdraw from white society and establish, under the National of Islam, a land of their own.

Malcolm X would also evince shades of Washingtonian conservatism. He railed against the cultural depravity of the black community, condemning black-on-black crime, drug abuse, alcohol abuse, and myriad other social pathologies plaguing the black community. In its place, he offered a vision of a black community heavily structured around the family and traditional conservative values of thrift, cleanliness, and proper deportment. He preached self-reliance, encouraging his audience to support any and all black businesses, especially those owned by Muslims, and establish businesses of their own. For Malcolm X—as well as Garvey, Washington, and a host of other early black conservatives, the secret to black empowerment was the creation of a strong and economically independent black community.

Commentators past and present often identify Malcolm X as the black radical nemesis of Martin Luther King Jr. There is, of course, a great deal of truth to this, as Malcolm famously countered King's declaration that nonviolent protest is the way to secure Negro freedom with the suggestion that blacks enjoyed a God-given right to defend themselves against white violence "by any means necessary." Mainstream civil rights advocates made the most of this juxtaposition, often using Malcolm X as foil to encourage the white establishment to accept their more modest demands.

In political terms, however, both King and Malcolm X were fundamentally radical in their views. Both sought revolutionary changes in American society. Both pursued strategies of racial empowerment. The more telling and frequently overlooked distinctiveness of Malcolm X and the Nation of Islam lies in their profoundly conservative nature. Whereas King and his followers embraced the liberal tradition, the Nation of Islam remained powerfully imbued with the tradition of black conservative thought.

The primary thrust of Nation of Islam conservatism was moral reform. Malcolm Little's dramatic transformation from the criminal "Detroit Red" to the upright and articulate leader Malcolm X exemplifies this approach. But Malcolm X was merely a participant in a much larger, programmatic effort undertaken by the Nation of Islam. As Louis Lomax famously recounted:

> They start out by convincing the ex-convict that he fell into crime because he was ashamed of being black, that the white man had so psychologically conditioned him that he was unable to respect himself. Then they convince the one-time prisoner that being black is a blessing, not a curse, and that in keeping with that blessing, he, the ex-convict, must clean himself up and live a life of decency and respect.

The result, according to Lomax, "is nothing short of miraculous":

> You never see a Muslim without a clean shirt and tie and coat.
> You never see a Muslim drink.
> You never see a Muslim smoke.
> You never see a Muslim dance.
> You never see a Muslim use dope.
> You never see a Muslim woman with a non-Muslim man.
> You never see a Muslim with a woman other than his wife.
> You never see a Muslim without some means of income.
> You never see a Muslim who will not stop and come to the aid of any black woman he sees in trouble.
> You never see a Muslim lapse back into crime.

The Nation of Islam's pursuit of moral reform recalls the plea of early black conservatives Jupiter Hammon and Richard Allen for blacks to lead chaste and temperate lives. Like early black conservatives rooted in the evangelical Christian tradition, the Nation of Islam believed that living an ethical and productive life was the surest path to exposing the hypocrisy of white America's disrespect for blacks. But whereas early black conservatives thought that an ethical and productive lifestyle for blacks would also demonstrate the failure of white Christians to live up to their shared ethical and religious ideals, members of the Nation of Islam preferred to believe that their morally upright lifestyle would serve as a proud declaration of their full humanity, and highlight the relative moral depravity of modern white society more generally.

The theological teachings, which emphasized morality, also championed the beauty and intellect of blacks. The teachings instilled a sense of pride and dignity among members of the Nation of Islam and empowered them to do for themselves. The Nation of Islam encouraged its members to open small businesses and practice economic solidarity. The Nation of Islam itself took the lead in this regard, opening up factories and purchasing farmland in Michigan to supply its members with jobs, goods, and food produced by and for blacks. For many members, the teachings of self-improvement and self-reliance provided a pathway to both spiritual and economic stability—neither of which depended upon white support.

The Nation of Islam's social conservatism also emulated old-style Washingtonian conservatism insofar as its teachings generally rejected the idea of engaging in active opposition to American law and politics of racial oppression. Nation of Islam members were instructed to fight back if attacked by whites, but they were warned against engaging in unprovoked confrontations. Instead, in true Washingtonian fashion, members were called upon to work hard, obey all laws, and generally avoid activist posturing. Indeed, Muslims were expressly prohibited from voting, running for office, or otherwise engaging in the American political process. Rebellion against white supremacy was to take place within their own hearts and minds and should be funneled into traditional black conservative aspirations of racial uplift and racial autonomy within white American society.

Contrary to popular opinion, this policy of political disengagement did not change with the ascension of Malcolm X. Despite his confrontational rhetoric, neither Malcolm X nor the Nation of Islam formally engaged in protests against white supremacy. Indeed, one might argue that active engagement with whites had no place in the inwardly focused Nation of Islam. The Nation of Islam had created a movement of escapism— one that was premised upon moral uplift, economic empowerment, and social withdrawal. Much as Washington's philosophy had done for previous generations of blacks, Nation of Islam teachings and community development provided blacks with an means of expressing their frustrations with white society without having to actually confront the source of their anxiety and problems. The Nation of Islam philosophy enabled blacks to strengthen themselves—both personally and as a community—so they might better weather the challenges of black life in white America.

Malcolm X was quietly critical of the policy of nonengagement by the

Nation of Islam, particularly in light of the rising militancy of the civil rights movement. Indeed, in 1963, Malcolm X's incendiary comments on the assassination of President John Kennedy led Elijah Muhammad to suspend him as head of the New York Mosque and to prohibit him from making public statements for ninety days. It was the organization's failure to engage in a larger political program that eventually led Malcolm X to leave the Nation of Islam.

To be sure, the Nation of Islam did not embody every feature of black conservative thought. Most black conservatives had an abiding faith in Western institutions and capitalism. Although the Nation of Islam believed in economic empowerment through capitalism, it rejected much of Western life, including democratic institutions of governments, courts, and the political process. Similarly, Nation of Islam members were distinctly unpatriotic. Whereas most black conservatives viewed themselves as "American" first and "black" second, Nation of Islam members believed the opposite, and further interpreted their religious teachings as prohibiting their service in the armed forces. In addition, the separatist ideology of the Nation of Islam was in direct contradiction to the "genuine" conservative views of, say, Edward Brooke, who viewed integration as essential to black empowerment. The infusion of anti-Semitism into Nation of Islam teachings by Louis Farrakhan in the late twentieth century likewise has no historical precedent in black conservative thought. Yet the Nation of Islam legacy of racial pride, self-reliance, moral reform, economic empowerment, and self-determination undoubtedly embrace the mood and consciousness of black conservatism—a point that even such a vocal opponent of black nationalism as George Schuyler had to concede.

## Black Conservatism and Black Power

Much like the Nation of Islam, the Black Power movement is rarely discussed in public conversation on black conservatism, albeit for different reasons. Part of the difficulty in situating Black Power under the rubric of black conservatism arises from the fact that the movement originated within the Student Non-Violent Coordinating Committee (SNCC, pronounced "snick"), a liberal, interracial student organization that worked closely with King's Southern Christian Leadership Convention to pursue liberal legal strategies of racial empowerment for blacks. A second difficulty arises because the Black Power movement has, in popular discourse, become confused with the radical, anticapitalist Black Panther Party and other radical organizations that appropriated the images, slogans, and basic political philosophy of black power. Thus Black Power has been largely viewed as a radical leftist movement that shares little with the black conservative tradition. However, when isolated from its liberal origins and radical offshoots, the Black Power movement reveals strong connections to the black conservative tradition.

## SNCC, Stokely Carmichael, and Rise of Black Power

On February 1, 1960, a small group of black college students from North Carolina A&T University refused to leave an all-white Woolworth's lunch counter in Greensboro, North Carolina, after being denied service. This single act of defiance sparked a wave of sit-ins in college towns across the South. Two months later, SNCC was created on the campus of Shaw University in Raleigh, North Carolina, to coordinate these efforts and promote more of the same. It was a liberal idealistic organization consisting of committed, interracial activists eager to participate in rallies, sit-ins, jail-ins, freedom rides, and voter registration campaigns throughout the South. Youth and idealism were its strongest assets, and white federal officials and the civil rights establishment admired the organization's zealousness but were wary of its maverick posture.

By the middle of the decade, however, the liberal idealism of SNCC gave way to frustration at the slow rate of progress toward racial equality. A pervading sense of disappointment and competing visions of racial empowerment fractured the group's abiding liberal philosophy. In 1966, the liberal, idealistic orientation of SNCC would be displaced by a new approach to racial empowerment—Black Power—engineered by the precocious and charismatic Stokely Carmichael.

Stokely Churchill Carmichael was born in 1941 in Port of Spain, Trinidad. His parents migrated to the United States one year later, leaving Stokely and his sisters in the care of his grandmother and other relatives. His early childhood in Trinidad was happily uneventful, and at the age of ten, Stokely and his sisters were reunited with their parents in New

York. Carmichael enjoyed a middle-class upbringing, residing in an integrated Bronx neighborhood and attending the prestigious, integrated Bronx High School of Science. Yet Stokely remained racially grounded, comforted by all-black family gatherings and frequent trips to Harlem, where he was exposed to the full array of African American cultural traditions.

In 1960, Stokely graduated from Bronx Science and enrolled at Howard University. As the nation's premier historically black university with a rich pedigree of graduating generations of leading black professionals, Howard served as the gateway to black middle-class orthodoxy. It was also a place of remarkable diversity and opportunity; the student population included a sizable number of Africans and Caribbeans as well as Americans from the urban North and rural South, and the school's setting in the nation's capital afforded students the full range of government institutions and influences. In this environment of dense political and professional activity, Carmichael learned of civil rights protests being undertaken by an integrated body of students known as the Nonviolent Action Group—Howard's SNCC affiliate.

Carmichael joined the group and began his career as a civil rights activist by accompanying a group of Freedom Riders on a "tour" of Mississippi in 1961. Carmichael, along with the other riders, was summarily arrested, and he spent forty-nine days in Mississippi jails. Energized by the moment, Carmichael would return to the Deep South each summer on behalf of the Nonviolent Action Group.

In 1964, Carmichael graduated from Howard University with a degree in philosophy, and he turned his attention full time to civil rights activism. He assumed the role of project director for SNCC's voter registration drive in Greenwood, Mississippi, and quickly developed a reputation as a vigorous organizer and charismatic and articulate speaker. Shortly thereafter, Carmichael turned his attention to Lowndes, Alabama, where he worked to coordinate rural black voters against the racially oppressive Democratic political machine. In Lowndes, Carmichael began to brush the traditional, interracial democratic ideals of SNCC against the grain, arguing that black voters should seek to solidify political power in the hands of an all-black political party. Carmichael brought his vision into fruition with the establishment of the Lowndes County Freedom Organization and adopted the image of a black panther to symbolize the organization's efforts. The organization held a nominating convention at a local Baptist church in May 1966, thereby ensuring that a Black Panther candidate would appear on the ballot the following November.

On the heels of his success in Lowndes, Carmichael was elected chairman of SNCC, much to the disappointment of Chairman John Lewis, who had directed the group's more moderate, integrationist efforts. Lewis had been an early adopter of King's strategy of nonviolence, and he perceived the changing politics of SNCC as a harbinger of bad things to come; he would eventually leave the organization. Many other SNCC activists did not share Lewis's views, however. Carmichael's experiment in black nationalism in Lowndes proved more appealing to SNCC organizers than had their previous efforts at integrated democracy, and the group applauded his efforts.

In June, Carmichael and SNCC would join efforts with King, the SCLC, and a host of other mainstream civil rights organizations to assist James Meredith's solo March Against Fear from Memphis, Tennessee, to Jackson, Mississippi—a march organized by Meredith to combat the pervasive fear of Mississippi blacks to exercise their constitutional rights. Meredith, who had made headlines four years earlier when he enrolled in the University of Mississippi, had since graduated from Ole Miss and left the state permanently. During the second day of his march, Meredith was shot multiple times by a disgruntled white Memphis contractor. Meredith, though injured, vowed to complete the march after a period of recovery. With Meredith hospitalized and incapacitated, Carmichael assumed the role of lead organizer for the remainder of the march.

Amid concerns that Carmichael's reputation as a black militant would undermine the credibility of the march, the NAACP and Urban League withdrew their support, leaving the bulk of the marching and organizing to SNCC with modest support from King's SCLC. Carmichael routed the march through Greenwood, Mississippi, where he had worked as project director for a voter registration drive just two years earlier. In Greenwood, Carmichael announced SNCC's new slogan—"Black Power" —and launched a movement that would fundamentally transform black political protest.

In a hastily planned speech in Greenwood, Carmichael began by establishing his reputation and credibility among the locals, pointing out his previous organizing efforts and personal relationships with members of the community. Gaining momentum and sensing the urgency of the crowd, he shifted gears and declared:

This is the twenty-seventh time that I've been arrested. I ain't go-ing to jail no more. The only way we gonna stop them white men from whuppin' us is to take over. What we gonna start sayin' now is Black Power!

Carmichael continued:

The white folks in the state of Mississippi ain't nothing but a bunch of racists. . . . What do we want?"

The crowd enthusiastically replied, "Black Power!"

## The Conservatism of Black Power

But what exactly did Carmichael mean when he invoked "Black Power"? His vision would coalesce in a "Position Paper on Black Power," first pub-lished in the *New York Times* in August 1966. Carmichael would explain why SNCC needed to change course and break with the civil rights es-tablishment's liberal policy. Although many would interpret the call for Black Power as a dramatic moment of radical militant engagement, the movement, at least as understood by its founder, embodied many of the essential precepts of black conservative thought.

For Carmichael, the essential flaw with prevailing liberal, integrative civil rights strategy was that it denied blacks the opportunity to liberate themselves in accordance with their own views of what racial progress entailed. Blacks had been duped into thinking that the liberal legal strat-egy of securing civil rights and promoting integration was tantamount to racial empowerment. As Carmichael explained: "In the beginning of the movement, we had fallen into a trap whereby we thought that our prob-lems revolved around the right to eat at certain lunch counters or the right to vote or to organize our communities. We have seen, however, that the problem is much deeper." The deeper problem, argued Carmichael, was a profound sense of cultural, political, and economic disempowerment occasioned by white supremacy. Blacks, Carmichael maintained, needed to close ranks and seize control of their own destiny. An "all-black proj-ect is needed in order for the people to free themselves," he remarked. "If we are to proceed toward true liberation, we must cut ourselves off from white people. We must form our own institutions, credit unions, co-ops, political parties, write our own histories."

Similar to the Nation of Islam, Carmichael's vision of Black Power required that blacks reject mainstream American culture and fashion an alternative space in which blacks could lead self-directed lives. "We reject the American dream as defined by white people," he argued, "and must work to construct an American reality defined by Afro-Americans." But why must that reality be segregated? Because, according to Carmichael, America was irredeemably racist. "When we view the masses of white people," he wrote, "we view the overall reality of America, we view racism, the bigotry and the distortion of personality, we view man's inhumanity to man: we view in reality 180 million racists." He elaborated:

> Whites are the ones who must try to raise themselves to our humanistic level. We are not, after all, the ones who are responsible for a genocidal war in Vietnam; we are not the ones who are responsible for neocolonialism in Africa and Latin America; we are not the ones who held a people in animalistic bondage over 400 years.

But what about the white members of SNCC, who had worked alongside Carmichael in his earlier efforts? Were they racists as well? According to Carmichael, they too were suspect. The myth of Negro inferiority and dependence was, in his view, deeply ingrained in white American culture. He believed that even whites sympathetic to the cause of black liberation "[have] these concepts in his mind about black people if only subconsciously" because "the whole society has geared his subconscious in that direction." As a result, white people could not fully understand or appreciate racial oppression. Nor could they understand what blacks truly desired by way of racial empowerment. According to Carmichael, "White people coming into the movement cannot relate to the black experience, cannot relate to the word 'black,' cannot relate to the 'nitty gritty,' cannot relate to the experience that brought such a word into being."

Equally problematic was the notion that white inclusion at the policymaking level reinforced prevailing stereotypes about the inability of blacks to lead their own cause. According to Carmichael, white participation "means in the eyes of the black community that whites are the 'brains' behind the movement and blacks cannot function without whites. This only serves to perpetuate existing attitudes within the existing society, i.e., blacks are 'dumb,' 'unable to take care of business,' etc. Whites are 'smart,' the 'brains' behind everything."

Most important, however, white participation also interfered with the ability of blacks to speak and think freely and to determine the course of their own destiny. "Blacks," Carmichael revealed, "feel intimidated by the presence of whites, because of their knowledge of the power that whites have over their lives. One white person can come into a meeting of black people and change the complexion of that meeting, whereas one black person would not change the complexion of that meeting unless he was an obvious Uncle Tom." Moreover, Carmichael pointed out that the intimidating effect experienced by blacks in mixed company was often "in direct proportion to the amount of degradation that black people have suffered at the hands of white people." For Carmichael, it was imperative that blacks be given an opportunity to organize themselves free of white interference—that a "climate [be] created whereby blacks can express themselves." Carmichael therefore called for the mass expulsion of whites from SNCC so that blacks might be in a better position to engage in self-definition and self-direction of the movement for racial empowerment. In Washingtonian fashion, Carmichael proposed that SNCC should be staffed, controlled, and, perhaps most important, financed by blacks. Financial independence was crucial, in Carmichael's view, to avoid "the tentacles of the white power complex that controls this country."

Carmichael did identify a role for sympathetic whites, however. Whites, he argued, could participate on a "voluntary basis," or perhaps the movement could "contract work out to them." But they were expressly precluded from participation "on a policy-making level." Whites who come into the black community with ideas of change, according to Carmichael, seemed "to want to absolve the power structure of its responsibility of what it is doing ... which is the worst kind of paternalism." Instead, Carmichael suggested that, in the spirit of "coalition" politics, whites seek to organize members of the white community:

> White people who desire change in this country should go where that problem [of racism] is most manifest. The problem is not in the black community. The white people should go into white communities where whites have created power for the express [purpose] of denying blacks human dignity and self-determination.

Carmichael added, "There can be no talk of 'hooking up' unless black people organize blacks and white people organize whites." Once this occurred, then "perhaps at some later date—and if we are going in the same direction—talks about exchange of personnel, coalition, and other meaningful alliances can be discussed." Carmichael advocated the immediate "re-evaluation of the white and black roles" so that "whites no longer designate roles that black people play but rather black people define white people's roles." He anticipated the allegation that his black nationalism was unadulterated racism, but he argued that whites who genuinely identified with blacks would see things somewhat differently. "The charge may be made that we are 'racists,'" he said, "but whites who are sensitive to our problems will realize that we must determine our own destiny."

Carmichael would later elaborate on these points in *Black Power: The Politics of Liberation in America,* co-authored with Charles Hamilton and published in 1967. According to its authors, "this book is about why, where, and what manner black people must get themselves together." In *Black Power,* Carmichael and Hamilton sought to situate the concept of Black Power in a large framework of political action. They advanced the idea of "black consciousness," arguing that the essential task was for blacks to assert their own humanity and engage in aggressive self-definition instead of simply adopting white societal views of blacks. They distinguished between individual racists acts and institutional ones—the collective acts of racial oppression carried out by white racist institutions and cultural practices—and argued that the thrust of black political strength ought to be directed at the latter. They rejected integration as political and cultural suicide and argued for a "politics of modernization" that entailed questioning old values and social institutions, searching for new and different forms of political structure to solve political and economic problems, and broadening the base of political participation to include more black people in the decision-making process. Responding to anticipated charges of racism, the authors defiantly declared: "In the end, we cannot and shall not offer any guarantees that Black Power, if achieved, would be non-racist.... The final truth is that white society is not entitled to reassurances, even if it were possible to offer them."

Carmichael's dramatic assertion of "black power" reverberated throughout the black community. His claim that blacks should seek economic independence by creating their own institutions inspired Roy Innis of the Congress for Racial Equality (CORE) to propose a new "social contract" in which he argued for a new black capitalism that would enable "the creation and acquisition of capital instruments by means of which we can maximize our economic interest." Carmichael's exhortation that "we must write our own histories" inspired broad-based race consciousness within education, leading to reform at the primary and secondary school levels and the creation of black studies programs on college campuses throughout the country. In 1969, Professor Nathan Hare published "Questions and Answers about Black Studies" in the *Massachusetts Review,* in which he proposed a curriculum and addressed concerns about forming such programs. Artists, eager to assert the notion that black culture and Black Power were one and the same, promoted a black arts aesthetic in which literature, art, and musical creation were understood as organically connected to the lives and traditions of black people. Their art embodied Black Power in cultural form, invalidated European and American claims of artistic superiority, and reaffirmed the essential beauty of black culture.

Despite the strident militancy of the rhetoric, Black Power proved strongly conservative in character. The core emphasis on self-determination and self-reliance reflected an embrace of age-old precepts of black conservative thought shared by marginal and mainstream black conservatives alike. Black conservatives had always understood that racial empowerment must entail the promotion of inner dignity and respect, and the Black Power movement notably seized upon this black conservative insight from its inception. Similarly, the idea that blacks should create and control their own institutions to enable self-help strategies of racial uplift embodied the conservative entrepreneurial spirit of James Forten, Booker T. Washington, and Marcus Garvey. The rejection of liberal legal strategies of civil rights and integration as the be-all-end-all approach to racial empowerment was not unlike the views held by Washington, Brooke, and members of the Nation of Islam. The same might be said of the inherent pragmatism of the Black Power movement, which sought to improve present African American reality rather than pursue abstract ideals to be realized in the indeterminate future.

At the same time, however, the Black Power movement's emphasis on overt political engagement, though perhaps consistent with Garveyism, proved a marked departure from the agnostic posture of the equally nationalist but perhaps more deeply conservative Nation of Islam. And although Carmichael, like Washington some seventy years earlier, desired to wield political power and exert influence on the trajectory of American race relations, his more forthright approach would, in all likelihood, have struck Washington as too aggressive.

It is true, of course, that the Black Power movement spurred nationalist radicalism on a much broader scale. Radical activists throughout the country seized upon the rhetoric of Black Power and the image of the black panther, and they appropriated the movement's ideas to suit their own political objectives. The Black Panther Party for Self-Defense, organized in Oakland, California, in 1966, was one of those organizations. Chairman Bobby Seale and Minister of Self-Defense Huey P. Newton advanced a "Ten Point" platform that embodied many of the Black Power precepts, including self-determination and the promotion of education centered on the black experience, but its particular emphasis on reparations and police brutality and its call for the immediate release of all black men then incarcerated proved to be a radical departure from the objectives that Carmichael imagined for the Black Power movement. The departure was only further reinforced by episodes of armed resistance by Panther members against "racist pig cops" in a grass-roots effort to "police the police," and the critique of capitalism and "politics of war" advanced by Minister of Information Eldridge Cleaver.

The Revolutionary Action Movement also drew upon the insights of Garveyism and Black Power in its call for "war with the white world." Like the Black Panther Party, the Revolutionary Action Movement was involved in grass-roots organizing and protests against police brutality, and, unlike the Black Power movement, its activists promoted the use of guerrilla warfare tactics against the racial and class oppressors. Like the Black Panther Party, activists in the Revolutionary Action Movement viewed themselves as being engaged in a revolutionary enterprise, "the pivotal point for the destruction of world imperialism," and they advocated the "war of Armageddon." Clearly, these ideas did not originate in the Black Power movement.

The existence of the Black Panther Party and the Revolutionary Action Movement reinforce the point that the 1960s and 1970s represented an era of experimentation in which activists sampled freely from the competing and contradictory wells of prevailing ideologies, formulating numerous pluralistic and revolutionary nationalist combinations. Their combinations proved far more radical and revolutionary than did the

Black Power movement—itself a combination of black conservative precepts and new world politics. Yet like its radical offshoots, the Black Power movement is a testament to the enduring appeal and significance of black conservatism in political thought.

The mainstream conservative philosophy of Senator Brooke, and the conservative nationalism of the Nation of Islam and the Black Power movement ensured that black conservatism remained a relevant part of the political landscape well into the 1970s. However, none of these proponents could foresee the explosion in black conservative thought that would occur in the subsequent decade and carry forth to the present day.

# SIX

# The Reformation of Black Conservatism

Black Neoconservatives, Their White Counterparts,
and How They Differ from Traditional Black Conservatives

By the close of the civil rights era, most blacks had abandoned conservatism as the dominant mode of political engagement. The majority of black voters now supported the Democratic Party and its liberal strategies for racial empowerment, which relied primarily upon federal intervention through civil rights enforcement and social welfare policy. Black support for mainstream conservatives continued to decline throughout the 1970s, despite Senator Brooke's reclamation efforts and attempts by the Nixon administration to moderate mainstream Republicanism with an uneasy embrace of affirmative action policy and formal recognition of organizations such as the NAACP and the National Urban League. Goldwater conservatism and the 1964 Republican "southern strategy" had deeply stigmatized mainstream conservatism in the eyes of many blacks, and the backlash was clear when Democrat Jimmy Carter received more than 90 percent of the black vote in the 1976 presidential election. As conservative journalist Tony Brown would sarcastically opine, for better or worse, most blacks had come to view the Democratic Party as the party of "less racism":

> The Democratic Party says this: "This white man is a Democrat; therefore he's a liberal and all liberals like blacks. This white man

is a conservative and a Republican, and at birth racist genes invade the body of any little white baby born who is going to be a Republican and/or conservative. Therefore vote less racism. Vote Democratic."[1]

Some commentators have described black conservatism in the immediate aftermath of the civil rights movement as divided into two camps: fundamentalist conservatives and antigovernment conservatives. The fundamentalists, according to this view, are social conservatives who tend to focus on traditional black family values, including moral and religious faith, as essential prerequisites to black empowerment. In this sense, black fundamentalist conservatives are not unlike white social conservatives, who draw inspiration from the "father" of white social conservatism, Edmund Burke. In this sense, "black" family values are not viewed as unique to blacks or the black experience, but simply a reflection or mild reinterpretation of traditional white family value systems. Notable modern examples of black fundamentalist conservatives include Joe Clark, the former Patterson High School principal whose work was dramatically captured in the mainstream film *Lean on Me;* conservative radio talk-show host Armstrong Williams; and former Reagan official, U.S. Senate candidate, and U.S. presidential candidate Alan Keyes.

The other camp—the antigovernment conservatives—are defined by their staunch opposition to direct government intervention in black life. Antigovernment conservatives are unwavering supporters of capitalism and are steadfast opponents of affirmative action and the welfare state. They are less concerned with moral or spiritual uplift, and more focused on producing a culture of self-help and self-reliance within the black community. Modern antigovernment conservatives, thought to include the likes of economists Thomas Sowell, Glenn Loury—at least the first incarnation (more on this later)—and Walter Williams, recall an earlier period of black conservative philosophy in which racial uplift was defined almost exclusively in market-oriented terms. Loury succinctly captured the antigovernment view when he wrote:

[Booker T. Washington] understood that when the effect of past oppression is to leave people in a diminished state, the attainment of true equality with the former oppressor cannot depend overly much upon his generosity; it must ultimately derive from an elevation of their selves above the state of diminishment.[2]

This neat categorization of black conservatism of the post–civil rights era, however, obscures the complexity of the black conservative tradition. Neither the mood of black conservatism nor the views of its proponents can be so easily reduced and digested in this fashion. Indeed, as the foregoing chapters make clear, black conservative thought has enjoyed the privilege of longevity precisely because it could be appropriated and deployed in a variety of political and cultural contexts.

What, then, did it mean to be a black conservative in the post–civil rights era? Can black conservatism of this period be defined in any coherent way? And if so, how might one describe the prevailing state of black conservative thought?

As a starting point, it is important to emphasize that, despite Senator Brooke's efforts to situate black conservatives within the larger context of "genuine" conservatism, experimentation, and expropriation of black conservatism into other fields of politics and culture, one can nevertheless identify certain enduring features or themes of black conservatism shared by all major proponents.

First, post–civil rights era black conservatives retained the inward focus of early black conservative thought, directing much of their energy to the task of self-critique of the black community. In contrast to the liberal focus on external causes of black disempowerment, black conservatives of this era preferred to identify areas within the black community that could be strengthened spiritually, morally, and/or culturally.

Second, black conservatives of this era genuinely believed that progress would only come about when blacks learned to do for themselves. Though they often disagreed on whether and to what extent white society could be called upon to ameliorate racial obstacles, black conservatives were unified in the belief that true empowerment must be sourced from blacks themselves.

Third, and consistent with the idea of self-help, black conservatives placed a premium on education in their approach to racial empowerment. Though they sometimes disagreed on the specific nature of that education (religious versus vocational, for instance), most if not all conservatives agreed that black progress hinged on the ability of blacks to acquire the intellectual and psychological wherewithal to provide for themselves and protect their own interests.

Fourth, black conservatives of this era shared the view that racial progress must entail some form of economic empowerment, though there may have been disagreement over whether such empowerment was to be secured exclusively through market means or through some combination of federal and/or state subsidy. However, all conservatives of this period understood that racial progress was incomplete with some degree of black economic empowerment.

Fifth, black conservatives generally adopted realistic views of American society and the prospect of racial empowerment. They rejected unanchored, idealistic theories about social equality, preferring to pursue pragmatic strategies that were directly responsive to present problems and designed to secure immediate tangible gains for blacks.

Finally, post–civil rights era black conservatives retained the core aspiration of black conservatism that people should strive to lead autonomous, self-directed lives. Indeed, the rejection of liberal alternatives turned precisely on this point: black conservatives were unapologetically opposed to becoming wards of the state. Like all other Americans, black conservatives viewed the sine qua non of empowerment to entail the capacity to direct one's own life affairs.

Though black conservatives generally subscribed to these basic attitudes and beliefs, expressions of black conservatism regularly transcended these. Some black conservatives, such as Senator Brooke, George Schuyler, and Nation of Islam members, tended to be more "fundamentalist" in their outlook—they placed a premium on family and moral values. Others, such as Black Power activists, did not. Moreover, there were sharp divergences among the fundamentalist conservatives, exemplified by a dramatic cultural gulf that separated the Nation of Islam's segregated, Islamic value system from the integrationist, mainstream family values endorsed by Brooke and Schuyler.

The range of antigovernment positions was equally varied. The Nation of Islam preferred political and cultural isolation from Western life and the influence of government. In contrast, Black Power advocates wanted to be free from government interference in the creation of a pluralistic black representational bloc, but they ultimately desired government intervention, albeit on terms decided upon by their representatives. Senator Brooke, however, rejected the segregated pluralism of the Black Power movement but agreed that government intervention, if it had to exist at all, ought to be directed in accordance with conservative precepts.

Beyond variation, contradiction existed within post–civil rights black conservative expression. Some black conservatives were patriotic and

"Americans" first, as was the case with Senator Brooke and Schuyler, and others were not, as was the case with the Nation of Islam and Black Power advocates. Some centered their politics on uplifting individuals, in the spirit of Brooke or Schuyler, whereas the Nation of Islam and Black Power movement viewed individual self-improvement as essential to securing "group" empowerment. Finally, some black conservatives endorsed "middle-class" morality and proper deportment as emblematic of racial empowerment, as was the case of both the Nation of Islam and Brooke, while others such as the Black Power advocates rejected the bourgeois values of American society.

It would be wrong, however, to interpret the theme, variation, and contradiction within black conservatism during the post–civil rights era as demonstrating an overall incoherence. To the contrary, one can and should interpret these features as emblematic of the vitality of the intellectual movement and the ongoing cultural significance of the conservatism in black politics. Black conservatism, though in decline, retained its essential appeal. In the late 1970s, as the novelty of the civil rights revolution began to wear thin, a new cadre of black conservatives would rise to public prominence. They would draw upon this important tradition— its themes, variations, and contradictions—and add new ideas of their own. The black conservative movement would be reborn and return to political prominence, but unlike its previous iterations, it would do so, by and large, without the support of the larger black community.

## The Fairmont Conference

On December 12 and 13, 1980—one month after Ronald Reagan's successful bid for the American presidency—leading white Republicans convened the Black Alternative Conference at the Fairmont Hotel in San Francisco, California. The conference was organized as part of a "search for new ideas and approaches to black and other minority problems" by those who "felt that the energy and creativity engendered by the old civil rights movement had run their course and spent themselves." The conference was nominally organized by economist Thomas Sowell, then identified as a potential Reagan nominee for secretary of the U.S. Education Department, who identified the participants as "those who have challenged the conventional wisdom ... people who have thought for themselves instead of marching in step and chanting the familiar refrains."

There is a certain irony to Sowell's comments, for although the people at the conference were not all self-identified conservatives, it was to clear that the purpose of the conference was to identify black conservatives sympathetic to the Reagan agenda on American race relations. As the preface to *Fairmont Papers,* the edited volume of the proceedings, makes clear, the search for new ideas was "part of a much broader rethinking of approaches to social policy, particularly those that relied largely on government intervention and on the centralization of authority and responsibility." Indeed, the conference itself was hosted and largely funded by the conservative Institute for Contemporary Studies, a research think tank with strong ties to the Reagan administration.

The conservative theme of the conference was unmistakable. Sowell, in his opening comments, began by advancing the conservative, antigovernment position:

> We need to look not at the noble preambles of legislation, but at the incentives created by that legislation. Very often, legislation intended to help the disadvantaged in fact pays people to stay disadvantaged and penalizes them to the extent that they make an effort to rise from disadvantage.

According to Sowell: "The issue is not that the government gives too much help to the poor. The problem is that the government creates too much harm to the poor." One example of "the losses that blacks suffer from the interventionist state" identified by Sowell was the loss of job opportunities that, he argued, were caused by minimum wage laws. "I think the greatest single loss is that the minimum wage laws promoted by labor unions protect their members by pricing black young people out of the market," argued Sowell. "There is no way to rise up the ladder if you can't get your foot on the ladder in the first place." Later in the proceedings, economist Walter Williams elaborated on this point:

> The minimum wage law discriminates against the lowest-skilled worker. Who are the lowest-skilled workers? The lowest-skilled of the teenagers. They are those kids who come from schools three to five years behind the national norm. And so if you were predicting unemployment effects of the minimum wage laws, you could confidently assume that there would be a higher number of black youths affected as opposed to white youths.

For Williams, government intervention was the biggest problem facing blacks. "We must ask questions," he argued, "about the country's legal structure in order to see if that legal structure aggravates and reinforces our handicaps." To illustrate, Williams offered the example of running a taxi service. Every state requires taxi operators to obtain a license, but the fee for that license ranged from $30,000 to $65,000. As a result, Williams said, very few blacks operated taxis is states with high licensing fees. By contrast, in the District of Columbia, Williams said, more than 80 percent of the taxis are run by blacks. Why? According to Williams, "It turns out . . . in Washington, D.C., the license costs less than $100."

Williams also cited regulation of the trucking industry as an example of how government harms blacks:

> A man named Jim Ward of Omaha, Nebraska, bid the lowest price on a contract to ship household goods of air force personnel. This black man was not awarded the contract . . . because he did not have Interstate Commerce authority to move goods across state lines [and] the contract was awarded to another man who, in fact, bid $80,000 more than Jim Ward for the project. Jim Ward did not need any "equal opportunity program." . . . What he needed was to have government get off his back.

In Williams's view, the greatest contribution that blacks could make would be to "lead us out of the impending hell of the growing social state—the state intervention—that we have in the United States."

Instead of government intervention, traditional conservative precepts of self-help and self-reliance were vigorously advocated. A young Clarence Thomas spoke on the need for educational reform and improvements in the academic performance of black youth. He recounted his own educational experiences, and lamented the fact that blacks continued to underperform, even at the schools he once attended. But unlike liberal school reform advocates, Thomas argued that blacks must first take responsibility for the problem:

> I believe the problem [of schools that poorly educate blacks] will definitely not be solved with an external answer. I do not believe that an institution can change its numbers, change its quotas, change its courses, or reduce its standards to make us better. I do

believe that we have some hope, some possibility of accomplishing something if we begin to internalize the solution to the problem, to think in terms of solving it ourselves.

But Thomas's theme of self-help and self-reliance extended far beyond education. He contended that simply taking responsibility would not necessarily ensure successful operation of the schools, but that failure to do would ensure that "we will not have any hope at all." Thomas concluded his remarks with a personal observation that blacks need to look inward for solutions, "not forgetting the preclusive practices that have occurred, but definitely putting the primary role, the primary responsibility for the solution to these problems, on ourselves."

Self-proclaimed conservative "outcast" and community activist Oscar Wright amplified these points, arguing that "you do not need new special laws to protect black people" and "you do not need social legislation for American citizens." What was important, according to Wright, is that "meaningful change must emanate from within the bowels of the black community."

Meaningful change, however, was not simply a matter of more liberal legal response or more leaders, the speakers contended. "We do not need more black leadership," said Chuck Stone, senior editor and columnist with the *Philadelphia Daily News.* "We need more economic leadership." Stone noted parallels between Reagan's professed economic agenda for blacks and the strategies for economic empowerment articulated by conservative black nationalists:

> This past July, when I interviewed Mr. Reagan at his home just before the Republican convention, one of things he said to me was that if you live in the ghetto and you need to buy a toothbrush, there is no reason why you shouldn't buy it from a black-owned drug store. I said, "Governor, you sound like a black nationalist." He smiled and he blushed. Nonetheless, those are the ideas we are hearing today. Those are the same ideas I heard at three national Black Power Conferences in 1966, 1967, and 1968—self-reliance, self-determination.

New economic leadership, according to Stone, might very well involve the embrace of traditionally black nationalist ideas as well.

For most participants, however, the vision of new black leadership was neither that of segregated Black Power nor that of the civil rights establishment. Indeed, participants bemoaned the fact that liberal black leaders tended to exaggerate the number of blacks who subscribed to liberal views and that these views were often the dominant ones projected through major media outlets. As Sowell argued:

> Blacks in this country support voucher systems two to one; blacks in this country prefer more strict enforcement of crime laws, are opposed to quota systems in employment or college admissions, and have never had a majority in favor of busing. And yet when I look at the TV news, an entirely different world is created before my eyes on that tube.

Sowell wondered aloud that "we can put Ben Hooks [of the NAACP] or Jesse Jackson on TV," but not information that would provide a clearer, more accurate portrait of the black community and its politics.

But as Martin Kilson, who would later prove to be one of the strongest critics of black neoconservatism, pointed out, supplanting the civil rights establishment would be a daunting task. "Diversifying the black leadership class," he argued, "is not going to be easy, precisely because the homogenized leadership policy of blacks was correct for its time." According to Kilson, a unified leadership was necessary during the civil rights movement because blacks faced "naked racism—institutionally fierce, violent at many times, and highly uniform."

But in the post–civil rights era, according to Kilson, racism was less and less an obstacle to black success. "We are in a new era now," he said. "Though racism is certainly not lying down in its casket, let alone being honorably buried, still it is much more residual today than in the past."

As a consequence, blacks now enjoyed the luxury of diversifying their leadership. In addition, there were good reasons beyond the decline of racism to promote diversity in black political thought:

> Why diversification? Three points: one, the left/liberal axis no longer has—if it ever did have—a monopoly on effective policy for black needs. Two, it is now clear that there is too high a cost associated with black policy in isolation from conservative initiatives in American political life. Three—and maybe above all— new coalitions are required by blacks.

These new coalitions required black leaders who could represent black interests in a manner that would achieve greater overall integration in mainstream social, political, and economic life in America. These new leaders, though black, would endorse "raceless" values to promote American success. "We need a new core of what I call trans-ethnic black political leaders, both liberal and conservative, but especially the latter," Kilson said. "And this conference just might be one the events that sparks this group of trans-ethnic black politicians."

One thought that was plainly on the forefront of participants' minds was, Now that they had declared their fidelity to the Reagan agenda, what was to happen next? Conservative journalist Tony Brown, in his comments to the conference, raised the issue directly. He began his comments speaking broadly about black/white politics and offering his assessment of how whites operate:

> White people are very simple to understand, and if you understand the analysis of whites I am about to give you, you can understand an analysis of politics beyond anything that we can learn in any college in this country. It is very simple: white people want something for something. White people do not know how to avoid quid pro quo. . . . And any time we—lacking power —design policies, programs, or other approaches to power that avoid the quid pro quo dictum, they simply cannot comprehend. They have no way to communicate with the powerless.

He went on to ask, rather pointedly, the question that was on everyone's minds: "I want to know what the Republican party is going to do for traditional black Republicans who have stood up for the Republican Party in the face of great hostility in the black community."

Edwin Meese III, then legal counsel to Ronald Reagan, was present and ready with a response. For Meese, the Fairmont Conference represented the culmination of sustained effort to court black Republicans since 1964. In 1968, the party founded the Heritage Groups Division to focus on minority issues, and it expanded that group in 1971 to include delegates from across the nation. In 1972, Republican Party Chairman George H. W. Bush created the National Black Republican Council, which by 1978 claimed thirty-one councils at the state level. These and an assortment of other outreach efforts had yet to generate the kinds of coalitions that white Republicans desired.

The Fairmont Conference, however, provided unprecedented access to leading black conservatives. Meese acknowledged as much. "The intellectual quality and the standard of excellence and the articulation of views here has not been matched by any conference that I have attended in the last ten years," he said. "With all that power gathered in one place, this has got to be the start of something really important." Meese then suggested the ways in which the Reagan administration might reward black conservatives:

> You are on the cutting edge of a whole lot of new coalitions. Here is an opportunity, since you are in at the start, to participate at a much higher level than has ever been achieved before in this country.

But what form would that participation take? According to Meese, the administration was not interested in securing "token" representation for black conservatives:

> The response will include black participation in government, but it will be different in some ways. I think Ronald Reagan is committed, as you suggest today, to putting blacks in non-traditional roles. There are going to be black people in high places on the White House staff, but they are not going to be there simply as ambassadors to other black people.

Meese went on to state, "We will further black political participation by way of the appointments process in the government itself." In the ensuing years, the Republican administrations delivered on this promise.

## Critical Departures from the Black Conservative Tradition

If the Fairmont Conference envisioned a new breed of black leadership, it also put forth a new vision of black conservatism. Black neoconservatives embraced the basic views of their post–civil rights brethren—self-critique, self-help, educational empowerment, economic empowerment, pragmatism, and social autonomy—but they departed from the tradition in a manner that would prove far more conservative. Many black neoconservatives viewed the civil rights revolution largely as a "success" and argued that race less determinative of black progress and empowerment. As a consequence, they uniformly advocated a return to the Washingtonian emphasis on capitalism and economic progress over civil rights. Unlike early conservatives, however, black neoconservatives did not see any value in practicing economic solidarity. They rejected the old ideas of segregated economies and communities and argued for thoroughgoing engagement by blacks in larger capitalistic society.

Black neoconservatives were also uninterested in the politics of self-definition that defined much of early black conservative thought. Black neoconservatives did not deny the importance of their race, but much as George Schuyler and Senator Brooke had, they preferred to view themselves as "American" first. They were less concerned about self-identity than about transcending race through the adoption of what they generally perceived as the "raceless" values of success. Many rejected groupthink along with the notion of group empowerment and instead advocated an emphasis on radical individualism that was reminiscent of Goldwater.

Many black neoconservatives emphatically rejected state intervention in the affairs of blacks, but not for the reasons that led to a similar rejection by early black conservatives. Early-twentieth-century black conservatives, living under a white supremacist government, were understandably wary of racist involvement in the direction of black community affairs. Mid-twentieth-century black conservatives were not only suspicious of the motives of government but viewed reliance upon the welfare state as harmful to the dignity of blacks. By contrast, black neoconservatives tend to object to government interference on the grounds that it is simply no longer necessary in an open capitalistic society in which race is of declining significance.

As a consequence, black neoconservatives tend to oppose traditional liberal welfare policies, including unemployment benefits, subsidized health care, subsidized small-business loans, minimum wage laws, and other forms of government economic regulation that affect poor and minority communities. But neoconservatives also object to other forms of liberal government intervention mounted in the name of promoting racial equality, including expanded civil rights protection, race preferences, and employment quotas. However, an interesting contradiction in philosophy arises in the context of law enforcement: black neoconservatives typically support radical government interference in black communities when it comes to enforcing crime laws.

The rise of black neoconservatism signals a dramatic rightward shift in black conservatism. The "genuine" conservatives of whom Senator

Brooke had spoken endorsed neither the radical antigovernment posture nor the radical individualism of the neoconservatives. Indeed, the moderate conservative view advanced by Brooke supported federal and state intervention for the express purpose of benefiting blacks as a group. For instance, Brooke supported the liberal desegregation remedy of busing in public schools as "necessary but temporary relief in the establishment of integrated schools," and proposed extended welfare relief in American cities while serving on the Kerner Commission on Urban Disorders. For conservatives such as Brooke, the radical antigovernment posture of Sowell, Williams, and other neoconservatives—and its corresponding emphasis on Goldwater-type individualism—were simply not part of the "genuine" conservative tradition. Indeed, many of the criticisms levied by Brooke against Goldwater's "hijacking" of the conservative movement in 1964 arguably apply with equal force against black neoconservatives.

This is a point that bears particular emphasis, given that modern black conservatism has become, by and large, synonymous with black neoconservatism. Black neoconservatism, in making such a pronounced shift to the right, was open not only to external liberal critique, but *internal* critique from the more traditional conservative position as well. In refashioning black conservatism for the 1980s and beyond, black neoconservatives arguably departed from the rich tradition of political thought that it claims as its roots.

Black neoconservatism departed from the black conservative tradition in another important way. Traditional black conservatism was "organic" in that it was developed and largely supported from within the black community. From Jupiter Hammon to Booker T. Washington to Marcus Garvey to the Nation of Islam, black conservatism had always been sourced from the lived experiences of blacks and crafted to protect and promote interests identified by members of the black community as important.

In contrast, black neoconservatism received little or no backing from the black community, a fact corroborated by the labels "outcast" and "dissenter" that black conservatives affixed upon themselves. Black neoconservatives found themselves in a position not unlike that of George Schuyler late in his career—a voice for black empowerment without an organic, black community base from which to operate. Although black neoconservatives had declared an urgent need to break with the reigning black civil rights leadership, it was quite clear that no black neoconservative enjoyed a mandate from the people to make that call. Indeed, one might argue that whoever made that call must be devoid of any authentic contact with African American community, as there was little reason to think that mass black support for liberal Democratic policy and the civil rights leadership was open to debate.

Black neoconservatives, operating at the periphery of both black American politics and the black conservative tradition, without an authentic black base of support, would nevertheless be nurtured and sustained by an inorganic array of political actors, think tanks and research institutes, and media outlets based outside the black community. Through these inorganic support networks, black neoconservatives were summarily legitimated through the bestowal of governmental largess, private funding, and national public exposure.

Consider the career trajectory of some of the blacks who attended the Fairmont Conference—Clarence Thomas, Clarence Pendleton, Samuel Pierce, Thomas Sowell, Glenn Loury, and Walter Williams. Shortly after the conference, Clarence Thomas was named to head the Equal Employment Opportunity Commission, Clarence Pendleton was named chairman of the Civil Rights Commission, and Samuel Pierce became the only black member of Reagan's cabinet with an appointment as secretary of Housing and Urban Development. Sowell, Loury, and Williams obtained positions at conservative think tanks such as the American Enterprise Institute, Cato Institute, and Hoover Institution that fell in line behind the Republican Party's new African American strategy. White conservative institutes and foundations such as the Manhattan Institute, the American Enterprise Institute, Olin Foundation, the Scaife Foundation, and the Bradley Foundation would provide financial security for many black neoconservatives, and underwrite the development of "autonomous" black conservative institutions, such as the J. A. Rogers Lincoln Institute for Research and Education in Washington, D.C. Connections with white conservatives would provide black neoconservatives with coverage in important conservative and neoconservative publications such as the *Wall Street Journal, Human Events, Washington Times, Commentary, Public Interest, National Interest, American Scholar,* and *The New Republic.* With the governmental support and financial backing of the white conservative elites, black neoconservatism gained exposure and political momentum at a remarkable pace. And it did so without the substantial backing of the black community.

# SEVEN

# The Rising Tide of Black Neoconservative Intellectualism

### The Blame Game, "Self-Help," Shelby Steele, and John McWhorter

Among black neoconservatives, it was the intellectuals that received consistent media attention throughout the 1980s and proved most effective in shaping the contours of black neoconservative thought. Interestingly, the most influential figures to emerge were all men: Thomas Sowell, Walter Williams, Glenn Loury, Shelby Steele, and more recently, John McWhorter. There were, however, a handful of women who joined the ranks as well. The most prominent were Illinois State University sociologist and Ayn Rand disciple Anne Wortham, and Harvard-trained Eileen Gardner, a researcher at the conservative Heritage Foundation in Washington, D.C. Wortham proved the more conservative of the two, exemplified by her critically acclaimed book *The Other Side of Racism,* which presented an extended and often argumentative dismissal of human rights and civil rights activism. Gardner, along with Claudia Butts, the Heritage Foundation's minority outreach director who would go on to serve briefly as the Bush administration's White House liaison to blacks, similarly worked to advance the new black conservative agenda. Whatever suspicions one might have regarding the gender imbalance among black conservative intellectuals, there is little doubt that the contribution of these five men in particular breathed new life into the black conservative tradition within American politics.

## Thomas Sowell

The best-known black neoconservative intellectual of the 1980s was Thomas Sowell. Born in Gastonia, North Carolina, Sowell spent much of his early childhood there in a highly segregated environment. He later moved with his mother and siblings to Harlem and attended the highly selective Stuyvesant High School. He dropped out of high school and struck out on his own at the age of 17 to escape a deteriorating home environment. He enlisted in the U.S. Marine Corps, where he served as a photographer and pistol instructor during the Korean War.

After his service, he enrolled in college at Howard University but eventually earned an A.B. in economics from Harvard College in 1958. He earned a master's degree in economics from Columbia University one year later, and a Ph.D. in economics from the University of Chicago in 1968. In his autobiography, *A Personal Odyssey,* Sowell would note that he chose the University of Chicago for his doctorate education in part because he wanted to study under George Stigler, who in 1982 would win the Nobel Prize in economics.

Over the past three decades, Sowell has taught economics at various schools, including Cornell, Amherst, and the University of California at Los Angeles, and he taught the history of ideas at Brandeis University. He has also been associated with a variety of research centers. He was project director at the Urban Institute from 1972 to 1974, a fellow at the Center for Advanced Study in the Behavioral Sciences at Stanford University in 1976–77, and an adjunct scholar of the American Enterprise Institute in 1975–76. Since 1980, he has been a senior fellow at the Hoover Institution of Stanford University, where he holds the fellowship named after Rose and Milton Friedman. During his distinguished career, Sowell has written twenty-five books and more than a hundred articles and essays.

Much of Sowell's economic analysis of racial issues is traceable to ideas on the inherent irrationality of racism and market-based solutions advanced by white conservative economists Milton Friedman and Gary Becker, under whom he trained while at the University of Chicago. Indeed, Sowell specifically invited Friedman to present his views on race at the Fairmont Conference. The thrust of Friedman's argument, presented in his 1962 book *Capitalism and Freedom,* is that, in a completely rational world—which Friedman conceded did not exist at the time he was writing—active opposition to black employment opportunities often, but not always, did not promote the economic interests of white employers and white workers. Racist behavior, Friedman argued, was economically irrational for two reasons. First, it excluded potentially valuable workers from employment, thereby reducing competition for jobs. In the absence of full competition, white workers would perform less efficiently, thereby reducing the overall quality of the goods produced and/or slowing the process of production—both of which impeded the maximization of profits by the employer. Second, in the absence of full competition, white workers could reasonably demand higher wages, thereby elevating the cost for each good produced and further eroding the employer's profits.

Maximization of profits would require that firms eliminate racial discrimination. However, Friedman opposed civil rights legislation that would effectively prohibit such conduct. Government intrusion, he argued, interfered with the proper workings of the market. Racism, he argued, was a "taste" that some economic actors and consumers might be willing to pay extra to indulge. In such circumstances, employers should enjoy the "freedom" to discriminate and satisfy this "taste." Friedman argued that the best policy, consistent with a market-centered approach, was to educate and persuade white employers and white workers to be rational; that is, to function in a manner that would promote their own best interest. Pure capitalism, and the relentless drive to maximize profits, would gradually erode the taste for racial discrimination. And this could best be accomplished, albeit slowly, without government intervention.

Thomas Sowell rose to prominence by promoting this idealized free market approach to racial empowerment. In his 1975 book, *Race and Economics,* and in many more books that followed, Sowell argued that government intervention, in the form of antidiscrimination laws and other employment regulations, has had negative consequences for disadvantaged people. Much like his mentor Thomas Friedman, Sowell insists that because racism is inefficient and economically irrational, market mechanisms alone are sufficient to erode racist behavior.

Sowell would later turn his economist's gaze on racial disparities in economic performance. In his 1983 book, *Economics and the Politics of*

*Race,* Sowell argued that variations in racial and ethnic success are a function of a differential distribution of values, attitudes, and other cultural traits among different racial and ethnic groups. He maintained that blacks suffer within a "culture of poverty" that hampers their ability to compete and succeed in American capitalist society.

This, of course, was nothing new to conservatives. For years, conservatives had argued that blacks suffered disadvantages—in education, skills, discipline, character, or geography—that impeded their ability to compete with whites. However, traditional conservatives understood that past racist practices played an important role in the development of this culture of poverty. They argued that blacks must take responsibility for their condition and should be forward looking and seek pragmatic solutions to the problems they faced, but, at the same time, they fully appreciated that their troubled circumstances were not entirely of their own making.

In contrast, Sowell remained dispassionate and "objective" regarding the plight of blacks. Although he was willing to call out the prevailing state of black pathology (he said that African Americans came out of slavery with "the enduring stigma of hard manual, or menial labor" that "has produced an anti-work ethic handicapping blacks"), much as would any traditional conservative, he did not suggest that the source of the pathology might lie in white America. Indeed, Sowell affirmatively resisted placing blame on anyone, except implicitly on blacks themselves. "The point," he argued, "is not to praise, blame or rank whole races and cultures. The point is simply to recognize that economic performance differences are quite real and quite large." Sowell would return to this argument in 2005 with the publication of *Black Rednecks and White Liberals,* in which he argued that the culture of poverty afflicting blacks in urban areas was actually an appropriation of the base "redneck culture" of southern whites, that is, "the cultural values and social patterns prevalent among Southern whites [that] included aversion to work, proneness to violence, neglect of education, sexual promiscuity, improvidence, drunkenness, lack of entrepreneurship, reckless searches for excitement, lively music and dance, and a style of religious oratory marked by strident rhetoric, unbridled emotions, and flamboyant imagery." The irony, in Sowell's view, is that white redneck culture, appropriated by blacks, has come to define "authentic" black behavior that is enforced through social norms within black communities and endorsed by "liberal alibis" who interpret black redneck behavior as "a sacrosanct part of black cultural identity."

Like most antigovernment conservatives, Sowell objected to government intervention to address racial disparities. A longtime critic of liberal interventionist economic policy, Sowell also opposed liberal educational reform, race preferences and affirmative action policy. In *Civil Rights: Rhetoric or Reality,* published in 1984, Sowell addressed the issues of school busing, affirmative action, and racial quotas head-on. The basic thrust of his position was that although some racial prejudice remains in this country, government intervention is not the solution. Instead, blacks, and all other Americans, for that matter, should seek to empower themselves through their own hard work in a free and open market.

In some ways, Sowell's objection to race preferences recalled objections previously advanced by white neoconservatives: namely, that by the end of the 1960s, discrimination was no longer a major obstacle to minorities' access to employment, education, and other social mobility mechanisms, and that affirmative action has not benefited the poor, who need it most, but has primarily benefited middle-class blacks and other minorities. Quoting statistics from the Moynihan Report, Sowell insisted that "the number of blacks in professional, technical, and other high level occupations more than doubled in the decade preceding the Civil Rights Act of 1964.... The trend was already under way." Sowell further argued that "The relative position of disadvantaged individuals within the groups singled out for preferential treatment has generally declined under affirmative action."

Sowell also reiterated the traditional white neoconservative objection that affirmative action fueled white resentment against minorities. As Sowell explained, "There is much reason to fear the harm that it is currently doing to its supposed beneficiaries, and still more reason to fear the long-run consequences of polarizing the nation.... Already there are signs of hate organizations growing in more parts of the country and among more educated classes than ever took them seriously before."

Sowell would also maintain that affirmative action eroded the self-esteem of beneficiaries and stigmatize minority success. According to Sowell, race preferences created a climate in which it would be assumed that achievement by blacks did not reflect individual worth, talent, or skill, but rather special consideration. "Pride of achievement," Sowell would write, is undermined "by the civil rights vision that assumes credit for minority and female advancement. This makes minority and female achievement suspect in their own eyes and in the eyes of the larger society." Sowell would reiterate this argument throughout much of his career, and in 2005, he published *Affirmative Action around the World,* in which he undertook a lengthy investigation of the actual consequences of affirmative action policy in the United States and in other countries where it has been in effect. Based upon his research, Sowell concluded that race preference programs worldwide had not met expectations and have often produced the opposite of what was originally intended.

## Walter Williams

Lesser known, but equally controversial, is Walter Williams. Walter Edward Williams was born March 31, 1936, in Philadelphia, Pennsylvania, and was raised there by his mother, Catherine, a day servant, after his father deserted the family when Walter was three. Following his graduation from Philadelphia public schools, Williams drove a taxi for two years, served in the Army, and enrolled at California State College in Los Angeles, where he received his undergraduate degree in 1965. He went on to study at the University of California at Los Angeles, where he received his master's in economics in 1968 and Ph.D. in economics in 1972.

After an eight-year teaching stint at Temple University in Philadelphia, Williams moved to George Mason University in Fairfax, Virginia, where he is currently the John M. Olin Distinguished Professor of Economics. Williams is the author of six books and more than 150 articles. He writes a nationally syndicated weekly column that is carried by approximately 140 newspapers and appears on several Web sites. In addition to serving as an occasional host for the *Rush Limbaugh Show,* Williams has made scores of radio and television appearances on *Nightline, Face the Nation,* the *MacNeil/Lehrer,* and *Wall Street Week.*

Like Sowell, Williams is a free-market conservative who believes that the vast majority of social and racial problems are best addressed through market means and without government intrusion. Like Friedman, Williams prefers to recharacterize racially charged words in economic parlance. Racial discrimination, in his view, is simply "informed preference." Prejudice, he argued, is simply a process of pre-judging, based upon existing information. Thus, an employer who declines to hire blacks is not racist but simply exercising an informed preference based upon preexisting, albeit limited, knowledge of generally inferior black educational attainment and work habits.

Beyond engaging in semantics, Williams is arguably more anti-government than Sowell. Throughout his career, he has vigorously argued the dangers of government action to effect economic and social change. In his 1982 work *The State against Blacks,* Williams offered his first book-length argument that the government, with its myriad social programs, has not been a good friend to blacks and indeed has been a strident enemy to social and economic black progress. Trumpeting deregulation and hands-off government, Williams revisited the issue over minimum wage legislation and discussed the state's strangulation of entrepreneurial spirit and economic opportunity. Returning to the subject of his talk at the Fairmont Conference, Williams spoke of the plight of the uneducated poor person in New York City seeking to become a taxi driver. Like his previous discussion, this one lamented the fact that, in the 1920s, one could buy a used car and turn it into a taxi business, but given today's taxi license regulations and fees, such an enterprise, for many poor minorities, is prohibitively expensive.

Reviewing *The State against Blacks,* Michael Novak wrote: "This clear and useful book prompts a general observation. Williams is one of several black scholars who are now enriching the economic profession with fresh inquiries into culture, family, and race. Their work is bound to have an impact on future discussions of differences in 'human capital' both in the United States and in the Third World."

Novak's words proved prophetic, as Williams would turn his attention to political and economic developments in South Africa. In the 1989 book *South Africa's War against Capitalism,* Williams explored the historic economic forces that shaped the internationally reviled apartheid regime of white minority rule there. According to Williams, contrary to popular belief, apartheid was not created as a means for white-owned businesses to exploit the work of the native black majority. Rather, he argued that in the early part of the twentieth century, business owners were inclined to hire blacks, but leaders of the communist and socialist movements decried the loss of white-worker jobs and supported the implementation of apartheid's explicit racial separation. After World War I, when many white South Africans returned home to see that their color-blind employers had hired black workers for their jobs at lower wages, the call for separate worker markets was again issued. Apartheid, he maintained, was not driven by greedy capitalists, but was a result of socialist government intervention in the marketplace. The larger point, which one finds throughout Williams's writings, is that that capitalism and free market forces, without the intervention of government, will engender the freest and least prejudicial society.

Like many black neoconservatives, Williams discounts the effects of racism in producing the culture of poverty in which many blacks find themselves. Unlike Sowell, however, Williams does not suggest that the problems were created by blacks themselves. He believes that most, if not all, of the problems faced by blacks are in some way rooted in racism. However, he firmly believes that many of these problems, including high unemployment, crime, illiteracy, and high illegitimate birthrates, are exacerbated or, worse, created by social programs that, though well-intentioned, have not been effective.

For Williams, this is true not only in employment, but also in education. Blacks often receive substandard education, according to Williams, because blacks attend inferior public schools. The poor quality of the schools, however, is not a function of insufficient funding. The problem, in Williams's view, is that the government has a monopoly on most children's education, and where a monopoly exists the quality of the product drops. "At the heart of the problem in public education," Williams wrote in *American Education Magazine* in 1982, "is a system of educational delivery which creates a perverse set of incentives for all parties involved.... At the core of the perverse incentives is the fact that the teachers get paid and receive raises whether or not children can read and write; administrators receive their pay whether or not children can read and write. Children (particularly minority children) receive grade promotions and diplomas whether or not they can read and write."

Welfare policy further deepens the deterioration of black youth, according to Williams. He argues that state handouts and unearned benefits subsidize behavior that society finds unproductive if not deplorable. He criticizes, for example, the provision of entitlements to women who give birth out of wedlock, claiming that the government is implicitly sanctioning an activity that contributes to the collapse of the black community. In general, Williams claims the welfare state stymies the development of values that are essential if parents are to properly rear moral, law-abiding children who can succeed in school and ultimately, as adults, contribute meaningfully to society. Writing in the *Christian Science Mon-*

*itor* in 1991, Williams remarked: "We don't have the decency to treat poor people the right way. We do to them what we would never do to someone that we loved. We want to give the poor money without demanding responsibility. Would you do that to your children? If we love our children, we teach them responsibility."

Not surprisingly, Williams, like Sowell and other antigovernment neoconservatives, also opposes affirmative action. Like, Sowell, Williams contends that liberal social policies such as affirmative action unintentionally provoke discrimination in situations where it did not exist before. According to Williams, the disproportionately few blacks at institutions of higher learning is ascribable not to discrimination but to the fact that blacks have historically underperformed against other groups on standardized tests. Many college administrators, in an effort to bolster black presence on campus, have compromised their academic standards of admission for blacks. The result, he contends, is not only a misguided policy but a counterproductive one. In a 1989 commentary that appeared in the *National Review,* Williams wrote: "Whatever justification may be given for such a practice, it cannot help but build resentment, bitterness, and a sense of unfair play among whites, as it has already in matters of hiring, promotions, and layoffs. Official policy calling for unequal treatment by race is morally offensive whether it is applied to favor blacks or applied to favor whites."

### Glenn Loury

If Sowell and Williams represent the extreme rightist views of black neoconservatism, more moderating voices are provided by Glenn Loury, an economics professor at Brown University who in the 1980s was an economist at Harvard University's Kennedy School of Government, and Shelby Steele, a senior fellow at the Hoover Institution.

Like Sowell, Loury believed that blacks suffered from a culture of poverty that impeded their ability to compete. In *Free at Last? Racial Advocacy in the Post Civil-Rights Era,* Loury wrote, "What is important to the alleviation of black poverty and racism is not the economic structure of the United States nor the racist behavior of whites, but African-Americans' behavior." Unlike Sowell, however, Loury's analysis adopted a more compassionate and tone. In "Economic Discrimination," Loury suggested that one could not address the problem of racial inequality in purely economic terms. Instead, he advocated an approach based upon "a combined recognition of historical conditions, and of certain structural features of social life in our country"—features that support racial discrimination. "The historical point," he emphasized, "is that due to slavery and racial caste, there has come into existence a distinct, insular, subgroup of our society that began with severe disadvantages (in comparison to others) in endowments of wealth, experience, and reputation so crucial to economic success." "The social structural point," he elaborated, "is that for as long as one can foresee, and without regard to legal prohibitions against racial discrimination in formal contract, we may confidently predict the practice of informal social discrimination—that is, discrimination in choice of social affiliation, which occurs partly along these racial lines." For Loury, this practice of discrimination in the social spheres suggested that there would be ongoing inequality of opportunity in the economic sphere. The reason, he argued, was that "full economic opportunity of any individual does not just depend upon his own income; it is also determined by the incomes of those with whom he is socially affiliated."

Not surprisingly, Loury would argue throughout his early years that progress by blacks depended upon their own moral and social standing within American society. "Further progress toward the attainment of equality," he maintained, "depends most crucially at this juncture on the acknowledgment of the dysfunctional behaviors which plague black communities and so offend others." But for Loury, acknowledgment of the problems was the first step toward actively remediating them, largely through self-help. In "Black Dignity and the Common Good," Loury declared:

> There is a great existential challenge facing black America today: the challenge of taking control of our own future by exerting the requisite moral leadership, making the sacrifices of time and resources, and building the needed institutions so that black social and economic development may be advanced.... If we are to be a truly free people, we must accept responsibility for our fate even when it does not lie wholly in our hands.

Echoing the Black Power movement, Loury suggested that to do otherwise—to lay blame on people in other quarters—could prove "quite dangerous, for it inevitably ends by placing the responsibility for maintenance of personal values and social norms among poor blacks on the shoulders of those who do not have an abiding interest in such matters."

Blacks, Loury maintained, must take responsibility for their own empowerment, regardless of whether they created the predicament in which they find themselves. "I am not questioning the existence of a link between behavioral difficulties and the effects of racism," remarked Loury, but "it is absolutely vital that blacks distinguish between the fault that may be attributed to racism as the cause of the black condition, and the responsibility for relieving that condition. No people can be genuinely free so long as they look to others for their deliverance." In the face of myriad social problems, including black-on-black crime, poverty, illegitimacy, and increasing dependence upon public welfare, Loury argued that it was mistake for blacks to blame racism and hold fast to the belief that such suffering will end when "America finally does right by its black folk." For Loury, such a response dodged the issue of black responsibility for blacks' welfare, "both at the level of individual behavior (the criminal perpetrator being responsible for his act), and at the level of the group (the black community being responsible for the values embraced by its people)." The solution, in Loury's view, was to "foster a sense of self-confidence and hope for the future among members of the black underclass." Although Loury did not dismiss the possibility that the federal government might "play a critical role in this process," he was adamant that "black business, academic, and political elites must press for improvement in their own people's lives through the building of constructive internal institutions, whether government participates or not."

But what form should this "press for improvement" take? According to Loury, blacks should look to Booker T. Washington:

Given the way in which the history of black Americans has evolved, it can now be seen that the animating *spirit* of Booker T. Washington's philosophy offers a sounder guide to the future for blacks than that reflected in the worldview of his critics. The problem of second-class political status for blacks, which so exercised DuBois and which he devoted much of his life to fighting against, has been resolved. But the problem of underdevelopment—the "brains, property and character" problem that Washington spent a lifetime trying to address—remains very much with us. Full equality of social standing in American society, the goal that blacks now seek, can never be attained until the fact of black underdevelopment is squarely faced and reversed. As Washington grasped intuitively, equality of this sort rests more on the performance of blacks in the economic and social spheres than it does on the continued expansion of civil rights.

For Loury, it was imperative for blacks to "question what it takes to stand truly equal among one's fellows" and to confront the "issues of dignity, shame, personal responsibility, character and values, and deservingness." This would entail what Loury described as "working on the inside game" of moral and social uplift within the black community. According to Loury, application of Washington's "philosophy of self-help, of good old-fashioned 'uplift'" and "working diligently to overcome the profound pathology to be found in some quarters of contemporary black life establishes what too often is only asserted—that blacks are indeed a great people struggling under terrible odds to overcome the effects of profound historic wrongs."

Only through self-help could blacks, in Washingtonian fashion, establish their social worthiness to compete in a capitalistic society because, as Loury said, "no one has a right to good standing among his fellows." Approaching one's problems through self-help would generate the sympathetic support of the rest of the political community. For Loury, it was "essential to establishing in the minds of whites what is true, which is that the bulk of poor blacks are deserving of the help they so desperately need. Making the effort to help yourself clearly conveys this message." In this way, self-help could provide a pathway to receipt of more thoroughgoing government support. As Loury suggested, "Self-help is not a substitute for government provision but rather an essential complement to it, ensuring that the state funded assistance is more effective, and that it is seen as legitimate by the political majorities that approve it."

Although Loury's conservative posture seemed more compassionate than Sowell's and Williams's, he nevertheless retained the dominant neoconservative antigovernment posture. In his testimony before the U.S. Congress on legislation that would become the Civil Rights Act of 1991, Loury made clear his belief that such legislation not only failed to address the real problems facing blacks but drew public attention away from the important questions of the day. According to Loury, the essential challenge facing blacks was that they were "disproportionately overrepresented" in the urban underclass, "where the problem of drugs, criminal violence, educational failure, homelessness, and family instability are manifest." Problems facing the black urban poor, he observed, "constitute the most important and intractable aspect of racial inequality in our time."

But in Loury's view, these problems did not lend themselves to easy legislative solutions. More important, these problems did not "derive in any direct way from the practice of employment discrimination," which was the target of the bill under consideration. Loury conceded that "the continued existence of these social problems contributes to the inability of those subject to them to compete effectively in the labor market." He also acknowledged that there were gross statistical disparities in employment between blacks and whites. But the existence of racial disparities in employment figures, alone were not compelling to Loury. "Gross statistical disparities," he pointed out, "are inadequate to identify the presence of discrimination, because individuals differ in many ways likely to affect their earnings capacities that are usually not measured and controlled for when group outcomes are compared. Thus, he concluded that "there is no basis for the expectation that antidiscrimination legislation will have anything but a marginal effect on these differences."

Rather than focus on the narrow issue of employment discrimination, Loury counseled Congress to consider that the "far greater threat to the attainment of full social and economic parity for racial minorities is posed by the trends affecting the social, educational and family life experiences of low-income urban communities." But rather than propose a novel approach for government assistance in this regard, Loury dismissed the possibility, observing that "these trends are more difficult to legislate against and do not as readily provide us with villains and heroes." Indeed, Loury intimated that white society bore little responsibility of creating these problems. "In my view," he said, "the problems of the so-called black underclass cannot be usefully ascribed solely to white racism, and they will not yield to political interventions in the form of stronger civil rights legislation." Indeed, Loury argued that greater government intervention through civil rights legislation might very well have the opposite effect: "To the extent that this focus on civil rights legislation as a remedy for the more general problem of racial inequality crowds from the public agenda a consideration of the broader causes of that inequality, I believe the long-term progress on the fundamental problem will be retarded."

Loury's skepticism about government intervention would inform his views on affirmative action as well. In his previous work, Loury had offered a range of conservative objections to affirmative action; that it violated the spirit of color blindness enshrined in the U.S. Constitution, that it encouraged race-conscious thinking, that it was directed at those who were least in need of a "boost," that it stigmatized its beneficiaries, that it encouraged the creation and perpetuation of racial stereotypes. But in a 1992 article, "The Effects of Affirmative Action on the Incentive to Acquire Skills: Some Negative Unintended Consequences," Loury offered a new reason to oppose affirmative action: namely, that government-imposed affirmative action actually worked to affirmatively underdevelop blacks. According to Loury, "A policy of affirmative action may alter the terms on which employers and workers interact with each other so as to perpetuate, rather than eliminate, existing disparities in productivity between minority and majority populations." The reason was that "the use of color as a basis for distributing opportunities may have the unintended effect of dulling the incentive to acquire skills for those who the policy is intended to benefit." He explained:

> Under affirmative action, employers may think they have to "patronize" minorities (i.e., not hold them to as high a standard) to meet governmental hiring requirements. Yet because this patronization can lower incentives for the acquisition of skills by minorities, it can perpetuate the racial skills differential which made the affirmative action policy necessary in the first place.

The patronizing effects of affirmative action, he concluded, served to exacerbate the deep effects of past discrimination.

In the mid-1990s, however, Loury would break ranks with his white conservative compatriots over the publication of three racially incendiary texts: Richard Herrnstein and Charles Murray's *The Bell Curve,* Dinesh D'Souza's *End of Racism,* and Stephan Thernstrom and Abigail Thernstrom's *America in Black and White: One Nation, Indivisible.* Each of these books, in one way or another, attacked blacks as genetically and/or culturally inferior to whites. Loury was critical of the authors' research methods and suspected that they were largely polemical texts masquerading as objective research. He soon realized that his own agenda was far different from that of these ultraconservative whites and that some reassessment of his earlier political beliefs might be in order. The culmination of that reassessment appeared in the 2001 publication of *The Anatomy of Racial Inequality,* in which Loury disavowed his early belief that color-blind racial policy and minimal government intrusion, coupled with self-help, might solve the race problem.

"The 'conservative line' on race in America today is simplistic," wrote Loury. Racial inequity is not the product of some inherent deficiency in the minds and hearts of African Americans. Rather, it is a social pathology "deeply rooted in American history," a pathology that "evolved in tandem with American political and economic institutions, and with cultural practices that supported and legitimated those institutions ... that were often deeply biased against blacks." Loury now rejected the complacency evinced by this conservative policy of indifference toward racial disparities, and he declared emphatically that racial inequality was "an American tragedy [and] a national, not merely a communal disgrace."

The root of the problem, according to Loury, was not "poor behavior," as he previously argued, but racial stigma. Racial stigma, according to Loury, is not so much about casual observations of blacks as it is about characteristics about the inherent nature of African Americans—about who, at the deepest level, they are understood to be. American blacks, according to Loury, have suffered the most from stigmatization as a result of the historical taint of slavery. Blacks, dishonored as a race by slavery, possess what he calls a "spoiled identity." It is the lingering effects of this spoiled identity that make it difficult for whites today to view blacks as individuals like themselves. This spoiled identity, reinforced by social structures, explains why African Americans, despite advances, are still at the bottom on many social and economic indices, and why whites are largely indifferent to evidence of racial disparity.

Thus, Loury concluded that the challenge to racial inequality must focus on the eradication of racial stigma and the assertion and acknowledgment of the essential humanity of blacks. This task, according to Loury, could not be undertaken with color-blind indifference. To the contrary, Loury argued that the promise of fairness, individual freedom, and dignity will remain unfulfilled without some form of intervention based upon race. Public policy must promote substantive racial egalitarianism that is directed squarely at remedying racial disparities rather than procedural equality designed to address concrete instances of "provable" racial discrimination.

## Shelby Steele

Loury's defection neither persuaded others to do the same nor deterred others from joining the ranks of black neoconservative intellectuals. Shelby Steele, a contemporary of Loury's, rose to prominence with the 1990 publication of *The Content of Our Character: A New Vision of Race in America*. Born in Chicago in 1946 to a biracial couple, Steele began his intellectual journey at Coe College in Cedar Rapids, Iowa, graduating with a degree in political science. He would go on to receive a master's degree in sociology from Southern Illinois University and a Ph.D. in English from the University of Utah. When *The Content of Our Character* was released, Steele was comfortably ensconced as an English professor at San Jose State College in California. He has been a resident scholar at the Hoover Institution since 1994.

The author of three critically acclaimed books, more than a hundred articles and commentaries, and the script for an acclaimed documentary (the Emmy Award–winning *Seven Days in Bensonhurst*), Steele is one of the most readily recognizable faces of black conservatism today. He has made countless public appearances, including appearances on current affairs news programs such as *Nightline* and *60 Minutes,* and his articles and commentaries appear in a variety of mainstream media publications, including the *New York Times, Wall Street Journal,* and *Harper's* magazine.

Like Loury, Steele is most concerned with what he sees as the manner in which liberal racial policy engenders a culture of dependency among blacks. In *The Content of Our Character,* however, Steele would argue that the culture of poverty was perhaps better understood as a culture of victimhood. For Steele, whites and blacks bore equal responsibility in nurturing and sustaining this sense of victimology. Steele suggested that many blacks retain a nagging sense of black inferiority. "You cannot be raised in a culture that was for centuries committed to the notion of your inferiority," Steele argued, "and not have some doubt in this regard—doubt that is likely to be aggravated most in integrated situations." Thus, blacks become overly preoccupied with racial discrimination, identifying it as the root cause of all of their problems, in order to cover "an unspoken black doubt about our ability to compete."

Whites, he maintained, suffered under the weight of intense guilt for the enormous injustices their ancestors imposed upon blacks. The combination of these two phenomena, according to Steele, created toxic policy that tended to view blacks as merely helpless victims. Much like Loury, Steele chose not to discount entirely the fact that blacks were and are often victims of white racism. "There is still racial discrimination in America," wrote Steele, "but I believe that the unconscious replaying of our oppression is now the greatest barrier to full equality."

The culture of victimhood, according to Steele, worked to destroy the impetus for black self-improvement. Because blacks were encouraged to see themselves as social victims, Steele argued that blacks were more inclined to look to external solutions for their problems, and less inclined to take responsibility and make changes within their own communities that would provide for greater social progress. According to Steele,

the victim-focused black identity encourages the individual to feel that his advancement depends almost entirely on that of the group. The individual "loses sight not only of his own possibilities but of the inextricable connection between individual effort and individual advancement.... Hard work, education, individual initiative, stable family life, property ownership—these have always been the means by which ethnic groups have moved ahead in America.... These 'laws' of advancement apply absolutely to black Americans also.... What we need is a form of racial identity that energizes the individual by putting him in touch with both his possibilities and his responsibilities."

Steele, in true neoconservative fashion, argued that blacks must seize control of their own destiny. "Whites must guarantee a free and fair society," he declared, "but blacks must be responsible for actualizing their own lives." Racism was no longer the barrier to black opportunity that it once was. Indeed, "the barriers to black progress in America today," argued Steele, "are clearly as much psychological as they are social or economic." According to Steele, civil rights leadership had bought into the culture of victimhood entirely and was leading blacks astray by demanding "concessions from government, industry, and society at large while demanding very little from blacks themselves by way of living up to the opportunities that have already been won."

Steele's emphasis on self-reliance and self-determination led him to criticize affirmative action policy. According to Steele, race preference programs were premised upon the idea of racial victimization and thus absolved blacks of individual responsibility to improve their own performance so that they might compete against whites on an equal footing. As a consequence, race preference programs undercut the integration of blacks into mainstream society. They "encourage dependency on entitlements rather than on our own initiative," he wrote. Rather than instill a sense of confidence, race preferences enlarged self-doubt among blacks and unfairly stigmatized blacks—including those who did not benefit from them—by suggesting that they are unable to compete against whites on an equal footing. Perhaps most troubling, in Steele's view, was that race preferences perpetuated the culture of victimhood by encouraging "blacks to exploit their own past victimization as a source of power and privilege."

The solution, according to Steele, was to reject government-sponsored, victim-oriented intervention into the social lives of blacks, and to encourage blacks to focus upon individual responsibility. Steele called for "a new spirit of pragmatism in racial matters where blacks are seen simply as American citizens who deserve complete fairness and in some cases developmental assistance, but in no case special entitlements based on color. We need deracinated social policies that attack poverty rather than black poverty and that instill those values that make for self-reliance." For Steele, self-help and personal responsibility provided the key to racial progress because "the promised land guarantees nothing. It is only an opportunity, not a deliverance."

The conservative themes first articulated in *The Content of Our Character* would pervade much of Steele's subsequent work. He would expand upon this thesis in 1999 in *A Dream Deferred: The Second Betrayal of Black Freedom in America,* in which he argued that too much of what has been done since the Great Society in the name of black rights has had far more to do with the moral redemption or self-satisfaction of whites than with any real improvement in the lives of blacks. According to Steele, the liberal racial policy of the 1960s had as its first and all-consuming goal the amelioration of America guilt rather than the careful development of true equality between the races. This created, in Steele's words, a "culture of preference" that betrayed America's best principles in order to give whites and America institutions a halo of racial virtue they could use against the stigma of racial shame. According to Steele, "The liberal looks at black difficulties—high crime rates, weak academic performance, illegitimacy rates and so on—and presumes them to be the result of victimizing forces beyond the control of blacks."

For Steele, liberal policy embodied a distinctly white supremacist view of blacks. It represented a "specific act of imagination" that not only viewed blacks as "outside the framework of individual responsibility," but one that also "imagine[s] them as inherently inferior." Steele elaborated:

> Double standards, preferential treatment, provisions for "cultural difference" and various kinds of entitlement all constitute a pattern of exceptionalism that keeps blacks (and other minorities) down by tolerating weakness at every juncture where strength is expected of others. . . . Then, after black weakness has been massaged, accepted, understood and felt for, people wonder why the infamous gap between blacks and whites on tests and other performance measures won't close. The answer, of course, is that nobody seriously asks that it be closed.

The reason, he argued, was that blacks and whites remained complicit in the maintenance of this culture of preference: "Whites agree to stay on this hook for an illusion of redemption, and blacks agree to keep them there for an illusion of power." But that illusion in fact perpetuates the powerlessness it is based upon. "Victimhood lasts only as long as it is accepted, and to exploit it for an empty sovereignty is to accept it," Steele cautioned.

Steele would once again return to these themes in 2005, with the publication of *White Guilt: How Blacks and Whites Together Destroyed the Promise of the Civil Rights Era,* in which he argues that blacks have been "twice betrayed": first, by slavery and oppression, and second, by group preferences mandated by the government that cause blacks to lose their self-esteem. "The great ingenuity of interventions like affirmative action has not been that they give Americans a way to identify with the struggles of blacks," he writes, "but that they give them a way to identify with racial virtuousness quite apart from blacks." The culture of victimization, Steele maintains, allows white Americans to see blacks as victims to ease their guilty conscience, while blacks attempt to trade on their victim status to extract further concessions from the liberal establishment.

Instead of relying upon "set-asides and entitlements," Steele argues that blacks should seek to develop a culture of "excellence and achievement." The culture of "excellence and achievement" in his view embodies "raceless" values of success. Thus, Steele, in effect, is arguing that to the extent that "blackness" is defined in terms of victimology, blacks should seek to transcend race. Commenting upon this component of Steele's conservatism in a 2002 *New York Times Magazine* profile, Loury commented that Steele's position was entirely consistent with his background:

> Shelby's position was that we had to completely transcend race.... How could it have been otherwise? His mother was a white woman. His wife is a white woman. When he looked at his own children's racial identity and wondered about an oppressive world that would say to those children, "Choose sides"—a dilemma I'd never faced—Shelby's angle of vision was really quite different from my own.

Not surprisingly, Steele does not view himself as a "black" conservative, preferring the label "free-market conservative"—one that allows him greater flexibility of racial and ideological affiliation.

## John McWhorter

Following closely in the footsteps of Steele is John McWhorter, a senior fellow at the Manhattan Institute, who earned a Ph.D. in linguistics at Stanford University in 1993 and has taught at Cornell and the University of California–Berkeley. He is the author of an assortment of academic texts on language and dialects, including *The Word on the Street,* which explores the nature of Black Vernacular English. Yet it is his writings on race, ethnicity, and cultural issues that have garnered the most attention. His stature among black neoconservatives has been solidified by his three books (*Losing the Race: Self-Sabotage in Black America, Authentically Black,* and *Winning the Race: Beyond the Crisis in Black America*), his many articles and interviews that have appeared in a wide range of publications (the *Wall Street Journal, New York Times, Los Angeles Times, Washington Post, National Review, City Journal,* and *Chronicle of Higher Education*), and his appearances on television and radio (*Meet the Press, John McLaughlin's One on One,* the *O'Reilly Factor,* and NPR's *Fresh Air*).

Much of McWhorter's work echoes the sentiments expressed by Shelby Steele and other neoconservatives. For instance, the three points of focus in McWhorter's first book, *Losing the Race*—the cult of victimology, cult of separatism, and cult of anti-intellectualism—offer an updated but largely anecdote-driven analysis of the culture of poverty and victimhood lamented by Steele, Loury, Sowell, and others. *Authentically Black,* a collection of essays that previously appeared in news and media outlets, also sounds familiar themes of black neoconservatism—self-reliance, self-help, the dangers of government intervention, and the like.

*Winning the Race* also treads familiar territory, but identifies McWhorter as perhaps even more moderate than Steele. He begins the book much as Steele began *A Dream Deferred,* with a critique of liberal racial policy of the 1960s that McWhorter claims turned black America "upside down" and "left us with a legacy much more damaging than anything racism left us." In a variation on Steele's analysis of how white and black guilt conspired to undermine black America, McWhorter argues that when "white radicals taught us to take a page from their new animus against The Suits and thumb our noses at The System and go on welfare because whitey wasn't devoted to us getting ahead, they sent us to hell."

Like Steele, Loury, and Sowell, McWhorter questioned whether receiving concessions from white America was in the best interests of blacks. However, he also shares the sense that held by those men that racism could not possibly explain all the problems experienced by blacks. Racism, McWhorter contends, cannot explain "millions of black people checking out of the job force forever, abandoning their children, letting a violent drug trade become the economic foundation of their communities, or even claiming in diversity seminars and classrooms and op-ed pages that their lives are defined by endless encounters with bigotry."

Consistent with the black neoconservative position, McWhorter writes that racism, though certainly alive and well, is but "an occasional nuisance that need not impede the black success we wish." The greater impediment, he maintains, is the absence of a culture of dignity and excellence. He waxes nostalgic about the 1960s, which he claimed embodied a healthier culture for blacks, despite the existence of harsh racial discrimination. In contrast, he is saddened by today's culture, in which the majority of black children are born out of wedlock, where blacks suffer from more crime and a weaker work ethic, where success is equated with "acting white," and where "black peer culture [views] school as something separate from black culture." The solution that McWhorter urges is predictable: blacks should choose leaders who reject victimhood and embrace the conservative ideals of self-help and self-reliance.

What is distinctive about McWhorter's book, however, is the occasional stumble when tracking the predicable neoconservative path. When discussing rap music, for instance, McWhorter does not engage in the ritual condemnation of the musical form. Though he says that rap "is the most overtly and consistently misogynistic music ever produced in human history," he adds, in a moment that, perhaps more than anything else, draws attention to the generational gap between him and his conservative counterparts, that hip-hop, whatever its failings, provides "a delicious beat."

McWhorter similarly departs from the "party line"—one which he often touted in his previous work—that blacks embrace a success-sabotaging culture out of their own volition. Much as did Glenn Loury, McWhorter suggests that blacks may very well be, in some ways, *victims* of white society's denial of opportunity. Blacks, he writes, are "a people deprived by history" of the social, economic, and psychological assets needed to lead self-directed lives. More important, like Loury, McWhorter evinces a sense of exhaustion in having to carry the mantle of black conservatism on his shoulders. When confronted by blacks who, in his view, subscribe wholly to the liberal policy of victimhood, McWhorter admits that he will "quietly shut down and . . . quickly agree with any further expression of fantasy." It is unclear whether he has begun the process of reexamining his own precepts or simply adopting a closing-ranks mentality that draws him closer to conservatives and further alienates him from the mainstream. In either case, McWhorter's ongoing lifework continues to lend credibility to black neoconservative ideas and ensures the longevity of the neoconservative intellectual movement for generations to come.

The effect of black neoconservative intellectuals on the trajectory of black conservatism cannot be overstated. These thinkers collectively resuscitated conservatism in black political thought and delivered black conservatism from the margins to the mainstream of American society. Not surprisingly, the rise in number of black neoconservative intellectuals was accompanied by a corresponding increase in the presence of black conservatives in public life that would forever change the face of black American politics.

# EIGHT

# The Public Face of Black Conservatism

## Revealing the Philosophies of Clarence Thomas, Colin Powell, and Condoleezza Rice

The conspicuous flourishing of black intellectual neoconservatism represents one important dimension of the resurgence of black conservative thought in American politics. The resurrection and repacking of traditional conservative precepts for modern-day application represents an important evolutionary step and has bestowed new legitimacy upon ideas that circulated within black communities for more than one hundred years. Whatever one might think about the virtues and merits of the black neoconservative position, it is clear that black conservatism is an important part of black politics today and will likely remain so for years to come.

But the arrival of black neoconservative intellectualism did not occur in isolation. In carving out intellectual space for extreme ideas within black conservative thought, black neoconservatism created a right-of-center void in American politics and culture that could be filled by more moderate black conservatives who, as operatives within the established corridors of government, could further legitimize the movement. Much like their intellectual counterparts, this cadre of new black conservative leaders lend credibility to conservative ideas and highlight their ongoing appeal to many blacks.

The rewarding of Fairmont Conference participants Clarence Thomas,

Clarence Pendleton, and Samuel Pierce as well as social conservative Alan Keyes with plum positions within the Reagan administration was followed by a range of high-level appointments by President George H. W. Bush. In 1989, Bush appointed Louis Sullivan as secretary of Health and Human Services, General Colin L. Powell as chairman of the U.S. Joint Chiefs of Staff, and Condoleezza Rice as director of the National Security Council. In 1990, Bush appointed Arthur Fletcher, the assistant secretary of labor under President Nixon, to replace Pendleton as chairman of the Civil Rights Commission. In 1991, he nominated Clarence Thomas to fill the Thurgood Marshall's pending vacancy on the Supreme Court. President George W. Bush would follow his father's lead in far more dramatic fashion in 2001, appointing Colin Powell as secretary of state, Roderick R. Paige as secretary of education, Condoleezza Rice as advisor to the National Security Council, Alphonso Jackson as deputy secretary to Housing and Urban Development, Claude Allen as deputy secretary of Health and Human Services, Leo S. Mackay Jr. as deputy secretary of Veterans Affairs, Larry D. Thompson as deputy attorney general, and Stephen A. Perry as administrator of the General Services Administration. Bush would later appoint Rice to replace Colin Powell as secretary of state; name Michael Powell, son of Colin Powell, as chairman of the Federal Communications Commission; and nominate conservative jurist Janice Rogers Brown to become a federal judge on the prestigious U.S. District Court for the District of Columbia.

Black conservatives also enjoyed success at the polls. In 1990, moderate conservative Gary Franks won a seat in the House of Representatives for the state of Connecticut in a district where blacks made up less than 5 percent of the eligible voters—a seat he held for three terms. Black Republican J. C. Watts won that year as well in his home state of Oklahoma, and in 1998 the House elected Watts as chairman of the House Republican Conference. In November 2001, Winsome Sears upset a twenty-year Democratic incumbent in her campaign for the 90th District seat of the Virginia House of Delegates, becoming the first black female Republican member of the legislature. Rather than seek a second term, Sears led an unsuccessful bid in 2004 to become the first black Republican to serve in U.S. Congress.

Black conservative politicians have continued to make headlines in spite of electoral defeat. In 2006, Ken Blackwell, a former secretary of state of Ohio, and Lynn Swann, an NFL Hall of Fame wide receiver, both made history as Republican nominees for governor in Ohio and Pennsylvania, respectively, despite losing their races to Democratic opponents. A similar situation arose in the 2006 Senate race. Former lieutenant governor of Maryland Michael S. Steele basked in media attention when he secured the Republican nomination for the Senate seat vacated by Paul Sarbanes, though he ultimately lost the race to Democratic congressman Ben Cardin. Keith Butler, a minister and former Detroit councilman, made headlines as the possible Republican nominee for Senate in his home state of Michigan, only to lose in the Republican primary against white Republican Michael Bouchard.

But among the ranks of black neoconservatives in government, by far the most recognizable members of the black conservative establishment are Clarence Thomas, Colin Powell, and Condoleezza Rice. How do these figures compare to their neoconservative intellectual counterparts? Do they exemplify black neoconservatism in practice? Or do they offer a more moderate take on black conservatism? As it turns out, they do a little of both. Moreover, the views and experiences of these figures highlight the complexities and contradictions within modern black conservatism and demonstrate that the boundaries of ideology are rarely as crisp and neat as we would like them to be.

## The Icon: Associate Justice Clarence Thomas

Associate Supreme Court Justice Clarence Thomas is perhaps the most enduring symbol of black conservatism in modern America. I traced some of the highlights of his early career above: a participant in the Fairmont Conference of 1980, Thomas was appointed by Reagan as assistant secretary for civil rights in the Department of Education and, within twelve months, as chairman of the Equal Employment Opportunity Commission. By the end of the decade he would be nominated the Federal District Court for the District of Columbia, and with two years of that appointment, receive President George H. W. Bush's nomination for a seat on the United States Supreme Court.

Thomas's Senate confirmation hearings brought national attention to black neoconservatives. But unlike Sowell, Loury, and others, Thomas had had a relatively short legal career, and he had not produced extensive writings that set forth his conservative beliefs. He was a darling of the Republican Party, but beyond the closely knit conservative circles in which he operated, little was known about him. As it turned out, his background would raise more questions than it answered.

In many ways, Justice Thomas is a most ironic icon of black conservatism, embodying much of the striking and occasionally choreographed contradiction that modern liberals despise about black neoconservatives. He is a man who claims to have risen from boyhood poverty, but there is ample evidence to suggest that Thomas enjoyed, by and large, a middle-class upbringing. He is an avowed opponent of affirmative action, but his life is, in some ways, one of affirmative action's greatest and most unapologetic success stories. He is a dyed-in-the-wool ideological conservative, yet his political roots lie in the black radical consciousness of late-1960s and early-1970s campus politics. He is a man who is critical of black elites and identifies strongly with everyday black people, but whose politics have left him largely estranged from the black community and a virtual outsider in his own family. He is a man known to be boisterous and outspoken among his peers, especially black conservatives, but he is conspicuously silent and disengaged on the bench. He counsels blacks to forgive past racial transgressions and simply move on with their lives, but he is known to hold deep grudges against those who personally disappoint him.

Perhaps the single greatest contradiction lies with the issue of affirmative action and race preferences. In 2003, Justice Thomas wrote a scathing dissenting opinion in a case in which the majority of the Court voted to uphold the use of race in law school admissions at the University of Michigan. Justice Thomas chastised the Court for allowing the state (here, the public university) to "discriminate" by taking race into account when deciding who should be admitted. Invoking Frederick Douglass, Justice Thomas counseled the university to "do nothing"—to cease its meddling and allow the students to rise or fall based upon their own merit. Thomas went on to argue that affirmative action stigmatizes its minority beneficiaries, inflames white hostility, and undermines the credibility and achievements of racial minorities, regardless of whether they actually received any benefit under the policy. In his view, affirmative action proved catastrophic to the life chances of racial minorities.

The dissent was classic Clarence Thomas opposition to affirmative action measures—the same oppositional stance that he had taken for much of his adult life. For many readers of the opinion, Thomas's position seemed consistent with his upbringing. After all, Thomas had, in the words of Justice Scalia, risen from *nothing.* He was a self-made man—proof that blacks could succeed without affirmative action.

Or was he?

In a recent unauthorized biography, *Supreme Discomfort: The Divided Soul of Clarence Thomas,* authors Kevin Merida and Michael Fletcher painstakingly make a case for seeing Thomas's "Horatio Alger" mystique as misplaced. Indeed, the authors suggest that at every critical step along his career progression, Thomas received some benefit because of his race. For instance, in the late 1960s, Holy Cross instituted a scholarship program in honor of the slain civil rights leader Martin Luther King Jr. When Thomas applied to transfer from Immaculate Conception Seminary to Holy Cross, he received one of these new scholarships earmarked for minorities, as well as a loan and a university job that, when combined, covered most of his university expenses.

Later, when Thomas was accepted at Yale Law School, affirmative action was by then an accepted practice in student admissions. Approximately 10 percent of the entering class at Yale Law School was reserved for minorities. Yale officials have neither confirmed nor denied that Thomas would have been admitted without affirmative action—a fact, which the authors note, "still galls [Thomas] more than three decades later."

John C. "Jack" Danforth gave Thomas his first job upon graduating from Yale. Danforth, a Republican and heir to the Ralston Purina fortune, was then the attorney general for the state of Missouri. Himself a Yale graduate, Danforth asked Guido Calabresi, one of his former law professors, to assist him in hiring promising recruits. According to Calabresi, "Danforth wanted somebody who was bright, preferably an African American." Calabresi recommended Thomas, who accepted Danforth's offer to join his office in Jefferson City, Missouri.

When Danforth won election to the U.S. Senate in 1976, Thomas left to work for Monsanto, a chemical company based in St. Louis. Danforth had recommended Thomas to Monsanto General Counsel Ned J. Putzell Jr., who was looking to hire an African American lawyer. According to Putzell, "I set about looking for a female [lawyer] and a black lawyer, and I ended up hiring both." But Thomas was unhappy at Monsanto, and when Danforth asked him to serve as a legislative aide, he jumped at the chance to leave.

After a short stint in that position, Thomas garnered the attention of

Edwin Meese III, who led Reagan's transition team following the 1980 presidential election. Thomas attended the Fairmont Conference shortly after the election, and he spoke candidly about his views on problems facing blacks and other minority communities. Soon after, he was named assistant secretary for civil rights in the Department of Education.

When, twelve months after taking that job, Thomas was asked to chair the Equal Employment Opportunity Commission (EEOC), there was no suggestion that Thomas was tapped for the job because of his race—at least not initially. However, following confirmation for his second term as chairman of the commission, William Bradford Reynolds, then serving as the Justice Department's assistant attorney general for civil rights, toasted Thomas at a celebratory reception as "the epitome of the right kind of affirmative action working the right way."

With Justice Thurgood Marshall's health failing, the Reagan administration looked for a conservative African American to appoint to the federal appellate bench, which the authors correctly note "is seen as a training ground for the Supreme Court." According to Reynolds, "Clarence was first discussed as a circuit court candidate when he was over at EEOC. And at that time, certainly a number of us who were involved identified him as a wonderful candidate for the Supreme Court." Reynolds then added, "I think everybody recognized that it would be next to impossible to name a nominee to the seat who wasn't black." When George H. W. Bush was elected president in 1988, Thomas was put on a short list of judicial candidates. In 1989, Thomas received the nomination and eventual confirmation to the federal appellate court for the District of Columbia.

Two years later, when Marshall announced plans for retirement, Bush nominated Thomas to replace him. Bush publicly denied that Thomas's race played any role in his selection. "The fact that he is black and a minority had nothing to do with this in the sense that he is the best qualified at this time," Bush said. "I don't feel he's a quota." Reynolds, however, saw things differently. "The politics of the situation," according to Reynolds, demanded that the administration "get the best-qualified person who is black whom we can put in that seat."

Contrary to Thomas's claims to have elevated himself by his bootstraps, so to speak, it seems all too clear that a great deal of his success came about *because of* rather than *in spite of* his race. But how does he reconcile his own status as affirmative action beneficiary with his public denunciation of race preference? Thomas has never directly answered the question himself.

The more telling point, however is that this deep contradiction lies at the heart of who Clarence Thomas is. He is a man for whom race has been a defining element, both personally and professionally, despite his best efforts to transcend his own race. James Baldwin once wrote in "Everybody's Protest Novel," "We take our shape ... within and against that cage of reality bequeathed us at our birth, and yet it is precisely through our dependence on this reality that we are most endlessly betrayed." This seems particularly true of Thomas, who, in many ways, remains sadly betrayed if not captured by the very thing he opposes.

Thomas's failure to publicly reconcile his troubled racial identity with his conservative philosophy would only serve to deepen his exile from both black and white society. A young Clarence Thomas enrolled at Immaculate Conception Seminary in August 1967—one of four African Americans—eager to join the priesthood. Yet a sense of betrayal would send him into a secular life within the year. The defining moment occurred on April 4, 1968, when Martin Luther King Jr. was assassinated in Memphis. Thomas recounts: "While walking into the dormitory, someone watching TV yelled that Dr. Martin Luther King has been shot. A fellow white seminarian who was walking up the stairs in front of me, upon hearing this, and without knowing I was behind him, replied after he heard that Dr. King had been shot, "That's good; I hope the SOB dies.'" Thomas withdrew from Conception at the end of the semester, enraged by the racism of his fellow seminarians, scornful of the empty promises of integration, and disillusioned with his faith. This defining moment of betrayal would prefigure his skepticism toward liberal solutions to race problems and strengthen his embrace of conservative political philosophy.

However, the greatest string of betrayals occurred as Thomas ascended to the Supreme Court. Thurgood Marshall set the tone during a packed news conference when he announced his resignation from the bench. When asked whether the president should nominate an African American as his replacement, Marshall responded that Bush should not use race as a cover to put the "wrong Negro" on the court. Marshall added, "My dad told me way back that there is no difference between a white snake and a black snake.... They'll both bite." As Thomas biographers Merida and Fletcher note, many regarded Marshall's comment as "an unmistakable reference to Thomas, who at that point, had already been touted as a leading candidate to fill the vacancy."

Thomas would later feel betrayed by the NAACP in the months leading up to his confirmation. Thomas met privately with the NAACP to allay criticisms that he was out of touch with the needs of black Americans. Following a productive exchange with Thomas, NAACP board members conceded that Thomas was impressive. According to Hazel Dukes, an influential board member that initiated the meeting, Thomas had "confirmed his 'blackness' and seemed to remember 'where he came from.'" One month later, after Bush has announced Thomas as his choice, the NAACP announced its formal opposition to Thomas, noting in a press release that Thomas "fails to demonstrate a respect or commitment to the enforcement of federal laws protecting civil rights and individual liberties."

Thomas undoubtedly felt betrayed by Anita Hill, a fellow Yale graduate and former coworker at the Department of Education and the EEOC who accused Thomas of sexually harassing her on the job. The allegations, replete with explicit details about Thomas boasting of his own sexual prowess and penis size, crass references to pubic hair, and repeated sexual overtures, proved devastating to Thomas' credibility and legitimacy. Hill's allegations opened the floodgates of inquiry into Thomas's history of using coarse language, telling raunchy jokes, engaging in sexual banter, and viewing of graphic adult videos. Particularly noteworthy was the discovery that Thomas, while chairman of the EEOC, had rented adult videos from Graffiti, a local sex shop in Washington's Dupont Circle. According to Merida and Fletcher, "It was there that Fred Cooke, the former D.C. corporation counsel, saw him at the checkout line during the late 1980s with a copy of *The Adventures of Bad Mama Jama*, a triple X-rated flick featuring the sexual exploits of a hugely overweight black woman with abnormally large breasts." Despite pressure from Hill supporters to come forward, Cooke ultimately elected to remain silent and allow Thomas's nomination to rise or fall on the merits. The story of Thomas and *The Adventures of Bad Mama Jama* made its rounds through Washington social networks but never received the full attention of the Hill-Thomas hearing participants. Soon thereafter, past acquaintances, familiar with the ex-seminarian's sordid tastes and past transgressions, would come forward with statements that lent credibility to Hill's allegations.

The sense of betrayal extended to his alma mater as well. Thomas was extremely disappointed by the lack of support he received from Yale Law School. The dean of the Law School did not publicly back Thomas's nomination before the Anita Hill allegations, and when asked about the veracity of Hill's allegations, claimed that both were telling the truth as each saw it. Though Yale Law School proudly displays the portraits of five former students and faculty members who went on to serve on the Supreme Court, Thomas's portrait is conspicuously absent because he has steadfastly refused to allow his portrait to be hung there. Unlike other members of the Supreme Court, who regularly visit their alma maters, Thomas has never returned to Yale during all his years on the bench, and he continues to devalue the importance of the education he received at Yale.

But his greatest disappointment with Yale was a personal one directed at Drew S. Days III, a Yale faculty member who formally opposed Thomas's nomination. The authors note that "the justice retains a special animus for Days," reporting on the comments of a white visitor to Justice Thomas, who "was surprised to hear Thomas characterize Days as another of those light-skinned blacks who look down on blacks like him and can never accept them as equals." This was the sort of criticism that Thomas would often hurl against a great many of his classmates at Yale, including William T. Coleman IV—the son of a prosperous lawyer who became the first black secretary of the Transportation Department— whom Thomas once described to a fellow student with blue-collar roots as being "not like us."

This string of betrayals and disappointments may help to explain why Thomas remains so publicly guarded, particularly among blacks and liberals. His life of exile as a lonely iconoclast is not simply a matter of personal choice, as many of his critics maintain, but rather a complex result of politics, personal preference, and psychological necessity. Following Thomas's confirmation, Claudia Butts, White House liaison to blacks under President Bush, declared, "Now is the safest time ever [for black conservatives] to come out of the closet." Yet Thomas himself seemed to disagree. During his time on the Court, Thomas has remained remarkably reserved in public. Unlike his conservative colleague Justice Scalia, Thomas rarely if ever presents his political views for public consumption.

Thomas's personal and professional odyssey, enabled by the contingent adoration of conservative whites, has left him powerfully conflicted. Detested by many members of the black community and not entirely comfortable among whites, Thomas had charted his own uneasy course to success. The young, sensitive boy—who according to his biographers was ashamed of his Negroid features and Geechee/Gullah accent—had grown into a man who seeks to transcend race through a thorough embrace of neoconservative ideas. At the same time, he strategically embraces racial identity when it suits his purposes—referring to his confirmation hearing as a high-tech lynching, or explaining his silence on the bench as a coping mechanism sourced from his self-consciousness as a sixteen-year-old black kid transferred to an all-white school. Thomas's racial identity, like the concept of race itself, proves slippery, protean, and prone to manipulation. He refuses to fit neatly within any predetermined category of racial identity. In the absence of some professed racial allegiance, it is no wonder that he resides at the periphery of both black and white society—a lonely, iconoclastic black neoconservative.

But what exactly makes Justice Thomas so conservative? Thomas was born in Pin Point, Georgia, a small community outside Savannah. His father abandoned his family when he was only a year old, leaving his mother, Leola Anderson, to take care of the family. At age seven they went to live with his mother's father, Myers Anderson, in Savannah. He had a fuel oil business that also sold ice; Thomas often helped him make deliveries. Thomas greatly admired his grandfather's grit and determination to be a self-made man, and Thomas would later acknowledge that he came to embrace the conservative principles of self-help and self-reliance though his grandfather.

Beyond this, however, Thomas himself reveals little about his personal political views, admitting only that he has some "libertarian leanings." However, his judicial philosophy of originalism and corresponding fidelity to the framers' intentions in crafting laws provide an important window into his thinking. His originalist take on the Fourteenth Amendment leads him to oppose affirmative action, exemplified in his stinging dissent in *Grutter v. Bollinger,* whereas the majority of the Court found affirmative action, under certain circumstances, constitutionally permissible. Furthermore, like most originalists, Thomas supports firm limits on federal government intervention and has an avowed preference for "state's rights." As a consequence, Thomas opposes a federally protected right to abortion, exemplified by his dissenting opinion in *Planned Parenthood v. Casey,* in which he advocated the reversal of *Roe v. Wade,* and his concurring opinion in *Gonzales v. Carhart,* in which he voted to uphold a federal legislative ban on partial-birth abortion but questioned whether Congress had the authority to do so.

His skepticism of federal government intervention led him to dissent in *Gonzales v. Raich,* a case that permitted the federal government to arrest, prosecute, and imprison patients who were using medical marijuana. However, in interpreting the Fourth Amendment, Thomas tends to support law enforcement over defendant's rights. In *Board of Education v. Earls,* Thomas, writing for the majority of Court, upheld drug testing for students involved in extracurricular activities and later, in *Samson v. California,* articulated the Court's view that random searches of recently paroled convicts were constitutionally permissible. Thomas also seems to afford greater latitude to the executive branch, particularly in the exercise of war powers, as he was the lone justice that entirely sided with the Bush administration in *Hamdi v. Rumsfeld* and was one of the few justices to dissent in *Hamdan v. Rumsfeld,* a case involving Guantanamo detainees.

Thomas's originalist interpretation of the rights afforded to citizens under the Eight Amendment proves equally narrow. Thomas believes that the Constitution places few limits on the use of capital punishment, exemplified by his opinion for the Court in *Kansas v. Marsh,* in which he indicated a belief that the Constitution affords states broad procedural latitude in imposing the death penalty, and in his dissenting opinions in both *Atkins v. Virginia* and *Roper v. Simmons,* two cases in which the majority of the Court held that the Constitution prohibited the application of the death penalty to certain classes of persons.

However, it was Thomas's dissent in *Hudson v. McMillian* that particularly outraged civil rights leaders and caused many of his supporters to question whether Thomas was "too conservative." Keith Hudson, a black inmate in a Louisiana prison, had sued prison officials after having been beaten by prison guards while shackled. He claimed that such treatment violated the Eighth Amendment's prohibition on cruel and unusual punishment. According to Thomas, Hudson's rights had not been violated because he had not sustained any significant injuries. "Abusive behavior by prison guards is deplorable conduct," opined Thomas, "but that does not mean that it is invariably unconstitutional." Thomas derided Hudson's invocation of the cruel and unusual punishment clause as "yet another manifestation of the pervasive view that the federal Constitution must address all ills in our society."

## The Soldier: General Colin Powell

Unlike Justice Thomas, whose disaffection with the black community and conservative judicial philosophy has tended to alienate mainstream and liberal blacks, Colin Powell's lifework imbues black conservatism with integrity and compassion. Born in Harlem in 1937, the son of Jamaican immigrants, General Colin Powell's lifetime of public service earned him countless awards and commendations, including a declaration as an honorary Knight Commander of the Order of the Bath by Queen Elizabeth II of the United Kingdom. The title of his autobiography is particularly apt, as Powell's life truly has been "an American journey."

Powell's journey from the rough streets of New York City to the White House is fascinating. His parents, both garment workers, were New Deal Democrats throughout his early childhood. He grew up admiring Franklin Roosevelt. Although his mother would remain a lifelong Democrat, his father by 1952 was supporting Republican Dwight Eisenhower. The Powell family would move to the South Bronx, and Colin— then pronounced *cah*-lin with the British inflection that Jamaicans used —enrolled in public schools. During World War II, Colin, then living on Kelly Street, learned of war hero Colin P. Kelly Jr., an Air Force pilot who had attacked the Japanese battleship *Haruna* two days after Pearl Harbor and posthumously won the Distinguished Service Cross. The war hero had pronounced his name *coh*-lin, and, because of his popularity among young boys, everyone began to refer to Colin as "Coh-lin of Kelly Street."

Colin could not have foreseen on that day that he too would become an American hero. After finishing school, Colin enrolled in City College of New York and joined the college ROTC program. The Army would take Powell from New York to Vietnam to Korea and to the Pentagon, then eventually to the White House, first as chairman of the Joint Chiefs under Presidents George H. W. Bush and William Jefferson Clinton, and later as secretary of state under President George W. Bush. Like a good soldier, Powell often kept his personal political views to himself.

This would change, beginning in the mid-1990s, when rumors circulated that Powell harbored political aspirations and was being recruited as a Republican nominee for president. Powell, recently retired, had authored an autobiography, *My American Journey,* in which he set forth his conservative philosophy.

"To sum up my political philosophy," wrote Powell, "I am a fiscal conservative with a social conscience." As consequence, "Neither of the two major parties [Republican or Democratic] fits me comfortably in its present state." For Powell, the ideology of both parties was too rigid. "I am troubled by the political passion of those on the extreme right who seem to claim divine wisdom on political as well as spiritual matters. On the other side of the spectrum, I am put off by the patronizing liberals who claim to know what is best for society but devote little thought to who will eventually pay the bills." Despite his misgivings about party affiliation, Powell would later openly affiliate with the Republican Party. Speaking at the Republican National Convention in August 1996, Powell declared all the reasons why he became a Republican:

> I became a Republican because I believe our party best represents the principles of freedom, opportunity, and limited government upon which our nation was founded. I became a Republican because I believe the policies of our party will lead to greater economic growth. I became a Republican because I truly believe the federal government has become too large and too intrusive in our lives. I became a Republican because I believe America must remain the leader of the free world.

Regardless of party affiliation, Powell's political philosophy proves far more conservative than compassionate. His fiscal conservativeness cannot be overstated. As Powell himself notes: "Everything I observe affirms my belief in free enterprise. It creates new wealth, generates new jobs, and enables people to live good lives, fuels demand, and triggers fresh enterprises, starting the cycle all over again." In terms powerfully reminiscent of Thomas Sowell and Walter Williams, Powell declared his belief that "government should not interfere with the demonstrated success of the free marketplace, beyond controls to protect public safety and to prevent distortions of competition by either labor or industry." Every tax dollar taken away from a consumer or business, according to Powell, "is a dollar that will be spent less efficiently than if left in private hands." Ultimately, all people benefit more from the capitalistic system than another, according to Powell ("I believe so strongly in job producing free enterprise because jobs are the best answer to most social ills"), a truth he sees evidenced by his own family's success: "My parents came to this country not looking for government support, but for job opportunities."

But it would be wrong to conclude that Powell endorses the radical antigovernment views of Sowell and Williams. Again, drawing upon his personal life journey, Powell praised the virtues of federal government intervention:

> I was a born a New Deal, Depression era Kid. . . . Government helped my parents by providing cheap public subway systems so that they could get to work, and public schools for their children, and protection under law to make sure their labor was not exploited. . . . I received free college education because New York taxed its citizens to make this investment in the sons and daughters of immigrants and the working class.

Despite this rather dramatic concession to the virtues of liberal reform that few other conservatives have been willing to make, Powell nevertheless views the current call for less government as entirely justified. Powell stated during the 1996 Republican Convention, at a time when welfare programs were undergoing a major transition to "workfare," that it is the "entitlement state that must be reformed, and not just the welfare state." The kind of jobs that paying a living wage "come from a faster-growing economy where the free enterprise system is unleashed to create wealth," he argued. "Government assistance is a poor substitute for good jobs."

But if Powell can be viewed as someone who disdains government intervention, he makes a notable exception in the area of civil rights. Here, one finds the social conscience element of Powell's conservative philosophy. As Powell explained, there is "one role I want government to be vigorous and active [in], and that is ensuring the protection of the Constitution to all Americans. Our Constitution and our national conscience demand that every American be accorded dignity and respect, receive the same treatment under the law, and enjoy equal opportunity." The reason, according to Powell, is his abiding respect for "the hard won civil rights legislation of the 1960s, which I benefited from" and the "courageous leaders who won these gains over the opposition hiding behind transparent arguments of "states' rights" and "property rights."

Unlike Justice Thomas, who often distanced himself from the black community, Powell understands the importance of asserting that connection if for no other reason than to legitimize one's conservative views among blacks. Of course, Powell's connection runs much deeper than politics. His military career had imbued him with a deep understanding of the sacrifices of all soldiers, black soldiers particularly. Speaking during the dedication of the monument to "Buffalo Soldiers," Powell reflected on the fact that African Americans had answered the country's every call from its infancy. "The fame and fortune that were their just due never came," he told the audience. "For their blood spent, lives lost, and battles won, they received nothing. They went back to slavery, real or economic, consigned there by hate, prejudice, bigotry, and intolerance." But for Powell, the Buffalo Soldiers symbolized the spirit of sacrifice that blacks should embrace more generally. "I am deeply mindful of the debt I owe to those who went before me. I climbed on their backs. I challenge every young person here today: don't forget their service and their sacrifice; and don't forget our service and sacrifice, and climb on our backs."

Unlike most black conservatives, Powell is unusually forthright about his racial heritage. Recounting a trip to a restored slave camp in Nigeria, Powell said, "I felt something stirring in me that I had not thought much about before." Powell had always understood his roots to be in Jamaica. But in a moment of remarkable directness, Powell recounted, "I now began to feel an earlier emotional pull, my link to Africa. Gazing down into those cattle pens for human beings, I could imagine the smells of packed bodies. A great-great grandfather of mine must have stood in a place as horrible as this." In his departure speech, Powell declared to his audience, "I am the son of Jamaicans who emigrated to the U.S. But today, I am something more. I am an African too. I feel my roots, here in this continent."

If there were any concerns about Powell's sincere connection with the black community, they were partially ameliorated when, during a speech delivered at the 2000 Republican Convention, Powell called upon white Republicans to reach out to blacks. As Powell noted:

> Recently, Gov. Bush addressed the annual meeting of the NAACP. He spoke the truth to the delegates when he said that the party of Lincoln has not always carried the mantle of Lincoln. I know that with all his heart, Gov. Bush wants the Republican Party to wear that mantle again.... He knows that that mantle will not simply be handed over, that it will have to be earned. The

party must follow the governor's lead in reaching out to minority communities and particularly the African-American community. And not just during an election year campaign. My friends, if we're serious about this, it has to be a sustained effort, it must be every day, and it must be for real. The party must listen to and speak with all leaders of the black community, regardless of political affiliation or philosophy. Overcoming the cynicism and mistrust that exists in the black community, and raising up that mantle of Lincoln, is about more than just winning votes, it is about giving all minorities a competitive choice.

In an August 2000 interview on the American Broadcast Corporation, Powell explained precisely what he meant with his appeal to Republicans. "By 'for real,'" Powell said, "I meant we have to get rid of the old Southern strategy of 25 years ago of pandering to certain constituencies at the expense of minorities. We have to make sure that is a consistent piece of our strategy and that we are working on it all the time, not just once every four years have an event. I don't want just the image of inclusiveness but policies that go to inclusiveness."

But what does Powell mean when he promotes inclusion? For Powell, inclusiveness requires the extinction of racial discrimination. As Powell remarked at the 1996 Republican Convention, "Where discrimination still exists or where the scars of past discrimination contaminate the present, we must not close our eyes to it, declare a level playing field, and hope it will go away by itself. It did not in the past. It will not in the future." Instead, he urged that we "open every avenue of educational and economic opportunity to those who are still denied access because of their race, ethnic background or gender."

In promoting equal opportunity, Powell is at pains to distinguish his opposition to affirmative action and race preferences. In his autobiography, Powell writes: "Equal rights and equal opportunity mean just that. They do not mean preferential treatment. If affirmative action means programs that provide equal opportunity, then I am all for it. If it leads to preferential treatment or helps those that no longer need help, I am opposed." For Powell, affirmative action was "equal consideration," and not "reverse discrimination": "Discrimination 'for' one group means, inevitably, discrimination 'against' another; and all discrimination is offensive." Powell notes, however, that treating unequal things equally is as unfair as treating equal things unequally: "If a history of discrimination has made it difficult for certain Americans to meet standards, it is only fair to provide temporary means to help them catch up and compete on equal terms." At the 1996 Republican Convention, Powell expressly stated his support for "affirmative action," though he left the term conveniently undefined. Powell would continue to equivocate on the question of affirmative action even at the 2000 Republican Convention, suggesting that white Republican opposition was disingenuous:

We must understand the cynicism that is created in the black community when, for example, some in our party miss no opportunity to roundly and loudly condemn affirmative action that helped a few thousand black kids get an education, but you hardly hear a whimper when it's affirmative action for lobbyists who load our federal tax code with preferences for special interests. It doesn't work. You can't make that case.

But if Powell's position on affirmative action and civil rights proves surprisingly liberal, his approach to bedrock issues of education, family, and morality reflect the inward quality of black conservative thought. Much like other black neoconservatives who call upon blacks to take responsibility for their own communities in crisis rather than seek external solutions, Powell suggested that the solution to social ills plaguing blacks begins with "the restoration of real families." "We need to restore the social model of married parents," he argued, "bringing into the world a desired child, a child to be loved and nurtured, to be taught a sense of right and wrong, to be educated to his or her maximum potential in a society that provides opportunities for work and a fulfilling life. Simple to say, difficult to achieve, yet the ideal toward which we must never stop striving."

The answer for crime-ridden communities, according to Powell, was equally simple: invest in your children. As Powell lamented at the 2000 Republican Convention:

I've seen kids destroying themselves with drugs, kids who see violence and crime as the answer to their hopelessness, kids who no longer believe in themselves and who don't see a reason to believe in America.... They are part of a growing population of over 2 million Americans behind bars.... Most of them are men

165

and the majority of those men are minorities. . . . The problem is as simple and as direct as this: We either get back to the task of building our children the way we know how, or we're going to keep building jails in America. And it's time to stop building jails in America and get back to the task of building our children.

Much as Booker T. Washington had argued a century before, Powell demanded that we give the "necessities" to our children. For Powell, this included the spirit of volunteerism—of giving "back to the community of which they are a part," so that children might learn that "what's important in life is giving to others, not whether your sneakers cost more than someone else's sneakers."

Building children also demands the inculcation of discipline and a strong work ethic. Powell is a strong proponent of the expansion of ROTC and Junior ROTC programs, which has led to accusations that he is trying to "militarize" education. Powell concedes that youths may be more inclined to enlist in the military as a result of participation in Junior ROTC programs, but he argues that the value of such programs transcends their use as recruitment tools. "Inner-city kids, many from broken homes, found stability and role models in Junior ROTC," he said, and they "got a taste of discipline, the work ethic, and they experienced pride of membership in something healthier than a gang." For Powell, such programs "can provide a fresh start for thousands of kids, particularly those from minorities living in crime-plagued ghettos."

Powell also supports education reform. He is on record as supporting standardized testing for students and testing for teacher qualification. However, Powell appears less interested in reforming public schools than in providing credible private alternatives—a position endorsed by white and black conservatives. He is a strong supporter of charter schools and of the use of private scholarship money to "give poor parents a choice that wealthy parents have." He also supports home schooling and prudent experimentation with voucher programs. As Powell explained at the 2000 Republican Convention: "What are we afraid of? Let's use innovation and competition, good old American innovation, good old American competition to help give our children the best education possible."

At bottom, however, Powell believes that progress turns less on programmatic efforts than on traditional—and transracial—family values, "values which must be lived and not just preached." Inculcating and reinforcing such values is the work of the family, religious community, schools, and the community at large. Consistent with Washington, Powell believes that only such values can provide families with "the strength to withstand the assaults of contemporary life—to resist the images of violence and vulgarity that flood into their lives every day." Such values include, at least for Powell, a sense of honor and corresponding sense of shame. "We say we are appalled by the rise of sexually transmitted disease, by the wave of teenage pregnancies, by violent crime. Yet we drench ourselves in depictions of explicit sex and crime on television, in movies, and in pop music," writes Powell. He believes that we should be willing to shame those who engage in such conduct or consume such depictions as a matter of course. "A sense of shame is not a bad moral compass. I remember how easy it was for my mother to snap me back into line with a simple rebuke: 'I'm ashamed of you. You embarrassed the family.' I wonder where our national sense of shame has gone."

Powell's strong opinions on family values and shame color his views on gays in the military. Indeed, Powell gave voice to the often unarticulated homophobia that exists in conservative black communities in his testimony before Congress on gays in the military. Despite attempts by proponents of lifting the ban to suggest that exclusion of gays was tantamount to exclusion of blacks in the past, Powell held fast to his position that "it would be prejudicial to good order and discipline to try to integrate gays and lesbians in the current military structure." As Powell explained, "Skin color is a benign, nonbehavioral characteristic. Sexual orientation is perhaps the most profound of human behavioral characteristics. Comparison of the two is a convenient but invalid argument."

When it came to matters of global impact, however, Powell proved more diplomat than soldier—a position that would come to define his term as secretary of state under President Bush. According to Powell:

America is trusted and respected as no other nation on Earth. This trust comes not only out of respect for our military, economic, and political power, but from the power of the democratic values we hold dear. The Cold War was ultimately won not by armies marching, but by triumphant democratic ideals that proved superior to every competing ideology.

Consistent with his conservative economic posture, however, Powell viewed the opening of markets in tandem with the promotion of democracy as the dominant role of the United States as leader of the free world. "Democracy, the rights of men and women, and the power of free markets are proving themselves around the world," he wrote. "We see it happening in Latin America, Asia, parts of Africa, and wherever else these principles have the opportunity to take root."

Powell's defense of the war in Iraq before the UN Security Council and the ensuing revelation of substantial falsehoods in his report not only tarnished America's reputation abroad but also impugned Powell's integrity and personal reputation as the Bush administration's leading light and voice of moderation. In many ways, Powell was a victim of his own making—a reliable soldier and loyal public servant until the end. Whatever one might make of those final days of his tenure as secretary of state, it is clear that Powell provides a compelling and compassionate example of black conservatism at work in the twenty-first century.

### The Enigma: Secretary of State Condoleezza Rice

Following Colin Powell's retirement from public service, Condoleezza Rice assumed the mantle of most prominent face of black conservatism in public life. She by then had been President George H. W. Bush's Soviet and East European affairs advisor during the dissolution of the Soviet Union and German reunification and had been national security advisor during President George W. Bush's first term of office. Rice made history as the first African American woman to serve as U.S. secretary of state. In 2004 and 2005, *Forbes* magazine recognized her prominence and influence in American life, ranking her first among the most powerful women in the world. In 2006, she held the number two spot. She is also one of only two African Americans to have been repeatedly ranked among the world's one hundred most influential people by *Time* magazine.

Yet to most Americans, Rice remains largely a mystery. Though accomplished in her own right (she is fluent in five languages and an accomplished classical pianist who once played alongside renowned cellist Yo-Yo Ma), she does not possess the infectious magnetism and charisma of Powell. A relentlessly private woman, Rice has successfully managed to keep her personal life and political views out of the public domain. Her public persona would appear to be defined almost entirely by the politics of the institutions that she serves. But appearances are often misleading and, in Rice's case, mask a rich complex of identity and politics that has come to define black conservative thought in the modern era.

Rice was born on November 14, 1954, in Birmingham, Alabama, and grew up in the neighborhood of Titusville. She is the only child of John Wesley Rice Jr. and his wife, the former Angelena Ray. John Rice was a guidance counselor at Ullman High School and minister of Westminster Presbyterian Church, which had been founded by his father. Angelena was a science, music, and oratory teacher at Ullman. Condoleezza's upbringing was quintessentially southern and middle class—a quiet, stable, Christian family life. The Rices were a loving and fiercely loyal family. As one of the Condoleezza's cousins would say, "Our family is suspicious of outsiders and their motives."

Despite her parents' best efforts to shelter her from the harsh reality of segregated life in Birmingham, Condoleezza experienced much of that reality firsthand. She recalls various times in which she suffered discrimination on account of her race, which included being relegated to a storage room at a department store instead of a regular dressing room, being barred from going to the circus or the local amusement park, being denied hotel rooms, and even being given bad food at restaurants. Also, while Condoleezza was mostly kept by her parents from areas where she might face discrimination, she was very aware of the civil rights struggle and the problems of Jim Crow Birmingham. The city was a hotbed of civil rights activity at this time, and it regularly received international attention because of the strong-arm tactics of its notorious police commissioner, Eugene "Bull" Connor. Marcus Mabry describes in his biography of Rice, *Twice as Good: Condoleezza Rice and Her Path to Power,* Rice's awareness of the racial turmoil in Birmingham. A neighbor, Juliemma Smith, told Mabry that Condoleezza ("Condi") "used to call me and say things like, 'Did you see what Bull Connor did today?' She was just a little girl and she did that all the time. I would have to read the newspaper thoroughly because I wouldn't know what she was going to talk about." Rice herself said of the segregation era: "Those terrible events burned into my consciousness. I missed many days at my segregated school because of the frequent bomb threats."

Threats turned into reality in September 1963, when on a quiet Sunday morning, the Sixteenth Baptist Church was bombed, killing four little girls. Two miles away, in the Westminster Presbyterian Church, Condoleezza recalls feeling the floor flutter beneath her feet. " I remember a sensation of something shaking, but just very slight." She would later learn that among the four girls killed was a friend and kindergarten classmate. Eight-year-old Condoleezza attended the girls' funeral with her parents. She doesn't recall much about the funeral other than "the small coffins" and "the sense that Birmingham wasn't a very safe place." Other bombings would ensue, including one of her neighbor's house, and John Rice, to his credit, arranged for blacks to patrol their own neighborhoods to protect against further incursions. Throughout these events, her parents did their best to instill a spirit of optimism in their daughter. As Rice would state in 1984, "They explained to me carefully what was going on, and they did so without any bitterness."

John Rice, for his part, refused to be confined by prevailing assumptions of race and place. A few days after President Johnson signed the Civil Rights Act of 1964 into law, Rice took his family out to enjoy a fancy dinner at a restaurant in downtown Birmingham that previously was barred to blacks—an event that, Condoleezza recalls, occurred largely without incident. John Rice would later become dean of students at the University of Denver, and after relocating his family in 1967 he promptly enrolled Condoleezza in St. Mary's Academy, a prestigious Catholic all-girls prep school where she was one of only three blacks in her class and was two years younger than most of her peers. He then turned his attention on the University of Denver, where he worked to recruit more black students. His efforts resulted in the creation of a course and lecture series called "The Black Experience in America," the first of its kind at the university. The list of speakers recruited by John Rice included a wide range of black thinkers, artists, and activists, including a young Louis Farrakhan of the Nation of Islam, composer Quincy Jones, SNCC organizer Fannie Lou Hamer, and Stokely Carmichael. Condoleezza attended many of these lectures and befriended many of the speakers, particularly Stokely Carmichael. Rice would recount: "He was a good family friend. And you know, he was actually wonderful to be around."

Given her childhood, one might expect that Rice would have pursued a career in civil rights activism. Instead, Rice would find her calling in politics and international affairs. This was the first clear indication of the self-discipline, independence, and will to power that would come to define much of Rice's conservative philosophy. She enrolled at the University of Denver and attended a course on international politics taught by Josef

Korbel, the father of future Secretary of State Madeleine Albright. This experience sparked her interest in the Soviet Union and international relations, and she fondly recalls Korbel as "one of the most central figures in my life." In 1974, at age 19, Rice earned her B.A. in political science. She would go on to earn a master's degree in political science from the University of Notre Dame and later, at the age of 26, a Ph.D. in political science from the Graduate School of International Studies at Denver.

The second sign was her defection to the Republican Party. Disappointed by President Carter's foreign policy, Condoleezza officially changed her party registration from Democrat to Republican in 1982. Rice would explain her motives in a speech delivered at the 2000 Republican Convention. "The first Republican I knew was my father, John Rice, and he is still the Republican I admire most," she said. "My father joined our party because the Democrats in Jim Crow Alabama of 1952 would not register him to vote. Republicans did." But Rice added that her father's reasons for joining the party were not her own:

> I found a party that sees me as an individual, not as part of a group. I found a party that puts family first.... I found a party that has love of liberty at its core. And I found a party that believes that peace begins with strength.

For Rice, individualism, inner strength, and determination represent her core values. She would elaborate on this theme later in the speech. "In America," she said, "with education and hard work, it really does not matter where you came from—it matters only where you are going." Rice viewed these values as embodying a certain truth that "cannot be sustained if it is not renewed in each generation—as it was with my grandfather." Reflecting shades of Booker T. Washington, Rice added: "But you know, that's not just my grandfather's story—that's an American story. The search for hope. The search for opportunity. The skill of good hard work."

Rice did not offer these ideas as a matter of politics. Six years earlier, in a commencement address at the University of Alabama, she sounded similar themes. "As an educated person," she instructed the graduates, "you have the tools to change your own circumstances for the better whenever you find them stifling, and along the way to change the lives of others too. But you have to believe—like many who had less reason to have faith in tomorrow but nonetheless did—that the locomotive of human progress is individual will. And then you only have to act on it, confident that you will succeed."

Rice's conservative belief in individualism, however, has created the perception that she, like Justice Thomas, prefers to distance herself from her racial identity. Unlike Powell, who had no difficulty asserting his racial identity as an African American, Rice appears often uneasy when it comes to her own racial identity. She shares the view held by many traditional and modern black conservatives that blackness is part of her culture and upbringing but is neither a defining nor confining element of her identity. When asked by Bill O'Reilly of Fox News' *O'Reilly Factor* whether "it hurts your feelings when some anti-Bush people say that you're a shill for [President Bush] and have sold out your race," Rice coolly responded: "Oh, come on. Why would I worry about something like that? Bill, the fact of the matter is, I've been black all my life. Nobody needs to tell me how to be black."

This view extends to her "public" recollection of life in Birmingham. During her Senate confirmation hearings for secretary of state, Rice observed that she grew up in the "old Birmingham of Bull Connor, church bombing, voter intimidation," and marches organized by Dr. King, but she emphasized that her appreciation lay with the outcome of that turmoil: that the "story of Birmingham's teachers and children is a story of triumph of universal values over adversity"—conservative values of "democracy," "liberty," "dignity" and "individual[ism]." An essential part of being black, in Rice's view, was subscribing to the traditional black conservative mantra of self-help, self-reliance, and pragmatic optimism.

Yet even for Rice, race plays an important role in her view of controversial issues such as affirmative action. She is, by most accounts, a beneficiary of affirmative action herself. Prior to completion of her dissertation at the University of Denver, Rice received a one-year fellowship from Stanford University, followed by an extraordinary offer to join the Stanford faculty as an assistant professor once she received her Ph.D. Former Stanford president Donald Kennedy conceded that "very few people go from a doctorate at the University of Denver to a first-class research university." He added that Rice's arrival at Stanford was attributable to her extraordinary talents, but, upon extending the offer, the chairman of the department confirmed that Rice was indeed an affirmative action hire. The chairman also pointedly informed Rice that less than a third of assistant professors get tenure, and "it will not matter to us one bit how you came here or what color you are or what gender you are; you'll have to win it on your own."

Rice later acknowledged that there was something "unusual" about the manner in which she was hired. But if her confidence was shaken by having been denoted an affirmative action beneficiary, she did not reveal it. When asked about these events, Rice stated, "I knew I had given a terrific job talk [a short lecture upon which appointment candidates are often evaluated]." She added, "I've always said that I can't go back and re-create myself as a white male. . . . As long as I'm never asked to do anything that I'm not capable of doing or competent to do, I'm not going to worry about other people's motivations for [offering me opportunities]."

Other opportunities at Stanford would follow. Rice would earn tenure amid suspicions that, contrary to the department head's claim to the contrary, affirmative action had played a determinative role. Whereas successful tenure candidates typically had two books and a few articles placed in prestigious academic journals, Rice received tenure based upon a single book and one journal article. She would later receive an extraordinary offer to become provost of the university, at age thirty-eight, without any prior university administration experience.

Not surprisingly, Rice is a supporter of affirmative action. She believes in the power of the individual to change his or her own circumstances, but she also views affirmative action as a crucial means of creating opportunities for individuals to succeed. But for Rice, affirmative action does have its limits. As Stanford provost, she sharply delineated those limits, mandating that affirmative action criteria should not be used when deciding whether to award tenure—despite the fact that such a practice had previously existed, at least informally, in certain departments, including her former department of political science.

She is also "mildly pro choice," according to Bill Sammon, a reporter with the *Washington Times*. Despite her religious and moral concerns about abortion, Rice indicated that her support for abortion rests on her belief in individualism—that a woman ought to have the right to choose her own destiny. This is, of course, a logical extension of the conservative mantra of individualism, the significance of which is often lost on right-wing opponents of abortion.

Rice's views on individualism and abortion also exemplify how conservatism, for Rice, is filtered through gender. Much as she is aware of her race, she is also aware of gender. Rice is occasionally the target of misogynist and sexist behavior and remarks by associates and by world leaders she encounters in her role as secretary of state. She's been called "honey" in internal meetings and asked to dance the tango with visiting foreign dignitaries. She's been lectured to by midlevel administrators in China and asked to wear modesty garments when visiting Saudi Arabia. Throughout all of this, Rice has remained serious and, more important, ensured that she is taken seriously.

There is one constituency that Rice continues to struggle with: the black community. In the wake of the botched federal relief effort following Hurricane Katrina and rapper Kanye West's impromptu remark that "George Bush doesn't care about black people," Rice was dispatched to perform Bush administration damage control. Yet she seemed unable to connect with the demonstrable suffering of the victims, particularly African Americans. She also refused to engage the perception, let alone the possibility, that the slow federal response had something to do with predominant race of the victims. "That Americans would somehow in a color-affected way decide who to help and who not to help—I just don't believe it," she said. Later, on the *Tavis Smiley Show*, Rice would argue that it was "just wrong" for people to suggest that the administration was not sensitive to the plight of suffering blacks. "This president has cared a great deal about minority populations," she said. Rather than engage the specific topic, Rice went to her talking points: "That's why he cared about home ownership. It's why he cared about black children not being warehoused in our schools, and that's why No Child Left Behind (the educational reform policy that Bush initiated) has been important to him." When host Smiley tried to get back on topic, asking her whether she believed that race and class played a role, Rice again spoke in uneasy generalities. "I do believe that we are dealing with the fact that there are pockets of America which are very poor and that some of those pockets of America have a bad combination of race and poverty," she said.

Rice's role as Bush administration apologist for lackluster Katrina relief served to reinforce the prevailing perception that her own brand of conservatism is synonymous with that of the administration. Unfortunately, her work as secretary of state only reinforces this perception. As secretary of state, Rice has championed the expansion of democratic governments. Rice stated that the 9/11 attacks were rooted in "oppression and despair" and that thus the United States must advance democratic reform and support basic rights throughout the Middle East. Despite her claim to have reformed and restructured the department, the overarching goal, which Rice describes as to "work with our many partners around the world ... [and] build and sustain democratic, well-governed states that will respond to the needs of their people and conduct themselves responsibly in the international system" is virtually identical to the position set forth by the administration during the previous term. As Eugene Robinson, a columnist for the *Washington Post*, asked rhetorically in 2005, "How did [Rice] come to a worldview so radically different from that of most black Americans?"

Blacks were not alone in this perception. California Democratic Senator Barbara Boxer criticized Rice's support for the war in Iraq. "I personally believe," she said, "that your loyalty to the mission you were given, to sell the war, overwhelmed your respect for the truth." In a 2007 Senate debate over the war, Boxer would amplify her concerns that Rice, much as she had done in connection with Katrina, expressed little sympathy for those who suffer as a result of the war. Boxer then offered a particularly personal jab at Rice, who remains single without any children:

> Now, the issue is who pays the price, who pays the price? I'm not going to pay a personal price. My kids are too old, and my grandchild is too young. You're not going to pay a particular price, as I understand it, within immediate family. So who pays the price? The American military and their families, and I just want to bring us back to that fact.

In fact, Rice has paid a price, and dear one. Like most black conservatives, Rice's unapologetic embrace of radical individualism and conservative values has left her estranged from the community that she deeply cherishes and respects on a personal level. She is, much like Justice Thomas and Colin Powell in this regard, a victim of her own conservative success. As support for the Bush administration continues to decline, it is unclear whether Rice has the will to announce and weather public criticism for her own political views. Regardless of whether she chooses to do so, her lifework exemplifies the pitfalls and possibilities of twenty-first-century black conservatism in public life.

# NINE

# The Influence of Infotainment

## How Bill Cosby, Chris Rock, Pundits, and Bloggers
## Lend Popular Credibility to Black Conservative Ideas

The increasing presence of openly conservative black public figures is a testament to the ongoing appeal of black conservative thought. But one might also point to the growing ranks of nontraditional supporters and proponents of black conservative precepts as further proof of its attractiveness. Much like their government counterparts, entertainers, pundits, and public supporters whose political voices supply America's hunger for "infotainment" bestow popular credibility and legitimacy on conservative ideas—ideas that often are initially shocking but ultimately prove delightful to their audiences.

## Entertainers and Pundits

In 2004, comedian-turned-social critic Bill Cosby lashed out in neoconservative fashion against what he described as "the lower economic and low middle economic [blacks who] are not holding up their end of this deal." The "deal," according to Cosby, was struck by those who had worked to achieve integration, symbolized by the Supreme Court's landmark decision in *Brown v. Board of Education,* and the successes of the civil rights movement. In Cosby's view, poor urban blacks had squandered these opportunities, and, given the myriad social ills plaguing black America, "you wouldn't think that any had done a damn thing."

Support for conservatism by entertainers and pop culture icons is nothing new. In 1964, former professional baseball star Jackie Robinson worked as a campaign organizer and official endorser of Republican gubernatorial candidate Nelson Rockefeller. Former National Football League star Roosevelt Grier affiliated with World Impact, a Los Angeles–based evangelical Christian organization, and rise to prominence in the 1970s and 1980s as a Republican celebrity figure. Later, Tony Brown, host of the popular PBS talk show *Tony Brown's Journal*, articulated his conservative take on American race relations and openly affiliated with the Republican Party in 1991. Most recently, in the 2006 election, hip-hip mogul Russell Simmons and boxing legends Don King and Mike Tyson offered their support for Republican senatorial candidate Michael Steele.

Yet Cosby's remarks, delivered on the fiftieth anniversary of the *Brown* decision before three thousand of black America's elite in Constitution Hall in Washington, D.C., struck a deep chord in the black American psyche. Cosby's comments were tinged with anger, frustration, and a degree of sadness—something wholly unexpected from the genial, aging comedian who introduced us to *Fat Albert and the Cosby Kids* and the Huxtables, and encouraged us all to enjoy Jell-O pudding pops. Cosby offered a disturbing portrait of a black community in profound crisis. He began by looking inward at the problems plaguing blacks:

> Ladies and gentlemen, these people [the civil rights establishment]—they opened doors, they gave us the right[s].... But today, ladies and gentlemen, in our cities we have fifty percent dropout [rates among young black men] in our neighborhoods. We have the [highest percentage of any American racial group with] men in prison. No longer is a person embarrassed because [she is] pregnant without a husband. No longer is a boy considered an embarrassment if he tries to run away from being a father.

Cosby's opening assessment in many ways echoes the conservative critiques of the "culture of poverty" advanced by Sowell, Steele, Loury, and McWhorter. But he was far from finished. Cosby soon criticized the immorality, criminality, and the lack of education rampant in the black community. Commenting on the breakdown of the black family structure, Cosby sarcastically noted in a tone strongly reminiscent of the George Schuyler: "Five or six different children—same woman, eight[,] ten different husbands or whatever. Pretty soon you're going to have to have DNA cards so you can tell who you're making love to ... you could have sex with your grandmother ... you keep those numbers coming, I'm just predicting." When it came to crime, Cosby did not offer black criminals any sympathy:

> Look at the incarcerated [population of black people], these people are not political [prisoners]. These people are going around stealing Coca-Cola. People getting shot in the back of the head over a piece of pound cake! Then we all run out and are outraged [declaring], "The cops shouldn't have shot him." What the hell was he doing with the pound cake in his hand?

The same level of contempt was leveled at the families of convicts: "I'm talking about these people who cry when their son is standing there in an orange suit [jailhouse uniform]. Where were you when he was two? Where were you when he was twelve [or] eighteen and how come you didn't know he had a pistol?"

But the topic of education would prove most troubling to Cosby— particularly in light of the fact that the event was to celebrate the *Brown* decision as a crowning achievement. Cosby observed:

> Everybody knows it's important to speak English except these knuckleheads. You can't land a plane with "Why you ain't ..." You can't be a doctor with that kind of crap coming out of your mouth. There is no Bible that has that kind of language. Where did these people get the idea that they're moving ahead on this? ... These people are fighting hard to be ignorant.

The ignorance of blacks, in Cosby's view, was a slap in the face the civil rights generation. "They've got to wonder what the hell happened," exclaimed Cosby. "These people who marched and were hit in face with rocks and punched in the face to get an education and [today] we got these knuckleheads walking around who don't want to learn English.... These people are not funny anymore." In a move that would perhaps shock many black conservatives, Cosby effectively disowned the black underclass:

That's not my brother. And that's not my sister. They're faking and they're dragging me down because the state, the city … have to pick up the tab on them because they don't want accept that they have to study to get an education.

Reflecting on the significance of the moment, Cosby said, "*Brown v. Board of Education*—where are we today … the white man, he's laughing—got to be laughing. Fifty percent dropout [rate]—rest of them in prison."

In a manner strikingly consistent with the rejection of victimhood by Steele and McWhorter, Cosby urged the audience not to buy into the notion that white racism caused these problems. "We can't blame white people," he stated, "*Brown v. Board* is no longer the white person's problems." Moreover, in a subtle dig at the black church, Cosby suggested that it would be a mistake for blacks to look for "deliverance" by anyone or anything other than blacks themselves. "You can't keep asking Jesus [to do] this for you. You can't keep asking that God will find a way. God it tired of you." To illustrate, Cosby offered the following vignette:

People putting their clothes on backwards—isn't that a sign of something going on wrong? Aren't you paying attention? People with their hats on backwards, pants down around the crack.… Are you waiting for Jesus to pull his pants up? Isn't it a sign when she's got her dress all the way up to the crack?

Cosby proved relentless in his critique. In a follow-up appearance at the annual convention of the Rainbow/Push Coalition and Citizenship Education Fund, Cosby defended his earlier remarks against criticisms that he was "airing dirty laundry" that was better left unsaid:

Let me tell you something. Your dirty laundry gets out of school at two-thirty every day. It's cursing and calling each other nigger as they walk up and down the street. They think they're hip. They can't read, they can't write. They're laughing and giggling and they're going nowhere.

The solution, according to Cosby, was for blacks to take responsibility for their problems, particularly their children, and take control of their individual lives. In a *Los Angeles Times* op-ed piece, Cosby wrote: "What we need now is parents sitting down with children, overseeing homework, sending children off to school in the morning, well-fed, clothed, rested, and ready to learn.... Change can only be set in motion when families and leaders get together and acknowledge that a problem exists. Where are the standards that tell a child: 'Stop! There is hope.' This has to happen at home."

Cosby's remarks inspired public debate on whether liberal social policy had failed black America. There were those, such as Michael Eric Dyson, who in *Was Cosby Right, or Has the Black Middle Class Lost Its Mind?* criticized Cosby for attacking a segment of the black community that was, for better or worse, ill equipped to deal with their own problems and lead the self-directed life that Cosby imagined for them. Others, such as Juan Williams, in *Enough: The Phony Leaders, Dead End Movements, and Culture of Failure That Are Undermining Black American—and What We Can Do about It,* applauded Cosby's efforts and advocated more of the cultural remediation work suggested by Cosby.

But if Cosby's remarks provided the crucial spark to ignite debate, the work of other black conservative commentators provided the kindling. Most of the leading neoconservative intellectuals enjoy tremendous access to print and news outlets, reflected in an informal 1992 survey conducted by *FAIR* (Fair and Accuracy in Reporting) magazine that ranked appearances and citations of leading black public intellectuals from January 1, 1984, to July 20, 1992. Atop the leader board were Thomas Sowell and Shelby Steele. Cornel West, the leading African American liberal thinker during this time, rang in with less than one sixth as many citations as Sowell.

The vibrancy of the infotainment medium also lent credibility to Cosby's comments. Armstrong Williams, a radio show host and commentator based in Washington, D.C., has steadfastly maintained that the black community is in crisis and that blacks should not look to help from sympathetic liberals to solve their problems. To do so, in Williams's view, is to embrace a destructive slave mentality. As he wrote in *USA Today* in 1994, "We need to break away from the crippling political orthodoxy that has kept ups begging for crumbs at the back stoop of the Democratic plantation." Larry Elder, a radio show host operating out of South Central Los Angeles, discounts racism as the efficient cause of problems facing blacks, writing in his book *The Ten Things You Can't Say in America* that black America's "biggest problem is not racism but illegitimacy."

Cosby, in other words, simply moved into the celebrity spotlight a conservative sentiment that had been percolating within the black community for years.

But it would be a mistake to assume that conservative sentiments are confined to aging comedians and infotainment pundits. Comedian Chris Rock, whose appeal among younger Americans has eclipsed that of Bill Cosby, has expressed similar ideas as part of his incendiary stand-up routine for nearly a decade. Putting the punch lines and profanity aside, one hears in Chris Rock many of the conservative themes advanced by neoconservative intellectuals and public figures.

Perhaps the earliest and most infamous occasion was in 1997, during Rock's *Bring the Pain* HBO special, in which he sought to distinguish between "niggers" and "black people." Rock began the segment with the dramatic declaration "I hate niggers." "I am tired of niggers. I wish they would let me join the Ku Klux Klan. I'd do a drive-by from LA to Brooklyn." Much like Cosby—but seven years earlier—Rock seemed both bewildered and exasperated by what he perceived to be the destructive cultural practices of urban blacks. "You can't have anything valuable in your house," he said. "Niggers will break in and take it all. You can't do anything without some ignorant-ass niggers fucking it up."

Rock's comments were met with resounding applause and cheers from the audience, which was mostly black. It was as if Rock had voiced an idea that his audience shared but did not dare to articulate. The audience seemed in some sense relieved by what Rock was saying—ideas that had been circulating within the black community for over a century. Rock continued:

> Everything white people don't like about black people, black people don't like about black people. It's like our own personal civil war. On one side, there's black people. On the other, you've got niggers. The niggers have got to go.

The source of Rock's exhaustion with "niggers" proved multifaceted. As an initial matter, Rock argued that "niggers" seemed to embrace a victim identity to such an extent that they believed that they should be rewarded for doing ordinary things. "They'll brag about stuff a normal man just does," explained Rock. "They'll say something like, 'Yeah, well I take care of my kids.' You're supposed to, you dumb motherfucker." Similarly,

Rock was unmoved by black men who sought credit for having never been to jail. "Whaddya want? A cookie?" wondered Rock. "You're not supposed to go to jail, you low-expectation-having motherfucker!"

Rock intended his comments to be funny and entertaining. At the same time, it is clear that Rock's routine was driven by serious and sincere conservative values of hard work, family, self-sufficiency, and law and order—the same values that provide the grist of cultural critiques by leading black neoconservative intellectuals and public figures. Rock would further demarcate the dividing line between niggers and blacks in connection with liberal welfare policy. He pointed out that "[e]very time you see a welfare story on the news, you always see black people." "Black people," he pointed out, "don't give a fuck about welfare. But niggers are shaking in their boots: 'They gonna take our shit.'" Sensing that his views ran counter to prevailing liberal wisdom about race in America, Rock gave voice to critics, noting that some black people may wonder "Man, why you got to say that? It ain't us, it's the media. The media has distorted our image to make us look bad." Rock's response to his imaginary critic proved revealing: "Please, cut the shit, okay? When I go to the money machine at night, I ain't looking over my back for the media. I'm looking for niggers!"

Rock's *Bring the Pain* routine vaulted him into the upper echelon of black comedic performers, and his smart and provocative critiques of black cultural practices drew wide praise from his audiences. It would also signal a turning point in his particular brand of comedy, as conservative critique of black culture would become a staple of his routine. In 1999, with *Bigger and Blacker,* Rock directed his acerbic wit at serious matters such as the decline in family values, poor educational performance, and the crisis of black leadership. One of the more conspicuous subjects he tackled was the crisis of parenting within the black community. He recounted an experience in a dance club—2 o'clock in the morning on a weekday—in which he met a woman who he later learned was the mother of two children. Rock was apoplectic as he wondered aloud why this parent was not at home with her children: "Is it your birthday? Did you get raise? Go home! ... You can get your kid on, or you can get your groove on, but you can't do both."

Then, Rock delivered a line that earned applause as well as a few boos: "Take care of them kids before they rob me in ten years." For Rock, there was an obvious connection between poor parenting and a number of other ills—especially poor academic performance and criminality among black youth. And like many black conservatives, he situated the problems within the larger context of declining family values, specifically the decline of two-parent households. "You can do it without a man," conceded Rock, "but that don't mean it is to be done. You can drive a car with your feet if you want to, but that doesn't make it a good fucking idea." Rock also lamented the declining role of fathers in the black community, reflected in the "mamma centric" orientation of black culture and music. "Nobody appreciates daddy," remarked Rock. "Nobody thanks daddy for knocking out the rent." For Rock, it was imperative to appreciate and celebrate fathers—particularly those that "handle their business." Fathers, in his view, provide not only financial stability but a disciplining and role-modeling presence. There is no greater weapon available to a mother attempting to correct a child's behavior, he said, than the words "I'm going to tell your daddy."

Rock sometimes has reminded his audiences that they ought not "make things bigger" than they really are when it comes to perceived racial insults. Rock conceded that racism still exists ("There ain't a white man in the room who'd want to trade places with me . . . and I'm rich!"), but he also claims that the most racist people in America are "old black men." Rock went on to explain that this was because, unlike most modern blacks, old black had men lived through "real racism" and not this "I can't hail a taxi bullshit." Much like black neoconservative intellectuals who criticize the culture of victimhood in which blacks often prefer to see themselves as racial victims despite the declining societal racial hostility, Rock subtly encouraged his audience to gain a sense of perspective on modern racism and its relatively modest effect upon the life chances of black Americans.

Rock would continue to advance his conservative politics of respectability in two segments of his 2004 HBO special, *Never Scared*. In the first, Rock declared his love for rap music, but noted that he is "tired of defending it." In the "old days," according to Rock, one could defend rap "intellectually" as a true art form. By contrast, modern rap, with its misogynistic and often vacuous content, proves largely indefensible. Shaking his head ruefully, Rock declared that "it's hard to defend 'I Got Ho's in Different Area Codes.' It's hard to defend "Move Bitch, Get Out of the Way.'" Rock went on to note his dismay at seeing women in nightclubs dancing to morally decadent songs, seemingly oblivious to the disrespectful content of the lyrics. His punch line was less a joke than an observation about the perceived crisis in black family values: "I feel sorry for the guys who have to pick a wife out of this bunch."

Rock also lashed out at the rampant consumerism within black communities and how blacks often confused being "rich" with being "wealthy." According to Rock's distinctions, "Shaq [NBA basketball player and multi-millionaire Shaquille O'Neal] is rich. The guy who signs his check is wealthy." Wealth, he pointed out, "will set us free. It is empowering. It allows you to uplift communities from poverty." "Rich," in contrast, "allows you to buy jewelry." Rock did not blame white society for the lack of wealth in the black community; rather, he identified the cultural habits of blacks themselves as the source of the problem. "Maybe if we didn't spend all our money on rims [for our cars], we might have something to invest." He chastised blacks for wasting money in the spirit of conspicuous consumption, observing that he often sees blacks with "TVs in the headrests of their cars—TVs are on, and nobody is sitting in the back seat."

Despite the pronounced socially and fiscally conservative themes in his stand-up routine, it is worth emphasizing that Chris Rock is by no means a knee-jerk conservative. In *Never Scared,* Rock angrily criticized President Bush for having "lied" about the war in Iraq and for promoting a patriotic fervor that carried with it the seeds of racism against Arabs and Latino immigrants. On the "most divisive issue in America"—affirmative action—Rock declared his view that blacks should not receive a job if they scored lower than whites, but if it's a tie, "fuck [whites because they] "had a 400-year head start." He was equally clear in his support of gay rights and a woman's right to choose whether to have an abortion. Indeed, if anything, Rock embraces a more nuanced form of issue politics, summarily rejecting what he called the "gang mentality" of political parties. People who subscribe to entire political platforms, such as Republicans and Democrats, or embrace uncritically prevailing conservative and liberal ideologies are "all idiots," he says. Instead, he counseled his audience: "Listen, then form your opinion.... No normal, decent person is only one thing." Being a decent person means, for Chris Rock, embracing conservative views on parenting, education, and law enforcement that put him in the unlikely company of leading black neoconservative intellectuals such as Sowell, Steele, and McWhorter, and black conservative public figures like Clarence Thomas and Colin Powell. More important, given the resounding applause he often receives when expressing these views, one can surmise that conservatism within the black community— at least on some issues—is far more popular and prevalent than one might suspect.

## Technology and the Expanding Reach of Black Conservatism

In addition to comedy and punditry, technological advances have enabled black conservative ideas to penetrate mainstream society on an unprecedented scale. Like their liberal counterparts, black conservatives have come to appreciate the manner in which the Internet enables rapid contribution to the world of ideas. For many black conservatives, the Internet introduces the possibility of serious intellectual engagement and robust exchange of ideas and perspectives. One discovers in many instances the grist of public conversation—thoughts and ideas, in various stages of development, offered for the engagement, consumption, refutation, and critique by interested members of the public.

Perhaps most fruitful in this regard is the use of Web logs—real-time online conversations. Web logs enable people to project their ideas into the public domain for the express purpose of shaping prevailing public discourse. The ease and pace of online publication allows participants to respond to matters of public importance as the events unfold and to enter public discourse on the ground level. In addition, the easy accessibility of online scholarship allows for the prompt retrieval, commentary, and formal and informal syndication by a multitude of individual readers, public and private institutions, and traditional and nontraditional media outlets. In this way, bloggers not only make a contribution to the world of ideas but provide an opportunity for the world to respond in a meaningful way.

One of the great benefits of Web logs is that one can obtain near-instantaneous feedback on an idea. In most instances, an engaging post will elicit a wide range of comments and criticisms, with the most serious responses leading to sustained conversation that can refine the original idea. Online discussion of ideas in this way provides an important check against the detachment and distant objectivity that one associates with scholarly research.

Many black neoconservatives, such as Thomas Sowell and Walter

Williams, provide a range of commentary accessible over the Internet. And there has been a mild explosion in the blogosphere, as an increasing number of Web sites dedicated to black conservative have become increasingly active. *BookerRising!* (www.bookerrising.blogspot.com) is one of these sites. Operated by Shamara Riley, *BookerRising!* positions itself as "a news site and media watchdog for black moderates and conservatives, regardless of party affiliation . . . particularly geared to those ages 45 and under." According to the Web site, BookerRising! is "inspired by Booker T. Washington's work" and is designed to "promote self-help, education, enterprise, democracy, and society as the seeds for Black America's future." "We won the civil rights movement," according to the Web site's mission statement. "It's now time for Stage II: further propelling black American success in this increasingly globalized era, via our 'seeds.'" *BookerRising!* subscribes to the black neoconservative aspiration of counteracting "negativity, victimology, and defeatism" within the black community—attitudes that, it says, are "too often thrust upon black Americans by schools, the media, and so-called leaders." But the site does not subscribe to the entire black neoconservative agenda. Indeed it declares its political orientation as "fiscally conservative" and "socially moderate."

Other sites, such as *LaShawn Barber's Corner* (www.lashawnbarber .com) carry on the blogger tradition contributing to the world of ideas. Barber, a self-proclaimed conservative and columnist for the *Washington Examiner*, has contributed essays to the *Washington Post, Washington Times, Christian Research Journal, Christianity Today, Today's Christian Woman, Beliefnet.com, National Review Online*, and *Townhall.com*. Her Web log, launched in 2003, addresses the full range of social issues, from crime to race preference to unemployment to health care to immigration. Of course, there is also a category that addresses "liberals."

The *Conservative Brotherhood* (www.conservativebrotherhood.org), whose slogan is "Keeping It Right," represents an online community of "African American writers whose politics are on the right hand side of the political spectrum." Their goal is to expand the dialogue on black politics "beyond traditional boundaries" in order to "contribute to a greater understanding of African Americans and America." The founder of the Conservative Brotherhood, Michael David Cobb Bowen, runs his own blog titled *Cobb* (http://cobb.typepad.com/cobb/2007/01/a_black_conserv.html). According to Bowen, he "writes from the perspective of a moderate conservative Republican representing the 'Old School' of African American culture and values." Raised in a middle-class black neighborhood in Los Angeles, the oldest of five children, by Catholic and Episcopalian parents who worked civil service jobs and engaged in grass-roots political activism, Cobb is part of a resurgence of black conservatism among the next generation of politically astute African Americans.

The rising Internet presence of black conservatives has also spawned grass-roots efforts to reclaim liberal blacks, among them *Republicans For Black Empowerment* (www.theblackgop.com), *The New Underground Railroad* (http://thenewundergroundrailroad.blogspot.com), and the Web log at Project 21 (www.project21.org). Every day, new voices enter the black conservative struggle to reclaim their liberal brothers and sisters. As blacks become increasingly connected over the Internet, public conversation on conservatism among blacks is likely to grow, which can only create new opportunities for conservatives to reach future generations of African Americans eager to find solutions to social problems and chart pathways for personal and collective empowerment.

# TEN

# The Significance of Black Conservative Thought in Modern American Life

I began this book with a question: What is a black conservative, and why would anyone ever choose to be one? The answer, it turns out, has less to do with prevailing Republican and Democratic Party platforms than with the lived experience of black people and their desire to lead full, meaningful, productive, and, perhaps most important, self-directed lives. Within any community, including the black community, there is disagreement over the means to achieve empowerment. Empowerment strategies take shape against the backdrop of social, political, and economic realities of a given moment. Political party platforms and positions are sourced from the instincts, attitudes, beliefs, and sentiments of the people—not the other way around.

For many blacks throughout American history, political views have been profoundly shaped by conservative precepts. These precepts evolved over time as blacks adapted, experimented, and combined them with other ideas to keep pace with the shifting political and cultural climate. Rooted in the black experience, but not constrained to any particular historic period, black conservative thought proves to be a remarkably robust and resilient organic intellectual tradition that demands our attention and respect.

### The Attraction of Modern Black Conservatism

The longevity of black conservative thought and the increasing prominence of modern black conservatives in the American public sphere are indicative of the attractiveness of modern black conservatism. But what accounts for its seductiveness? Why are blacks increasingly drawn to this movement?

There is, of course, no definitive answer to this question. As the foregoing chapters demonstrate, the black conservative tradition embodies a host of ideas, variations, and contradictions that, over time, have attracted and alienated blacks for a wide range of reasons. Nevertheless one can point to a handful of features of modern black conservatism that may shed some light on its appeal to contemporary blacks.

First and foremost, black conservatism vindicates the deeply held desire of blacks to view themselves as architects of their own destiny. For most of their history in America, blacks have been the victims of devastating modes of institutional and private racial oppression—from slavery to lynching to segregation to modern forms of subtle, unconscious racial bias. At the same time, liberal strategies for racial empowerment have often retained this external focus, requiring blacks to seek relief from victimizing whites by turning to sympathetic whites. Whether viewed as the object of oppression or a group worthy of liberal sympathy, blacks seem effectively denied the "right" to lead autonomous, self-directed lives.

Many blacks today are weary of being viewed as victims and the perennial object of liberal charity. White liberals and the civil rights establishment remain deeply invested in the idea that blacks continue to suffer under the weight of racial oppression. Many blacks are increasingly turned off by this image of black society, and interpret efforts to sustain this image as dishonest and ultimately destructive. Although racism undoubtedly persists in American society, many blacks today appreciate the wealth of political, social, and economic opportunities that exist for blacks in this country. The myriad success stories of upwardly mobile blacks attest to the fact that American capitalism, whatever its faults and limitations, can provide a means of social economic empowerment, and that the protection of basic rights of equality can ensure that pathways to success remain open. As a consequence, many blacks are eager to trade in their badges of racial victimhood and cease being special favorites of the law and white liberals via affirmative action and race-based set-asides.

Modern conservatism proves appealing because it embodies the over-arching American aesthetic of freedom through strength. Many blacks, individually and collectively, look forward to the day when they might assume the rank of ordinary American citizens who pursue their own, autonomous lives with pride, dignity, and respect.

The pursuit of pride, dignity, and respect points to a second and related attractive feature of black conservatism. Blacks who are weary of being cast in the role of racial victim also want to demonstrate their capacity to lead self-directed lives by engaging in self-help and promoting the virtue of self-reliance. Many blacks are coming to the view that as race becomes less determinative of their life prospects, success becomes, more or less, a function of one's own individual will and initiative. Not surprisingly, liberal strategies of empowerment, particularly welfare policies and those directed at group-based relief, are increasingly viewed with skepticism because they do not appear to provide an incentive for individuals to help themselves. This is not to suggest that blacks no longer view themselves as group: many still do. Rather, blacks are beginning to view racial empowerment through the prism of the individual. Put differently, group empowerment is thought to come about through the multiplication of individual success stories.

The individual success of many blacks provides a third reason that many blacks may find black conservative thought appealing. The economic success experienced by many blacks has buoyed their belief in American capitalism, but it has also fueled a desire to solidify and conserve the wealth they have attained. Not surprisingly, many socially conservative blacks are increasingly drawn to conservative fiscal policy in the form of a reduced welfare state, lower tax burdens, and support for initiatives directed at stimulating and solidifying economic gains in individuals and wealth-generating institutions.

The emphasis on morality and family values provides a fourth point of attraction. For many blacks, the moral depravity that has infected segments of the black community has reached an unacceptable level. Many blacks are increasingly appalled by the drug use, criminality, sexual promiscuity, child illegitimacy, and other ills associated with urban black communities. Perhaps more disturbing to many blacks, however, is that such images of black moral depravity are packaged and distributed within mainstream culture as representative of black society as a whole. Upwardly mobile blacks are finding that these images are not only internalized by their own children and communities, but by white youths as well —neither of which bodes well for the future leadership of America.

Given black conservatism's roots in the Christian evangelical tradition, it is not surprising that many blacks, especially those that retain a strong connection to the black church community, would find modern conservatism appealing. Throughout the 1990s, a number of proponents of traditional family values rose to prominence as leading voices of black conservatism, including Alan Keyes; Mildred Jefferson, founder and former chairman of the National Right to Life Committee and former chair of the National Right to Life Crusade; Greg Keath, then leader of two groups, Rescue Black America and the Alliance for Family; the Reverend Cleveland Sparrow, founding member of the National Coalition for Black Traditional Values; and Ezola Foster, founder of the Los Angeles-based Black Americans for Family Values. More recently, Bishop T. D. Jakes, whose Potter's House church in Dallas, Texas, boasts thirty thousand members and attracts more than a hundred thousand visitors during his annual "Megafest Revival," has joined the ranks of black conservatives who promote traditional family values.

Blacks concerned about failing schools and the concomitant poor performance of children who attend them may also find themselves drawn to modern black conservatism. Public schools, particularly in poor and urban areas, have been in crisis for more than two decades. Many blacks share the conservative belief that education—including education that imparts the life skills of discipline, sacrifice, and hard work—is an essential building block of individual and collective success in American life. There is a growing sense among many blacks that traditional liberal approaches to improve education by increasing funding will not solve the problem. By contrast, conservatives have largely spearheaded innovation in school reform through greater accountability regarding student and teacher performance, support for charter schools, voucher programs, and other privately funded alternatives.

Finally, blacks may be drawn to modern conservatism because of its forward-looking spirit of pragmatic optimism. For many blacks, the novelty of the idealistic society envisioned by civil rights advocates has worn thin and has given way to a reality in which formal equality is secure but racial disparities in health, wealth, and society persist. Whereas liberals tend to look to past practices of racial discrimination to explain present-day difficulties, many blacks perceive conservatives as focusing their energies on devising pragmatic, workable solutions. Rather than lament the permanence of racism, modern conservatives focus on opportunities for growth and the possibilities that are presently available to blacks to achieve their own success. The spirit of pragmatic optimism is succinctly captured in the first and last of Colin Powell's "13 Rules of Life": "1. It ain't as bad as you think. It will better in the morning" and "13. Perpetual optimism is a force multiplier."

### Reasons to Be Skeptical of
### Modern Black Conservatism
### —An External Liberal Critique

But if modern black conservatism proves appealing, there are also reasons to be skeptical. One reason is that modern black conservatism tends to understate the power—both positive and negative, but especially the latter—that race continues to exert on people's lives. Many black conservatives discount the importance of affirmative action policy in promoting the success of blacks, despite their own positive experiences as affirmative action beneficiaries. They argue that the harms of such policy outweigh the benefits, but as William Bowen and Derrick Bok illustrate in their study of affirmative action beneficiaries in *The Shape of the River: Long-Term Consequences of Considering Race in College and University Admissions,* the majority of blacks they interviewed concluded otherwise.

Modern black conservatives' assumption that race plays a diminished role in negating or minimizing one's life chances is equally dubious. Take prison populations, for example. Black men are disproportionately represented among the two million inmates in American penal institutions. Modern conservatives, black and white, would have you believe that this is a result of disproportionate criminality among black men. But this assumes that law enforcement officials investigate and prosecute or (equally important) decline to prosecute cases in a racially consistent and "color-blind" manner. The reality, of course, is that at every stage of the criminal justice system, those who are in charge exercise discretion. They choose which areas to patrol, which laws to enforce, which offenders to warn, which offenders to arrest, which cases to file, which cases to dismiss, which evidence to consider, which argument to believe, which argument to discount, and which sentence to impose. Given the pervasiveness of attitudes, assumptions, and beliefs about the cultural inferiority, moral depravity, and criminal predisposition of blacks—particular poor black men, who make up the majority of those blacks charged with crimes—it is hard to conclude that the justice meted out by our criminal courts is truly color-blind.

Moreover, many conservatives incorrectly assume that all blacks experience acts of racial insensitivity and callousness in the same way. The reality, of course, is that class difference profoundly affects not only the frequency of racist acts that one experiences but also the effect of those acts. Wealth has a way of allowing black elites to buy their way out of racially problematic situations through neighborhood choice, school choice, social networks, and the like. The proliferation of upscale, racially segregated, suburban enclaves of blacks, documented in Sheryl Cashin's *The Failure of Integration: How Race and Class Are Undermining the American Dream*, exemplifies this phenomenon. Wealth not only creates mobility options that most blacks do not possess; it also provides a buffer against racial slights. For blacks living in economic crisis, racial slights reinforce a sense of relative powerlessness. This is not to suggest that wealthy blacks do not feel the sting of racism. Indeed, a racial slight may prove particularly troubling when experienced against the backdrop of relative privilege. Nevertheless, there is good reason to believe that it is far easier to wash down a racial insult with a glass of champagne.

There is also good reason to be skeptical of the antigovernment mantra of black conservatives. Many of the tangible gains in the lives of black people were brought about, directly and indirectly, through government intervention. Indeed, it is impossible to imagine blacks thriving today without the passage of the Thirteenth, Fourteenth, and Fifteenth Amendments to the Constitution, the full range of antidiscrimination laws, as well as laws that protect against the exploitation of labor. Most conservatives argue that the market, free of government intrusion, will discipline people's racial choices—that there is a cost associated with racial discrimination, and that persons who wish to pursue either their business or personal affairs in the most efficient manner will limit their own discrimination to the optimum level. But American history has proved that whites on a mass scale were more than willing to bear this cost, even to their own detriment. That's why it became necessary to vigorously enforce rights designed to create the possibility for equal opportunities for blacks and, for good measure, to institute affirmative action policy to ensure that blacks would actually be in a position to pursue such opportunities.

Another reason to be skeptical of modern conservatives relates to family values. Conservatives often present themselves as protectors of family values, but liberals have often championed policies and programs designed to elevate the importance of family in American life. Indeed, the radical expansion of the welfare state orchestrated by liberals was designed to provide social relief for families and their children when market-based approaches failed them. There is, of course, important and substantial disagreement between liberals and conservatives over which family values should be promoted. But it worth emphasizing that conservatives do not enjoy a monopoly on this issue. Conservatives may seek to promote "traditional" family values, but the tradition of promoting policy that values American families is a liberal one.

Emphasis on individualism by black conservatives suggests another reason to be skeptical. For many modern black conservatives, the pursuit of individualism is closely linked with the pursuit of color blindness in American society. All too often, this leads to the minimization or rejection of a professed racial identity in favor of a more generic American one. Many blacks, by contrast, view racial identification as a crucial element of their personal identity—an aspect that should be accented and celebrated, not masked. Individualism, as endorsed by some modern black conservatives, ironically serves to deprive certain blacks of their individual capacity to define themselves as they choose.

Moreover, racial identification and color consciousness do not necessarily produce tragic outcomes at every turn, as many modern black conservatives suggest. It is true, of course, that color consciousness serves to reinforce the salience of the racial line that has divided America for much of its history. But as black conservatives are fully aware, racial identity can and often does provide economic solidarity and supportive communities. Many modern black conservatives are willing to forsake "community" for freedom premised upon rugged individualism, whereas liberals imagine freedom coming about through pluralism and democratic engagement.

### Reasons to Be Skeptical of Modern Black Conservatism —An Internal Conservative Critique

In addition to liberal criticism of modern black conservatives, there is reason to believe that traditional black conservatives may not necessarily subscribe to the tenets of modern black conservatism. Modern black conservatism departs from the tradition in a number of ways that might give more traditional black conservatives pause. First, unlike traditional black conservatism, the modern variant is neither sourced from nor supported by large numbers of African Americans. Modern black conservatives do not have an organic black constituency but instead draw their support primarily from conservative whites and their network of institutions. As a consequence, many traditional black conservatives may share the liberal intuition that modern black conservatives lack the credibility to speak on behalf of the true needs of the black community.

Second, traditional black conservatives, like their liberal counterparts, may reject the rugged individualism of black neoconservatives. An essential feature of the black conservative tradition, from Booker T. Washington to Stokely Carmichael, was that blacks should take pride in their racial heritage and look to their own traditions and customs as a source of empowerment. They engaged in self-critique, highlighting failures within the black community, but they never suggested that blacks ought to relinquish their own heritage and customs and embrace "raceless" values of success.

Finally, although many traditional black conservatives rejected the idea that government intervention was the solution to their problems, they did so based upon the valid assumption that a government that actively promoted their racial subjugation was unlikely to prove helpful in their empowerment efforts. During and immediately after the civil rights revolution, black conservatives moderated their opposition, in large part because government had proved it could be reliably called upon to intervene in the name of racial justice. The efficiency arguments by black neoconservatives against government intervention fundamentally misinterpret the black conservative stance against government intrusion. Thus traditional black conservatives may be in stronger agreement with liberals when it comes to federal and state intervention to promote the social and economic empowerment of blacks.

## Reasons to Give Black Conservatives Our Attention

Whatever doubts or suspicions one may have about modern black conservatism, there nevertheless is good reason to give modern black conservatives and the black conservative tradition our attention. In years past, liberals commanded the black political and culture stage, and black conservatives resided at the periphery of American society. They were, by all accounts, largely inconsequential, as the conservative ideas they espoused had little demonstrable effect upon the trajectory of American politics and race relations.

However, the twenty-first century marks the dawn of a new political reality in this country. Black conservatism is plainly on the rise as conservatives are quickly becoming the most visible and prominent voices within African American politics, culture, and society. As a consequence, black conservative thought will increasingly influence policy that will define the social, political, and economic future of African Americans. For individuals who take social justice matters seriously—especially those that affect the African American community—the ability to secure progressive change in American race relations will increasingly hinge upon the depth of one's understanding and engagement with the source of black conservative ideals in general and the black conservative perspective on racial empowerment in particular.

For this reason, liberals can no longer afford to dismiss modern black conservatism as marginal or inconsequential to public conversation on racial issues. They must learn to engage in sincere, constructive, and intelligent discussion across ideological lines. We live in a society in which people of color, and African Americans in particular, not only continue to struggle to realize their full political, social, and economic potential, but risk losing the societal gains achieved by previous generations. Liberals may disagree with the black neoconservative agenda for racial empowerment, but both liberals and conservatives agree that something must be done to improve the lives of everyday black people. For those who take seriously the attainment of political, social, and economic empowerment for all African Americans, it is imperative to move beyond ideological wrangling and acknowledge that both liberals and conservatives possess a rich arsenal of ideas for racial empowerment.

At the same time, both liberals and conservatives must understand that neither has the entire solution to the problems facing blacks at their fingertips. Both the liberal and the conservative traditions of racial empowerment have entailed real sacrifices and trade-offs. The traditional black conservative emphasis on the achievement of cultural and economic stability spurred the development of black business and institutions and certainly produced economic growth within black communities. But early black conservatives failed to see that social and political rights were necessary to stabilize and secure the enjoyment of those gains and that no amount of material success could ameliorate the growing social and political isolation experienced by blacks, let alone protect them against lynchings, beatings, threats, and everyday acts of racial callousness. Similarly, liberal legal strategies of racial empowerment that focused on securing civil rights proved successful, but they were not able to create a strong cultural and economic foundation upon which to build wealth and stability over the generations. It is vital that both conservatives and liberals appreciate the complex manner in which both liberal and conservative ideas can be understood to advance as well as undermine prospects for racial empowerment.

In these pages, I have endeavored to provide a deepened and long overdue account of black conservative thought—a legacy of black empowerment that has existed since the founding of our Republic. I have written this book not out of political affection for conservatives, but to remedy a blind spot in American political history—one that would deny the intellectual and human agency of black conservatives and denigrate their efforts, historic and contemporary, to help themselves and others lead fulfilling and self-directed lives. The extended legacy of black conservatism highlights the rich diversity that has always existed within African American political thought. My hope is that this discussion will explode any perception of blacks as a cultural and political monolith and help liberals and conservatives to appreciate the intellectual and cultural connections that modern black conservatives share with the larger political tradition of black conservatism.

Each generation can and should be called upon to push the limits of political imagination, to explore new and interesting political possibilities. The changing political and cultural landscape demands nothing less from any of us. In an era in which black Americans are finding a greater degree of comfort in conservatism, liberals must acknowledge and adapt to this new political reality or risk mass defection by members of its most loyal constituency. For better or worse, pushing the limits of political imagination for an increasing number of African Americans has come to mean revisiting the past—going back to the black conservative tradition—to reclaim the future. If we are to fully understand why black conservatism remains a coherent and compelling alternative for many African Americans today—even if our ultimate goal is to dissuade them from joining this resurgent movement and to champion liberal empowerment strategies—we owe it to ourselves and the future of America to travel with them.

# Acknowledgments

No author writes a book without the support of others. First, I wish to thank my friend and literary agent Jacqueline Hackett for pushing me to take my casual thoughts on black conservatives more seriously. I also wish to thank the fine staff of editors and assistants at Beacon Press, especially Gayatri Patnaik and Tracy Ahlquist, and authors Cornel West, Debra Dickerson, Peniel Joseph, and Ira Katznelson for their gracious contributions to this project.

Beyond these individuals, there were a wide range of folks who contributed substantively to this project, provided crucial motivation, or otherwise enabled its completion. They include Paul Butler, Spencer Overton, Fred Lawrence, Roger Trangsrud, Cynthia Lee, Bob Cottrol, Dan Solove, Roger Fairfax, Shavar Jeffries, Kent Syverud, Randall Kennedy, Gerald Early, John Baugh, Tomiko Brown-Nagin, F. Scott Kieff, Troy Paredes, David Konig, John Haley, Dan Ellis, Kimberly Jade Norwood, Peter Joy, Bob Pollack, Phil Berwick, Prashant Kolluri, and those members of the law faculty of Washington University in St. Louis who participated in the faculty workshop where I first presented my ideas on black conservatism for public consumption.

I also wish to thank a special group of friends and neighbors who, in some way or another, ensured that I remained focused on this project, despite a multitude of distractions. They include Diana Embrey, Gretchen and Alex Placzek, Tracey Johnson, Elif and Murat Bilgin, Melvin Davis, Reuben Charles, and Hugh and Linda Weisenstein.

In addition, I wish to thank my parents, Alfred and Mary Bracey, for their ongoing support and patience. And I am grateful to longtime (notice

## Acknowledgments

that I didn't say "old") friends of family, such as Jacob and Gwen Adams and Eldridge and Eloise Jackson, who prompted me to discuss and often rethink portions of the book based upon their experiences as blacks who actually lived through periods of American history discussed in the book.

Finally, and most important, I want to thank my wife, Susan, who was the prime motivator for my writing this book, and my son, Lawson, whose arrival provided a proper incentive to bring this project to a close.

# Notes

## Introduction

1. Georgia E. Conic, *An Exploration of Conservative Ideology in African American Political Thought, Attitudes, and Behavior*, Ph.D. diss., Wayne State University, 2005 (Ann Arbor, MI: UMI Dissertation Services, 2006), p. 79.
2. The Pew Research Center for the People and the Press, *The 2004 Political Landscape: Evenly Divided and Increasingly Polarized*, available at http://people-press.org/reports/display.php3?PageID=749.
3. *The American National Election Studies Guide to Public Opinion and Electoral Behavior, 2002 & 2004*, available at www.umich.edu/~nes/nesguide/2ndtable/t3_1_1.htm.
4. Wes Allison, "Black Conservatives Gather Momentum," *St. Petersburg (Fla.) Times*, Feb. 28, 2005.
5. A 2004 CNN Gallup Poll indicated that 11 percent of African Americans voted for President Bush—up from 9 percent in 2000. The poll is available at www.cnn.com/ELECTION/2004/pages/results/states/US/P/00/epolls.o.html.

## Chapter One: The Origins of Black Conservative Thought

1. Although the exact date of Hammon's death has never been confirmed, the preface to a Quaker reprint of one of Hammon's poems in 1806 implied that he was deceased at the time of publication.
2. See the biographical article on Hammon by Lisa Clayton Robinson in *Africana,* ed. Kwame Anthony Appiah and Henry Louis Gates Jr. (New York: Basic Civitas Books, 1999); and Jeffrey Stewart, *1001 Things Every-*

*one Should Know about African American History* (New York: Doubleday, 1998).

3. Indeed, Hammon does not even appear in the most recent version of *The Norton Anthology of African American Literature* (ed. Henry Louis Gates and Nellie Y. McKay [New York: W. W. Norton, 1997]), which compiles the work of more than one hundred authors.

4. Jupiter Hammon, "An Address to the Negroes in the State of New York," in *Jupiter Hammon and the Biblical Beginnings of African American Literature,* ed. Sandra A. O'Neale (Metuchen, NJ: American Theological Library Association and Scarecrow Press, 1993), p. 240.

5. Forten's relationship with Garrison ran much deeper than the occasional letter. Indeed, Forten almost completely funded Garrison's abolitionist newspaper, the *Liberator,* during its first year. Garrison subsequently obtained funding from other white abolitionists, but it is worth noting that Forten backed Garrison's efforts when abolitionism was not particularly popular among whites.

### Chapter Two: The Dawn of the Twentieth Century

1. Genna Rae McNeil, *Groundwork: Charles Hamilton Houston and the Struggle for Civil Rights* (Philadelphia: University of Pennsylvania Press, 1983), p. 134.

### Chapter Three: Shades of Black Conservatism

1. Quoted in James O. Young, *Black Writers of the Thirties* (Baton Rouge: Louisiana State University Press, 1973), pp. 64, 151.

2. Ibid., p. 38. From Benjamin Brawley, *Negro Builders and Heroes* (Chapel Hill: University of North Carolina Press, 1937).

3. Quoted in Juan Williams, *Enough: The Phony Leaders, Dead-End Movements, and Culture of Failure That Are Undermining Black America—And What We Can Do about It* (New York: Crown, 2006), p. 142.

4. Quoted in Henry Louis Suggs, "The Washingtonian Legacy: A History of Black Political Conservatism in America, 1915–1944," in Peter Eisenstadt's *Black Conservatism—Essays in Intellectual and Political History.* (New York: Garland, 1999), p. 95.

5. Bethune quoted in B. Joyce Ross, "Mary McLeod Bethune and the National Youth Administration," in *Black Leaders of the Twentieth Century,* ed. John Hope Franklin and August Meier (Urbana: University of Illinois Press, 1982), p. 197.

6. Quoted material is from Marcus Garvey, "The Negro's Greatest Enemy,"

*Current History* (September 1923), reprinted in *Marcus Garvey and the Vision of Africa,* ed. John Henrik Clarke (New York: Vintage, 1974).

7. E. Franklin Frazier, "Garvey: A Mass Leader," in *Marcus Garvey and the Vision of Africa*, ed. John Henrik Clarke (New York: Vintage), pp. 236–241.

8. For a summary of these exchanges, see Lawrence W. Levine, "Marcus Garvey and the Politics of Revitalization," in *Black Leaders of the Twentieth Century,* ed. John Hope Franklin and August Meier (Urbana: University of Illinois Press, 1982), pp. 133–134.

## Chapter Four: The Agonistic Voice of Midcentury Black Conservatism

1. Schuyler was apparently referring to Tippu Tip, an East African slave trader whose real name was Hamed Bin Muhammad. Born in Zanzibar, Tip reportedly commanded a merchant army that routinely raided surrounding villages to capture women as concubines and people of both sexes as plantation workers and porters.

2. See "The Black Muslims in America—An Interview with George S. Schuyler, Malcolm X, C. Eric Lincoln, and James Baldwin (1961)" in *Rac[e]ing to the Right—Selected Essays of George S. Schuyler,* Jeffrey B. Leak, ed. (Knoxville: University of Tennessee Press, 2001).

## Chapter Six: The Reformation of Black Conservatism

1. The various quotations from the Fairmont Conference that appear in this chapter are taken from *The Fairmont Papers—Black Alternatives Conference, San Francisco, December 1980,* ed. Bernard Anderson et al. (San Francisco, CA: Institute for Contemporary Studies, 1981). This quotation, from Tony Brown, "Politics, Power, and Horse Trading: The Broad Opportunities," appears on p. 129 of that volume.

2. Glenn Loury, *One by One, from the Inside Out: Essays and Reviews on Race and Responsibility in America* (New York: Free Press, 1995), p. 73.

# Bibliography

The bulk of the material contained in this book is drawn from the writings of black conservatives themselves. Although these major works are all cited in the text, I also list them below. In addition, I have made liberal use of other scholars' research on historical and contemporary figures and discussions of the periods in which they lived. Works of this nature are also listed in this section. A handful of articles, speeches, videos, and websites proved particularly helpful in fleshing out the ideas in this book, and they are specifically mentioned below. Material relied upon but not listed was generally drawn from readily accessible databases, news reports, and reference works.

## Books

Allen, Richard. *The Life, Experiences, and Gospel Labours of the Rt. Rev. Richard Allen.* Philadelphia: Martin & Boden, Printers, 1833.

American Anti-Slavery Society. *Anti Slavery Record, Appendix* (1835). Washington, D.C.: Negro University Press, 1936.

Anderson, Bernard, et al. *The Fairmont Papers—Black Alternatives Conference, San Francisco, December 1980.* San Francisco, Calif.: Institute for Contemporary Studies, 1981.

Baldwin, James. "Everybody's Protest Novel." In *Notes of a Native Son.* Boston: Beacon Press, 1955.

———. *Notes of a Native Son.* Boston: Beacon Press, 1955.

Boston, Thomas D. *Race, Class, and Conservatism.* Boston: Allen & Unwin, 1988.

Bowen, William, and Derrick Bok. *The Shape of the River: Long Term Consequences of Considering Race in College and University Admissions.* Princeton, N.J.: Princeton University Press, 2000.

Brooke, Edward W. *The Challenge of Change: Crisis in Our Two Party System.* Boston: Little, Brown, 1966.

Brotz, Howard, ed. *African American Social and Political Thought 1850–1920.* Piscataway, N.J.: Transaction Publishers, 1992.

Brundage, W. Fitzhugh, ed. *Booker T. Washington and Black Progress.* Gainesville: University Press of Florida, 2003.

Carmichael, Stokely, and Charles Hamilton. *Black Power: The Politics of Liberation in America.* New York: Vintage, 1967.

Cashin, Sheryll. *The Failure of Integration: How Race and Class Are Undermining the American Dream.* New York: Public Affairs, 2004.

Conic, Georgia E. *An Exploration of Conservative Ideology in African American Political Thought, Attitudes, and Behavior.* Ph.D. diss., Wayne State University, 2005. Ann Arbor, Mich.: UMI Dissertation Services, 2006.

DeYoung, Karen. *Soldier: The Life of Colin Powell.* New York: Knopf, 2006.

DuBois, W.E.B. *The Philadelphia Negro: A Social Study.* Philadelphia: Published for the University, 1899.

———. *The Souls of Black Folk.* Chicago: A. C. McClurg & Co., 1903.

———. *Writings.* New York: Library of America, 1986.

Dyson, Michael Eric. *Is Cosby Right, or Has the Black Middle Class Lost Its Mind?* New York: Basic Civitas Books, 2005.

Eisenstadt, Peter, ed. *Black Conservatism—Essays in Intellectual and Political History.* New York: Garland, 1999.

Elder, Larry. *The Ten Things You Can't Say in America.* New York: St. Martin's Griffin Press 2001.

Faryna, Stan, Brad Stetson, and Joseph Conti, eds. *Black and Right—The Bold New Voice of Black Conservatives in America.* Westport, Conn.: Praeger, 1997.

Fauset, Jessie Redmon. *There Is Confusion.* Boston: Northeastern University Press, 1989.

Felix, Antonia. *Condi—The Condoleezza Rice Story.* New York: Newmarket Press, 2002.

Forten, James. *Letters from a Man of Colour on a Late Bill before the Senate of Pennsylvania.* Philadelphia, 1813.

Franklin, John Hope, and August Meier, eds. *Black Leaders of the Twentieth Century.* Urbana: University of Illinois Press, 1982.

Friedman, Milton. *Capitalism and Freedom.* Chicago: University of Chicago Press, 1962.

Garvey, Amy Jacques, and Marcus Garvey. *The Philosophy and Opinions of Marcus Garvey.* London: Cass, 1967.

Gates, Henry Louis, and Nellie Y. McKay, eds. *The Norton Anthology of African American Literature.* New York: W. W. Norton, 1997.

**Bibliography**

Goldwater, Barry. *The Conscience of a Conservative*. Shepherdsville, Ky.: Victor Publishing, 1960.

Gosnell, Harold. *Negro Politicians: The Rise of Negro Politics in Chicago*. Chicago: University of Chicago Press, 1935.

Harlan, Louis R. *Booker T. Washington—The Wizard of Tuskegee, 1901–1915*. New York: Oxford University Press, 1983.

Howard-Pitney, David. *The African American Jeremiad—Appeals for Justice in America*. Philadelphia: Temple University Press, 2005.

Hurston, Zora Neale. *Their Eyes Were Watching God*. Urbana: University of Illinois Press, 1991.

Hutchinson, George. *The Harlem Renaissance in Black and White*. Cambridge, Mass.: Belknap Press, 1995.

Ikonne, Chidi. *From DuBois to Van Vechten, The Early New Negro Literature, 1903–1926*. Westport, Conn.: Greenwood Press, 1981.

Johnson, James Weldon. *Black Manhattan*. Salem, N.H.: Ayer, 1990.

———. *Complete Poems*. New York: Penguin Books, 2000.

———. *Writings*. New York: Penguin Putnam, 2004.

Joseph, Peniel E. *Waiting 'Til the Midnight Hour—A Narrative History of Black Power in America*. New York: Henry Holt & Co., 2006.

Keyes, Alan L. *Masters of the Dream: The Strength and Betrayal of Black America*. New York: Morrow, 1995.

Leak, Jeffrey B., ed. *Rac[e]ing to the Right—Selected Essays of George S. Schuyler*. Knoxville: University of Tennessee Press, 2001.

Lomax, Louis E. *When the Word Is Given: A Report on Elijah Muhammad, Malcolm X, and the Black Muslim World*. Cleveland, Ohio: World Publishing, 1963.

Loury, Glenn. *The Anatomy of Racial Inequality*. Cambridge, Mass.: Harvard University Press, 2002.

———. *One By One, from the Inside Out: Essays and Reviews on Race and Responsibility in America*. New York: Free Press, 1995.

Mabry, Marcus. *Twice as Good—Condoleezza Rice and Her Path to Power*. Emmaus, Pa.: Holtzbrinck, 2007.

Marable, Manning. *Black Leadership*. New York: Columbia University Press, 1998.

McKay, Claude. *Complete Poems*. Urbana: University of Illinois Press, 2004.

McNeil, Genna Rae. *Groundwork: Charles Hamilton Houston and the Struggle for Civil Rights*. Philadelphia: University of Pennsylvania Press, 1983.

McWhorter, John H. *Losing the Race—Self Sabotage in Black America*. New York: Free Press, 2000.

McWhorter, John H. *Authentically Black: Essays for the Black Silent Majority*. New York: Gotham Books, 2003.

————. *Winning the Race: Beyond the Crisis in Black America.* New York: Gotham Books, 2005.

Merida, Kevin, and Michael Fletcher. *Supreme Discomfort: The Divided Soul of Clarence Thomas.* New York: Doubleday, 2007.

Moore, Jacqueline M. *Booker T. Washington, W.E.B. DuBois, and the Struggle for Racial Uplift.* Wilmington, Del.: SR Books, 2003.

Moton, Robert Russa. *What the Negro Thinks.* New York: Garden City Publishing, 1942.

Mwakikagile, Godfrey. *Black Conservatives: Are They Right or Wrong?* Palo Alto, Calif.: Fultus, 2004.

O'Neale, Sondra A. *Jupiter Hammon and the Biblical Beginnings of African American Literature.* Metuchen, N.J.: American Theological Library Association and Scarecrow Press, 1993.

Persons, Georgia. *Dilemmas of Black Politics: Issues of Leadership and Strategy.* New York: HarperCollins, 1993.

Powell, Colin (with Joseph E. Persico). *My American Journey.* New York: Random House, 1995.

Schuyler, George S. *Black and Conservative.* New Rochelle, N.Y.: Arlington House, 1966.

————. *Black No More.* Boston: Northeastern University Press, 1989.

————. *Slaves Today.* New York: AMS Press, 1969.

Sowell, Thomas. *Affirmative Action around the World: An Empirical Study.* New Haven, Conn.: Yale University Press, 2004.

————. *Black Rednecks and White Liberals.* San Francisco: Encounter Books, 2005.

————. *Civil Rights: Rhetoric or Reality.* New York: Morrow, 1984.

————. *Economics and the Politics of Race.* New York: HarperCollins, 1983.

————. *A Personal Odyssey.* New York: Free Press, 2002.

————. *Race and Economics.* New York: D. McKay Co., 1975.

Steele, Shelby. *The Content of Our Character: A New Vision of Race in America.* New York: St. Martin's Press, 1990.

————. *A Dream Deferred: The Second Betrayal of Black Freedom in America.* New York: HarperCollins, 1998.

————. *White Guilt: How Blacks and Whites Together Destroyed the Promise of the Civil Rights Era.* New York: HarperCollins, 2006.

Tate, Gale T., and Lewis A. Randolph, eds. *Dimensions of Black Conservatism in the United States—Made in America.* New York: Palgrave, 2002.

Toomer, Jean. *Cane.* New York: Modern Library, 1994.

Van Deburg, William L., ed. *Modern Black Nationalism—From Marcus Garvey to Louis Farrakhan.* New York: New York University Press, 1997.

Van Vechten, Carl. *Nigger Heaven.* New York: Knopf, 1926.

Washington, Booker T. *The Story of My Life and Work*. Naperville, Ill.: J. L. Nichols & Co., 1900.

———. *Up from Slavery*. Garden City, N.Y.: Doubleday, 1963.

———. *Working with Hands*. New York: Arno Press, 1969.

Washington, Booker T., and Robert Park. *The Man Farthest Down: A Record of Observation and Study in Europe*. Garden City, N.Y.: Doubleday, 1912.

West, Cornel. *Keeping Faith—Philosophy and Race in America*. New York: Routledge, 1993.

———. *Race Matters*. Boston: Beacon Press, 1993.

Wideman, John Edgar. *My Soul Has Grown Deep: Classics of Early African American Literature*. New York: One World/Ballantine, 2002.

Williams, Armstrong. *Beyond Blame: How We Can Succeed by Breaking the Dependency Barrier*. Darby, Pa.: Diane Publishing, 1995.

Williams, Juan. *Enough: The Phony Leaders, Dead-End Movements, and Culture of Failure That Are Undermining Black America— And What We Can Do about It*. New York: Crown, 2006.

Williams, Oscar R. *George S. Schuyler: Portrait of a Black Conservative*. Knoxville: University of Tennessee Press, 2007.

Williams, Walter. *South Africa's War against Capitalism*. New York: Praeger, 1989.

———. *The State against Blacks*. New York: New Press, 1982.

Winch, Julie. *A Gentleman of Color—The Life of James Forten*. New York: Oxford University Press, 2002.

Wintz, Cary D., ed. *The Harlem Renaissance 1920–1940, The Critics and the Harlem Renaissance*. Vol. 4. New York: Garland, 1996.

Wortham, Anne. *The Other Side of Racism*. Columbus: Ohio State University Press, 1981.

## Articles, Letters, and Documents

Allen, Richard. Articles of the Free African Society, May 17, 1787.

———. Preamble of the Free African Society, April 12, 1787.

Allison, Wes. "Black Conservatives Gather Momentum." *St. Petersburg Times*, Feb. 28, 2005.

Asumah, Seth N., and Valencia C. Perkins. "Black Conservatism and the Social Problems in Black America—Ideological Cul de Sacs." *Journal of Black Studies* 31, 1 (2000): 51–73.

Carmichael, Stokely. "Position Paper on Black Power." *New York Times*, Aug. 5, 1966.

Crowe, Nick. "Rap's Last Tape." *Prospect Magazine*, March 2004.

Kilson, Martin. "The Anatomy of Black Conservatism." *Transition* 59 (1993): 4–19.

King, Colbert I. "Fix It Brother." *Washington Post,* May 22, 2004.

Letter of James Forten to Nathaniel Rogers, March 29, 1839.

Megalli, Mark. "The High Priests of the Black Academic Right." *Journal of Blacks in Higher Education* 9 (1995): 71–77.

Mutch, David. "Black Conservatives Articulate Alternative View of Civil Rights." *Christian Science Monitor,* Sept. 23, 1991.

*Poulson's American Daily Advertiser,* March 2, 1822.

Robinson, Eugene. "What Rice Can't See." *Washington Post,* Oct. 25, 2005.

Smith, Robert C., and Hanes Walton Jr. "U-Turn." *Transition* 62 (1993): 209–216.

Williams, Walter. "Profile." *American Education Magazine,* July 1982.

## United States Supreme Court Cases

*Atkins v. Virginia,* 536 U.S. 304 (2002)

*Board of Education v. Earls,* 536 U.S. 822 (2002)

*Brown v. Board of Education,* 347 U.S. 483 (1954)

*Buchanan v. Warley,* 245 U.S. 60 (1917)

*Giles v. Harris,* 189 U.S. 475 (1903)

*Gonzales v. Carhart,* 127 S.Ct. 1610, 550 U.S. ___ (2007)

*Gonzales v. Raich,* 545 U.S. 1 (2005)

*Grutter v. Bollinger,* 539 U.S. 306 (2003)

*Hamdan v. Rumsfeld,* 126 S.Ct. 2749 548 U.S. ___ (2006)

*Hamdi v. Rumsfeld,* 542 U.S. 507 (2004)

*Hudson v. McMillian,* 503 U.S. 1 (1992)

*Kansas v. Marsh,* 126 S.Ct. 2516, 548 U.S. ___ (2006)

*Planned Parenthood v. Casey,* 505 U.S. 833 (1992)

*Plessy v. Ferguson,* 163 U.S. 537 (1896)

*Roper v. Simmons,* 543 U.S. 551 (2005)

*Samson v. California,* 126 S.Ct. 2193, 547 U.S. ___ (2006)

## Speeches

Allen, Richard. Address to the Free People of Colour of These United States. September 1831. In *Minutes of the Proceedings of the National Negro Conventions,* 1830–1864, ed. Howard Holman Bell. New York: Arno Press, 1969.

Powell, Colin. Speech delivered at the 1996 Republican National Convention. Available at www.pbs.org/newshour/convention 96/floor_speeches/powell.html.

**Bibliography**

———. Speech delivered at the 2000 Republican National Convention. Available at http://transcripts.cnn.com/TRANSCRIPTS/0007/31/se.20.html.

Rice, Condoleezza. Speech delivered at the 2000 Republican National Convention. Available at www.cnn.com/ELECTION/2000/conventions/republican/transcripts/rice.html.

## Videos

Rock, Chris. *Bigger and Blacker.* New York: Home Box Office, 1999.

———. *Bring the Pain.* New York: Home Box Office, 1997.

———. *Never Scared.* New York: Home Box Office, 2004.

## Web Sites and Online Sources

"The American National Election Studies Guide to Public Opinion and Electoral Behavior, 2002 & 2004." Available at www.umich.edu/~nes/nesguide/2ndtable/t3_1_1.htm.

Booker Rising! www.bookerrising.blogspot.com

Cobb (Michael David Cobb Bowen), http://cobb.typepad.com/cobb/2007/01/a_black_conserv.html

Conservative Brotherhood, www.conservativebrotherhood.org

LaShawn Barber's Corner, www.lawshawnbarber.com

McPherson, Lionel. "The Loudest Silence Ever Heard." *FAIR (Fairness and Accuracy in Reporting) Magazine,* July/August 1992, available at www.fair.org/index.php?page=1488.

The New Underground Railroad, http://thenewundergroundrailroad.blogspot.com

The Pew Research Center for the People and the Press. "The 2004 Political Landscape: Evenly Divided and Increasingly Polarized." Available at http://people-press.org/reports/display.php3?PageID=749.

Project 21, www.project21.org

Republicans for Black Empowerment, www.theblackgop.com

"2004 CNN Gallup Poll—Voters in Presidential Election, 2000 and 2004, by Race." Available at www.cnn.com/ELECTION/2004/pages/results/states/US/P/00/epolls.0.html.

# Index

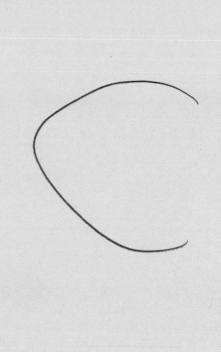